Deprivation and Education

Deprivation and Education

M. L. Kellmer Pringle, B.A., Ph.D.
Director, National Bureau for Co-operation in Child Care

Longmans

Longmans, Green & Co Ltd
48 Grosvenor Street, London W.1

*And associated companies, branches and representatives
throughout the world*

© M. L. Kellmer Pringle 1965
First published 1965

*Printed in Great Britain by
Richard Clay (The Chaucer Press), Ltd.
Bungay, Suffolk*

Contents

217618

1. Introduction

The publication of this series of research papers in one volume has been prompted by three circumstances: first, the demand for off-prints, both from this country and abroad, has continued, even for the early articles, and the supply was exhausted some time ago. Secondly, in recent years there has been an increasing interest in, and emphasis on, the central importance of language development for intellectual growth and educational progress (Hoggart, 1958; Opie and Opie, 1959; Bernstein, 1960 and 1961; Luria, 1961; Riessman, 1962; Vygotsky, 1962; Lewis, 1964; Home Office, 1964). Thirdly, the Children and Young Persons Act 1963 provides local authorities with new and wide powers: it enables them to safeguard at a much earlier stage than was permissible previously, the welfare of children in their own homes, and it empowers them to carry out research into methods for doing so most effectively. Two aims in particular are written into the Act, namely to reduce the number of children who are being taken into or kept in care, and to bring about a decrease in the number who are brought before juvenile courts. But, even more important, prevention in the widest sense of the term has now become possible. Local authorities are being asked to consider estab-lishing family welfare centres in recognition of the fact that 'there is a field of home behaviour where family welfare councillors can perhaps give help to parents who know things are going wrong but are not sure what to do for their children' (Home Office, 1964).

It is therefore a matter of urgency to formulate as comprehensive a concept of prevention as possible before the pattern of the services to be developed becomes too narrow or set. The main theme of this collection of papers seems to be of some relevance to this task.

The term 'deprivation' is commonly used to denote three different conditions: first, the child who is living in residential care, either for long periods or permanently, is deprived of normal family life; second, if a child is unloved and rejected by his parents, especially his mother, he is likely to suffer emotional deprivation; and third, the child who is growing up in a home which is culturally and educationally extremely unstimulating, will be handicapped by environmental deprivation. Of course these three conditions are not mutually exclusive, but at present there are no estimates available to indicate the likely number of children within each of these categories or how many may be affected by two or all three types of deprivation. The overall number of children in care (using the term in the technical sense of the word) is by no means negligible—over 70,000 or as high as the total number of children suffering from physical handicap. If we add to this the other two groups of deprived children this figure may well have to be trebled.

It is generally accepted now that each of these three conditions may be detrimental to emotional and social development. Far less is known about the likely effects of deprivation in all its forms on language development, intellectual growth and educational progress. Yet these are just as important for a child's all-round development and adjustment.

The reasons which led to the investigations described in the following chapters were threefold: first, there had been comparatively little systematic study of the language development and scholastic attainment of children living in residential care; secondly, teachers of such children were of the opinion that many of them showed serious learning problems in school; and thirdly, in recent years there has been growing awareness that in this scientific and technological age, a nation's reservoir of intelligence is among its most important raw materials. It has become essential, therefore, to search for 'pools of unrealised ability'. If we need to find and train more teachers, more social workers, more technicians and so on, then potential ability can neither be wasted nor ignored. And language development is basic for general intellectual development. Similarly, it is now recognised that children whose language development remains stunted will later on also become seriously backward educationally. Of course the most critical period for the fostering of language and speech is during the preschool years. Since all children whose language development remains needlessly limited will inevitably be underfunctioning both intellectually and educationally, they represent a waste of potential ability.

The series of studies reported here have been mainly concerned with children living in residential care and who have been separated from their families for considerable periods of time. To begin with, a comprehensive enquiry was made into the development and achievements of some unselected samples of children aged 8, 11 and 14 years, who were living in residential care (chapters 2 and 3). Wherever possible, comparisons were made with the abilities and attainments of children who lived with their own families. In addition three hypotheses were tested regarding the results of deprivation: namely, that its ill-effects would be more marked (a) if the first separation from the mother occurred at an early age; (b) if deprivation had been severe (i.e. no contact whatever with the family); and (c) if the period of residential care had been prolonged.

Marked backwardness in language development was found, not only among both boys and girls, but also at each of the three age levels studied. The relationship, if any, between language development and emotional adjustment, was then explored by an intensive clinical study of two groups selected from the main sample (chapter 4). The subjects were children rated either as 'notably stable' or 'severely maladjusted' on four independent assessments. Both groups had been separated from their mothers at an early age and had remained in residential care for a large part of their lives. The salient finding of this investigation was a confirmation of the central importance of the nature of emotional relationships available to a child. All the children in the stable group had had the opportunity or the ability to build up and maintain an enduring relationship with a parent figure, who was not necessarily a blood relation. This suggested that a stable, continuing relationship with an adult in the 'outside world' decreased a child's susceptibility to maladjustment.

To test this hypothesis, another study was designed (chapter 5). In a large Children's Home, the housemothers, responsible for groups of ten to fourteen children, were asked to rank them from the most stable and easy to handle, to the most difficult problem child. Detailed information was also obtained on the frequency and regularity of contact each child had with adults outside the Home. As had been predicted, a statistically significant relation was found between optimum contact with an adult and emotional stability in the child. Then an intensive clinical study was made of a sample of the most stable and most maladjusted children, to explore further any qualitative differences in their attitudes to themselves and to other people.

In view of the very high proportion of children in residential care who were found to be seriously backward educationally, it was suggested that remedial education may have something to offer. An opportunity to explore the effectiveness of this educational approach with deprived and maladjusted children was provided by Miss Leila Rendel, the Director of the Caldecott Community. She made it possible to establish a remedial unit and to evaluate the results of two years' work (chapter 6).

The last investigation was concerned with the effects of early deprivation on the speech development of preschool children (chapter 7). A quantitative and qualitative analysis was made of the differences in spoken language between young children in residential care and a matched group who were living with their own families. The latter were found to be in advance of the deprived group on all quantitative aspects. Some suggestive qualitative differences were also found.

In reviewing the research which has been carried out in the decade following the publication of Bowlby's pioneering monograph *Maternal Care and Mental Health*, the hope is expressed that this new work 'will at least provide a stimulus to further research into a problem that is of the greatest importance not only for the care of children but also for the social life of the whole community (Ainsworth et al., 1962). The same hope underlies the publication of this volume.

The book consists of two parts: the first (chapters 2–7) contains the reports of the investigations described above. These were carried out in collaboration with some of my senior students between 1954 and 1961. In the second part the practical implications of the research findings are considered in relation to policy and practice in the field of child care and education (chapters 8–14). The last two chapters have been specially written for this book. In chapter 16, an attempt is made to delineate the concept of prevention in child care and to outline the aims of a comprehensive, preventive service for children's psychological welfare. Finally, all the practical suggestions and recommendations which have been put forward are summarised in chapter 17.

References

AINSWORTH, M. D. *and others* (1962) *Deprivation of maternal care; a reassessment of its effects.* (Public health papers, 14.) Geneva, World Health Organisation.

BERNSTEIN, B. (1960) 'Language and social class', *British Journal of Sociology*, **11**, 271–6.

BERNSTEIN, B. (1961) 'Social structure, language and learning', *Educational Research*, **3**, 163–76.

HOGGART, R. (1957) *The uses of literacy; aspects of working class life, with special reference to publications and entertainments.* London, Chatto & Windus.

HOME OFFICE (1964) *The needs of young children in care; a memorandum prepared by the Home Office in consultation with the Advisory Council on Child Care.* London, H.M.S.O.

HOME OFFICE (1964) *Report on the work of the Children's Department 1961–1963.* (H.C. 155.) London, H.M.S.O.

LEWIS, M. M. (1963) *Language, thought and personality in infancy and early childhood.* London, Harrap.

LURIA, A. R. (1961) *The role of speech in the regulation of normal and abnormal behaviour.* London, Pergamon Press.

OPIE, I. and OPIE, P. (1959) *The lore and language of schoolchildren.* Oxford, Clarendon Press.

RIESSMAN, F. (1962) *The culturally deprived child.* New York, Harper & Row.

VYGOTSKY, L. S. (1962) *Thought and language.* New York, Wiley.

2. Intellectual, emotional and social development of deprived children*

with Victoria Bossio

Introduction

In the current literature, the term 'deprived' is used to describe a child who, for one reason or another (such as ill-health, death or desertion of one or both parents), is unable to live with his own family but is being brought up in an institution (Home Off., 1946; United Nations, 1952; Ford, 1955). The term is also used for children who, although now living in their own homes, have early in life been separated from their parents, particularly the mother, or who are unloved and rejected by her. Like institutionalisation, such 'maternal deprivation' is considered to be detrimental to children's development (Bowley, 1947; Fitzgerald, 1948; Bowlby, 1951).

This investigation is primarily concerned with the effects of deprivation due to institutionalisation, although some attention is given to the problem of separation and maternal deprivation. In recent years considerable research has been devoted to these topics yet there have been comparatively few systematic investigations of unselected groups of deprived children. There has been a tendency for special categories such as preschool or hospitalised children, or for certain aspects, such as emotional adjustment or social maturity to be studied. Our aim has been to attempt a comprehensive enquiry into the development and achievement of some unselected samples of deprived children, to examine the interrelationship between their abilities and attainments and to make a comparison with ordinary children wherever possible.

Previous studies

Enquiries in this field began with a series of investigations of similar design, aiming to survey the intellectual development of orphanage

* First published in *Vita Humana*, 1958, 1, 2, 65–92.

children (Fernald, 1918; Terman and Wagner, 1918; Calif. State Bd, 1918; Gobb, 1922). The findings suggested that they were mentally retarded compared with ordinary children. Crissey (1937) found a general tendency for I.Q.s to decrease with increasing length of institutional residence. There are many studies of preschool children, particularly young babies, which lend support to the theory that early individual care and maternal love are essential for optimal growth (Gindl and Hetzer, 1937; Crissey, 1937; Rheingold, 1943; Spitz, 1945; Spitz and Wolf, 1946; Levy, 1947; Simonsen, 1947). A series of investigations of the amount of crying showed that babies cried least under home care and most under ordinary hospital conditions (Aldrich, Sung and Knop, 1945, a, b, c; Aldrich, Norval, Knop and Venegas, 1946). When the latter were modified to permit increasing nursing care, there was a substantial decrease in the length and amount of crying. The investigators suggested that such excessive crying is likely to have important implications for emotional adjustment as well as speech development.

Goldfarb (1943 a, b, 1945 and 1947) aimed to test the hypothesis that the experience of living in the highly impersonal surroundings of residential nurseries during the first few years of life, has far-reaching and often permanent effects upon a child's whole personality. Two groups of forty children were studied, all of whom had been separated from their own mothers within the first nine months of life. One group lived in an institution until about 3 years of age, the other group was placed permanently in foster-homes, soon after separation from their mothers. In all other respects the groups were carefully matched. Among the developmental aspects studied were mental and social growth, personality adjustment and language ability. Except for social competence, the foster home group was markedly superior to the institutionally reared children. The latter were then fostered out and it was found that when they had settled down, their social development tended to show a slower rate and often there was some definite regression. Goldfarb suggests that this may be due to the traumatic, or at least unsettling, effect of being removed from their familiar environment into a foster home. An alternative and, he believes, more likely explanation is that this comparatively high social competence had been produced and maintained by the very conditions of institutional routine. When this was replaced by the more individual care given in a foster home, 'the thin shell of social maturity collapsed'. Goldfarb described the general behaviour of the institution children as passive, apathetic and asocial, and concluded that his data confirm the hypothesis of personality impairment.

Though Goldfarb's samples were rather small, other and quite differently conceived investigations lend support to his contentions Theis, 1924; League of Nations, 1938; Lowrey, 1940; Bowlby, 1946). A study of the personality development and social maturity of a large number of children drawn from eight different institutions, led Edmistone and Baird (1949) to very similar conclusions. The emotional adjustment of their institution children was significantly below that of ordinary children while they compared favourably with regard to social competence.

As a result of the Second World War there have been many reports regarding the effects on children of evacuation, homelessness and separation from their parents. Different investigators in different countries agree that emotional difficulties and deviations in personality development are due mainly to the disturbance in, and break up of, family relationships rather than the more obvious phenomena of war, such as bloodshed and destruction (Carey-Trefzer, 1949; Burlingham and Freud, 1954). These studies are, however, based mainly upon clinical assessments.

Except for three investigations (Lawrence, 1929; Burt, 1944 and 1947) which deal rather marginally with the effects of deprivation, systematic enquiries in Great Britain began only after the war. Bodman and others (1950) concluded from a comparative study of 15-year-old institutionalised and ordinary children that constitutional factors are at least as important as environmental factors in the development of social maturity; and that deprived children are behind normal ones in this aspect of growth. This is the only study where institution children are reported to be below average in social competence.

Bowley (1951) found a severe degree of emotional maladjustment among children from broken homes, especially where the break-up occurred in early childhood. Lewis (1954), in a study of 500 children referred to a Reception Centre for investigation and placement, reports an uncommonly high incidence of emotional disturbance, namely 75 per cent. Of these 32 per cent were delinquent. On the other hand, intelligence quotients were higher and the proportion of able children greater than reported by other investigators. It seems, however, that Lewis's sample is not altogether representative of what are usually called 'deprived children': a third of her cases were still living in their own homes and had been referred to the Centre for behaviour problems; 20 per cent had already been examined and treated at Child Guidance Clinics; 50 per cent of the total sample had been placed in substitute homes which had proved unsuccessful; 25 per cent had been in three to six different substitute homes. Thus a large proportion consisted of the most difficult section of emotionally disturbed children or those whose placement had proved a failure.

Mean I.Q.s above average have also been reported in a study of children who had been in a sanatorium (Bowlby and Ainsworth, 1956). Though separated from their parents, they were not deprived of love and attention. They were visited as frequently as permitted and their families were hoping and waiting for their return. A group of children were selected who had been patients in a sanatorium for periods of months or years (average length 18 months) because of tuberculosis. All had entered the sanatorium before the age of 4 years. At the time of the investigation they were living with their parents and attending an ordinary day school. A control group was chosen from the same school and class, matched for sex and age; each ex-sanatorium child was matched in this way with three controls. No significant differences in intelligence were found, but the sanatorium children were significantly less well adjusted than the controls. The investigators conclude that while separation has had some detrimental effects, in many cases the children's maladjustment was due to other factors, primarily the nature of the mother–child relationship before and after separation.

Summarising, it may be said that there is considerable support for the hypothesis that deprived children are more maladjusted, less intelligent but socially more mature than those living in their own homes. It seems that, to some extent at least, intellectual limitations and personality difficulties can be attributed to the effects of deprivation itself. These effects are clearly discernible at an early age.

The investigation
The aim of this investigation was twofold: first, to study the development and achievement of deprived children, comparing these, as far as possible, with those of the ordinary school population. In addition to the three aspects discussed in this paper, language development and reading attainment were investigated. These results will be

reported in a subsequent chapter. The second aim was to test three hypotheses regarding the results of deprivation: that its ill-effects are more marked (1) where the first separation from the mother occurred at an early age; (2) where separation has lasted for a long time; and (3) where deprivation has been severe.

The subjects

Altogether 188 children were studied by group and individual methods. Of these, 142 lived in one institution and they constituted the main experimental sample. Only this group will be dealt with here but the results for the 46 children living in another Home were closely similar to those of the main sample. Both institutions were large but organised into Cottage Homes, each of which housed 30 to 40 children. At the time of this study, boys and girls lived in different Houses, so that brothers and sisters were always separated. As the children were further grouped according to age (0–2 years, 2–5 years, 5–9 years and so on), even siblings of the same sex were often living in separate Houses.

All children aged 8, 11 and 14 years were selected for study. These ages were chosen as certain educational milestones are reached then: between 7 and 8 years, promotion from the Infant to the Junior School; at 11, selection for secondary education; and by 14 years of age, children are in their last year at school, when not only finding the first job, but also leaving the institution, are problems to be faced. It was thought that any difficulties commonly experienced by

Table 2.1. Age and sex distribution

	Boys		Girls	
	N	%	N	%
8-year-olds N = 50 Mean = 8–2	24	48	26	52
11-year-olds N = 50 Mean = 11–0	27	54	23	46
14-year-olds N = 42 Mean = 14–2	29	69	13	31
Total N = 142	80	56	62	44

deprived children, were likely to become more apparent or accentuated at times of change and crisis: thus they might be more readily observed and assessed.

The age and sex distribution of the main sample is shown on table 2.1. The number of girls decreased as age increased, and this also held true for the total population in this institution. It may be due to the fact that girls are more frequently chosen for boarding out and for adoption; therefore the older girls will tend to be a less representative cross-section of deprived children than the boys.

Fifty-five per cent of the children in the total sample had siblings in the same institution or in care somewhere else, and 27 per cent were illegitimate. The latter figure is very much higher than the percentage of illegitimate births in the general population.*

The reasons for admission into care were grouped under the following main headings:

a. illness or death of one or both parents, extreme poverty or eviction to non-payment of rent—circumstances which do not imply any rejection of the child (20 per cent of cases);

b. divorce or separation of the parents, neglect, ill-treatment or abandonment of the child (44 per cent of cases);

c. mental illness, insanity or criminal offence of one or both parents (20 per cent of cases);

d. the child being beyond the control of his parents or guardians— in some cases a pretext to enable the parents to get rid of an unwanted child (16 per cent of cases).

The experimental design

To assess the differential effects of deprivation, each age group was sub-divided into the following categories: first, 'early' or 'late entrants', according to whether the first separation from home took place before or after the age of 5 years. This borderline was chosen since the child comes to accept daily and regular time away from his mother and from home after he starts to attend school at the age of 5 years; furthermore, the period before this age is by many considered to be most important for forming the basic patterns which determine the capacity for making and maintaining emotional relationships in later life.

* In England and Wales, according to the Registrar General the illegitimate birthrate was 42 per thousand total live births in 1937. It increased during the war, reaching a peak of 93 in 1945, but it fell to 66 in 1946 and then continued to fall to 54 in 1948 and 51 in 1949.

B

Secondly, the length of institutional residence was expressed as a proportion of a child's chronological age, to allow for direct comparison between the three age groups; thus 'long stay' children were defined as having spent more than one-third of their lives in care, while 'short stays' had been away from their families for less than that time. This classification did not differentiate between continuous and intermittent periods in care, but merely indicated the total length of separation. Thirdly, to consider the effect of both these variables simultaneously, the age samples were regrouped into the following four subcategories:

a. early entrants/long stay;
b. early entrants/short stay;
c. late entrants/long stay;
d. late entrants/short stay.

Lastly, severity of deprivation was defined in terms of the contact, maintained by parents, foster parents or relatives. Three subdivisions were made: 'mildly deprived', 'deprived' and 'severely deprived'. Children in the first group regularly received letters and parcels, were visited and taken on outings, holidays, etc.; the second group was contacted by parents or relations only at the request of the Children's Officer; the third group had very little or no contact at all with their families since admission to the institution.

Thus the effect of five variables was studied: age, sex, age at first separation, total length of institutional residence and severity of deprivation. Although the groups and subgroups into which each age sample was divided were rather small, it was hoped that some differences, or at least suggestive trends, might emerge.

To obtain further evidence on the hypothesis that the effects of deprivation are most serious where separation occurs early and lasts a long time, the more extensive approach was supplemented by some intensive case studies. From the total sample those children were selected who had been most or least adversely affected by a severe separation experience. The following criteria were stipulated for selection: the first removal from home to have taken place before the age of five years and separation to have lasted for more than a third of the child's life. To exclude possibly complicating factors of low or high intelligence, the choice was confined to children of average ability (i.e. I.Q. range 85–114). Only those were chosen who were classed either as 'notably stable' or as 'severely maladjusted' by all the following assessments: (*a*) the Bristol Social Adjustment Guides, filled in by the class teachers; (*b*) the Bristol Social Adjustment Guides filled in by the house-parents; (*c*) the personality test and (*d*) the clinical observations made by the investigator throughout the testing and interviewing. These criteria were fulfilled by eleven 'severely maladjusted' and five 'notably stable' children. The findings from this more detailed examination of the interrelationship between deprivation and personality reactions will be presented at a later stage.

Tests and other measuring devices used

Because of the different ages, certain tests could not be used with all the children. Where this was the case, the age group which was given the particular test, is indicated in brackets. In this chapter the results from the following tests and assessments will be discussed:

Group tests

1. Cornwell Orally presented Group Test of Intelligence for Juniors (8- and 11-year-olds).
2. Moray House Picture Intelligence Test (8-year-olds).
3. Sleight Non-verbal Intelligence Test (11-year-olds).
4. Raven's Progressive Matrices (14-year-olds).
5. Simplex Intelligence Scale (14-year-olds).

Individual tests and assessments

1. Wechsler Intelligence Scale for Children.
2. Doll's Vineland Social Maturity Scale.
3. Raven's Controlled Projection Test for Children.
4. Bristol Social Adjustment Guides:
    a. for Day School Staff;
    b. for Residential Home Staff.
5. Interview, using a formalised recording schedule.

The minimum interviewing time was a total of four hours but this was exceeded where a child was either too voluble or else reluctant to cooperate. Information about the children's home background, educational and health history before entering the institution and reasons for admission, was obtained from the case records.

Statistical techniques used

In view of the different ages it was decided to present the data in the form of quotients. This at once allowed for direct comparisons between the age groups and between the various categories and subcategories. Objections have been raised to the use of quotients but the small loss in accuracy, which might result from their use, was more than compensated for by the greater ease in the handling and interpretation of the results.

The differences found between the various groups and subgroups were tested for significance by the following techniques:

a. the t test (the small sample formula), when only two group means or two percentages were being compared:

b. the analysis of variance technique:

i. the simple method (Lindquist, 1940) when more than two groups of children were being compared and where each group consisted of children of the same age, and

ii. the pooled results method (Clarke and Clarke, 1954), when two or more groups of children were being compared and where each group consisted of children of more than one age level;

c. the chi-square test of independence in contingency tables, when the comparison was based upon frequencies within a group.

Results

a. *Intelligence*

According to both the verbal and non-verbal group tests, this sample of deprived children was of dull intelligence (table 2.2). On the WISC Full Scale, the mean I.Q. of each age group was within

Table 2.2. Distribution of the group verbal and group non-verbal intelligence quotients

| | Verbal quotients | | Non-Verbal quotients | |
	Mean	Sigma	Mean	Sigma
8-year-olds	Cornwell		Moray House	
N = 45 *	82·13	10·02	84·71	14·01
11-year-olds	Cornwell		Sleight	
N = 50	85·32	13·33	85·78	14·38
14-year-olds	Simplex		Raven's Matr.	
N = 42	80·36	17·06	77·62	20·00

* The results of five children in this group had to be disregarded as they could not follow the directions, either leaving the papers blank or covering them with meaningless scribbles.

the average range (i.e. I.Q. 85–115), although below the mean for the ordinary population (table 2.3). The overall proportion of children of average intelligence was closely similar for the deprived

Table 2.3. **Distribution of intelligence quotients on the WISC (full scale)**

	Mean	Sigma
8-year-olds N = 50	86·22	10·64
11-year-olds N = 50	94·10	14·56
14-year-olds N = 42	89·07	13·50
Total N = 142	89·84	13·32

and ordinary children—79 per cent and 82 per cent respectively; however, the proportion of educationally subnormal and dull children was considerably higher, and that of bright and very able children considerably lower than among children generally (table 2.4).

Age and sex differences. The 11-year-olds were the relatively brightest group, but only the difference between the mean intelligence quotient of this group and the 8-year-olds was statistically significant beyond the 5 per cent level (table 2.3). Boys received consistently higher scores than girls in each age group as well as in the total sample. These differences were not, however, significant except for the 14-year-olds (at the 1 per cent level).

Differences according to the three criteria of deprivation. Regarding the age at the first separation, 'early entrants' showed consistently lower mean scores in all three age groups and this difference was statistically significant for the total sample beyond the 5 per cent level of confidence. On the other hand when the children were regrouped according to the length of institutional residence, no differences in mean quotients were found.

When both these variables were considered simultaneously, the mean quotients for the subcategories 'early entrants'/'short stay' and 'early entrants'/'long stay' were lower than the mean quotients for the 'late entrants'/'short stay' and the 'late entrants'/'long stay' and these differences proved significant beyond the 5 per cent and 1 per cent level respectively (table 2.5). It is worth noting that in each age group as well as in the total sample, the mean quotient of the 'early

Table 2.4. Distribution of WISC (full scale) intelligence quotients compared with the expected frequencies*

	Educ. subnormal –69		Borderline 70–79		Dull-normal 80–89		Average 90–109		Bright-normal 110–119		Superior 120–129		Very superior 130 +	
	N	%	N	%	N	%	N	%	N	%	N	%	N	%
8-year-olds N = 50	4	8	7	14	17	34	22	44	—	—	—	—	—	—
11-year-olds N = 50	2	4	6	12	13	26	19	38	9	18	1	2	—	—
14-year-olds N = 42	3	7	7	17	14	33	16	38	2	5	—	—	—	—
Total N = 142	9	6·3	20	14	44	31	57	40	11	8	1	0·7	—	—
Expected frequencies	2·2%		6·7%		16·1%		50%		16·1%		6·7%		2·2%	

* See Manual of Directions, Wechsler Intelligence Scale for Children, table IX, p. 16.
Percentage of deprived children within the average range (I.Q. 80–119) = 79 per cent.
Percentage of ordinary children within the average range (I.Q. 80–119) = 82 per cent.

entrants'/'long stay' was below the mean quotient of the 'early entrants'/'short stay' children. Though these differences were not statistically significant, they pointed in the expected direction. Among the 'late entrants' this trend was reversed in each age group and in the total sample, the 'long stay' having higher quotients than the 'short stay' children. Again these differences were not statistically significant but the trend was consistent.

Table 2.5. Differences in WISC (full scale) quotients according to the age at first separation and the length of institutional residence

	Early-long	Early-short	Late-long	Late-short	F ratio
8-year-olds					
Mean	84·70	86·25	89·11	86·67	0·35
Sigma	9·19	11·00	13·96	10·72	d.f. = 3 and 46
11-year-olds					
Mean	91·21	91·50	98·27	95·00	0·57
Sigma	13·89	15·81	15·62	14·37	d.f. = 3 and 46
14-year-olds					
Mean	83·00	88·00	91·70	89·09	0·62
Sigma	11·44	10·09	15·87	13·19	d.f. = 3 and 38
Total					
Mean	86·72 *	88·25 †	93·03 *	91·22 †	10·98 †
Sigma	11·59	12·11	15·36	13·37	d.f. = 3 and 6

* Statistically significant beyond the 1 per cent level.
† Statistically significant beyond the 5 per cent level.

Lastly, regarding severity of deprivation, the mean quotients for the 'severely deprived' were lower than those of the 'deprived' which in turn were below those of the 'mildly deprived' children in each age group. For the total sample the differences between the 'severely deprived' and 'deprived' and between the 'severely deprived' and 'mildly deprived' proved significant beyond the 5 per cent level.

b. *Emotional development*
The data from Raven's Projection Test, the Bristol Social Adjustment Guides and the clinical observations were not analysed for sex differences or for the three criteria of deprivation; these devices for measurement and assessment are not considered sufficiently precise quantitatively to warrant refined statistical analysis.

Raven's Controlled Projection Test. The children's responses to this test did not conform closely to those given by the normative group. Thus the mean coefficients of conformity fell considerably below the expected mean of 100 (table 2.6). The differences between the age

Table 2.6. **Distribution of coefficients of conformity**

	Mean	Sigma
8-year-olds N = 50	51·02	10·17
11-year-olds N = 50	53·12	14·03
14-year-olds N = 42	49·69	10·92
Total N = 142	51·37	11·83

groups were not statistically significant. Conversely, a large number of the replies fell into the 'unique response' category. Each protocol contained on an average five such responses, the range being from 1–15. A content analysis of these 'unique responses' showed that they seem to fall into four groups:

1. 'Don't know' type of answer (40 per cent).
2. Rejection or avoidance of the question, either by not replying at all or taking an excessively long time over the reply (21 per cent).
3. Answers expressing overtly fear, anxieties, aggression, ambivalence or guilt (37 per cent).
4. Bizarre responses of a schizoid type (2 per cent).

Analysis of the responses showed that the hero of the deprived children's stories is similar to that of ordinary children with regard to his spare-time occupations, his attitudes to authority and the kind of stories, lies and jokes he tells. Similarly there was nothing noteworthy regarding his choice of future occupation. The hero differed markedly from that of ordinary children in his friendships, attitudes towards his parents, personal feelings and worries. Thus he preferred to be with his parents or relatives rather than playing with other children; quarrels between his parents worried him and he tended to blame himself as being their cause; often he thought he had been sent away as a punishment for being naughty; the hero frequently felt lonely and longed for his parents and/or siblings. Replies were most often avoided or delayed in connection with questions linked, explicitly or implicitly, with family situations. Nightmares and a desire to buy presents for adults and friends were mentioned much more frequently than in the stories of ordinary children.

Perhaps the most outstanding feature of the stories was the very idealised picture painted of the hero's mother. For example, not once was she blamed for the quarrels between the parents, even when in reality the child was bound to know that it was his mother who had ill-treated and rejected him or who had deserted the home. This is in marked contrast to the normative group, whose members blamed the hero's mother almost as frequently as the father for parental disharmony.

The Bristol Social Adjustment Guides. Stott's (Stott, 1956) threefold classification of 'normal or emotionally stable'; 'unsettled'; 'definitely maladjusted' was used. At the day school, the incidence of both un-settledness and maladjustment was somewhat higher than at the residential Home (tables 2.7 and 2.8). These differences were small

Table 2.7. Proportion of children classed 'emotionally stable', 'unsettled' and 'maladjusted' at the day school

	Stable		Unsettled		Maladjusted	
	N	%	N	%	N	%
8-year-olds N = 50	17	34	16	32	17	34
11-year-olds N = 50	19	38	15	30	16	32
14-year-olds N = 42	13	31	14	33	15	36
Total N = 142	49	35	45	32	48	33

only and not significant statistically ($\chi^2 = 0.63$, d.f. 2). The highest incidence of normal, stable behaviour was shown by the 11-year-olds at school and in the Home. Though the differences between them and the other age groups were not significant ($\chi^2 = 0.52$ and 0.49 respectively, d.f. 4) they suggest that the more intelligent group contains also the relatively largest number of emotionally stable children. Again using Stott's classification, an analysis of the various categories of unsettled and maladjusted behaviour was made; this showed that the most common symptoms were those denoting

Table 2.8. Proportion of children classed 'emotionally stable', 'unsettled' and 'maladjusted' at the residential Home

	Stable		Unsettled		Maladjusted	
	N	%	N	%	N	%
8-year-olds N = 50	19	38	15	30	16	32
11-year-olds N = 50	21	42	15	30	14	28
14-year-olds N = 42	15	36	14	33	13	31
Total N = 142	55	39	44	31	43	30

anxiety about adult interest or affection, and general educational backwardness (table 2.9). A considerable number of children were 'unforthcoming'—a condition which, according to Stott, is 'characterised by a lack of confidence with people and with things or situations'.

Table 2.9. Incidence of symptoms of emotional disturbance shown on the Bristol Social Adjustment Guides, day school and residential forms * (Total sample, N = 142)

Symptoms	Frequency †	
	N	%
Anxiety or uncertainty about adult interest or affection	92	65
General educational backwardness	89	60
Restlessness or inability to concentrate	71	50
Unforthcomingness	48	34
Depression	35	25
Withdrawal	21	15
Hostility to adults or to other children	28	20
Unconcern for adult approval	21	15

* Only those children who were reported to show a symptom both at the school and in the residential Home were included in this table.
† Many children showed more than one symptom.

Clinical observations. Most children cooperated well during the individual testing. However, many showed a change in attitude when the personality test was administered, becoming tense, sullen or refusing to reply altogether to some of the questions. For example, a

7-year-old boy, who was so anxious to be seen by the examiner that he came far too early and then was quite cheerful and at ease, grew restless and anxious when the Raven's test was being given. Eventually he asked whether he could go and fetch a friend to stay with him while he finished the story. An 11-year-old girl who had conversed quite normally, refused completely to answer the questions of the personality test but offered to write them down. A 14-year-old boy who had talked quite fluently, began to stammer and his speech deteriorated steadily throughout the test. According to the school report, he stammers a great deal in class but rarely when talking to his friends or on the playing field.

Similarly, many of the children seemed ill at ease during the interview and the impression was gained that they found difficulty in dealing with an unstructured situation involving personal contact with an adult. At the same time, symptoms of maladjustment were in evidence which had not been so apparent during the rest of the examination. These seem to fall within the following categories:

1. Infantile or regressive behaviour.
2. Compulsive or self-punishing symptoms.
3. Over-anxiety to gain attention or affection.

Some 40 per cent of the children showed one or more regressive symptom; the most frequent ones were: baby talk, jealousy of other children, excessive curiosity and finger sucking (sometimes two or more fingers at a time). Self-punishment and compulsive behaviour such as nail biting, nose picking, body scratching, inappropriate giggling and laughter and various bodily movements and twitches were shown by 53 per cent. Among the symptoms denoting anxiety to gain attention or affection, the following were most frequently observed: an excessive desire to please, boasting and showing off, an over-affectionate, clinging attitude involving touching or standing close to the examiner. Such behaviour patterns were shown by 60 per cent.

Attitudes towards other people. Lastly, based on all the data discussed above, an attempt was made to group the children according to their predominating emotional attitudes and reactions towards other people. Those showing marked inconsistencies of behaviour in different situations were placed in a separate group. For the rest three broad but well differentiated behaviour patterns could be distinguished:

1. Normally affectionate; friendly to adults and children and very fond of his parents (real or substitute).
2. Over-affectionate and clinging, craving love and attention, yet unable to attach himself to anybody; tending to be jealous of other children.
3. Affectionless and withdrawn; indifferent to social stimuli; often aggressive and suspicious towards other children as well as adults, including his parents.

Though a considerable number of children fell into the 'normally affectionate' category, a still larger number were either 'over-affectionate' or 'affectionless'. Inconsistent emotional reactions were shown most frequently by the adolescent group (table 2.10).

Table 2.10. Proportion of 'normally affectionate', 'over-affectionate', 'affectionless' and 'inconsistent' children

	Normally affectionate		Over-affectionate		Affectionless		Inconsistent	
	N	%	N	%	N	%	N	%
8-year-olds N = 50	20	40	22	44	3	6	5	10
11-year-olds N = 50	19	38	24	48	3	6	4	8
14-year-olds N = 42	13	31	13	31	6	14	10	24
Total N = 142	52	37	59	42	12	8	19	13

c. *Social development*

The mean S.Q. of each age group was near or just slightly above the mean for the ordinary population. A comparison* between social and intellectual development showed that almost half the children were accelerated socially, while the degree of retardation was negligible (table 2.11). It has been suggested (Dunsdon, 1947; Pringle, 1950) that while external demands may lead to precocity in social development, this is often achieved at some cost, indicated by emotional disturbance, including delinquent manifestations. To test this hypothesis, each age group was divided into two groups: children whose S.Q.s were above their I.Q.s and those whose S.Q.s and I.Q.s were equal. Similarly, a twofold classification, based on the results

* The comparisons between I.Q.s and S.Q.s were based on standard scores.

from the Bristol Social Adjustment Guides, was made into stable
children and those who were either unsettled or maladjusted. The
incidence of unsettledness and maladjustment in the total sample

**Table 2.11. Distribution of social quotients and incidence of acceleration
and retardation**

	Mean	Sigma	Acceleration		Retardation	
			N	%	N	%
8-year-olds						
N = 50	102·08	13·63	30	60	—	—
11-year-olds						
N = 50	100·66	15·28	12	24	2	4
14-year-olds						
N = 42	104·67	6·78	27	64	—	—
Total						
N = 142	102·34	12·72	69	48·5	2	1·4

was higher among the socially accelerated children than among
those whose S.Q.s and I.Q.s were closely similar (table 2.12).
Though not statistically significant (C.R. = 1·35 for d.f. of 138), the
trend was in the expected direction.

**Table 2.12. Incidence of unsettled or maladjusted behaviour among
children whose S.Q.s are above their I.Q.s and those whose S.Q.s and
I.Q.s are similar ***

		Unsettled or maladjusted		Stable	
		N	%	N	%
8-year-olds	N = 50				
S.Q. > I.Q.	N = 30	20	67	10	33
S.Q. = I.Q.	N = 20	11	55	9	45
11-year-olds	N = 48 *				
S.Q. > I.Q.	N = 12	7	58	5	42
S.Q. = I.Q.	N = 36	21	58	15	42
14-year-olds	N = 42				
S.Q. > I.Q.	N = 27	19	70	8	30
S.Q. = I.Q.	N = 15	8	53	7	47
Total	N = 140				
S.Q. > I.Q.	N = 69	46	67	23	33
S.Q. = I.Q.	N = 71	40	56	31	44

* Only two children had social quotients significantly below their intelligence
quotients and they were excluded from this table.

Age and sex differences. The differences between the means of the age groups were not significant. However, the mean of the 11-year-olds was the lowest and the incidence of acceleration compared with intellectual development was also least in this group (table 2.11). Girls received slightly higher scores than boys except in the 14-year-old group, but none of the differences was significant.

Differences according to the three criteria of deprivation. Regarding the age at the first separation, 'early entrants' showed consistently lower mean scores but the differences were not significant. When the children were regrouped according to the length of institutional residence, no differences in mean quotients were found.

When both these variables were considered simultaneously, again no significant differences were found. Lastly, regarding severity of deprivation, the mean quotients for the 'severely deprived' were lower than those of the 'deprived' which in turn fell below those of the 'mildly deprived' children. The trend in the age groups was similar. However, only the differences between the mean S.Q.s of the 8-year-old 'severely deprived' and 'mildly deprived' and between the 'deprived' and 'mildly deprived' were statistically significant (beyond the 1 per cent level).

Discussion of the findings

a. *Intelligence*

During the group testing, many children looked worried, found it difficult to follow directions and quickly lost interest. The high incidence of unsettledness and maladjustment and the craving for individual attention shown by many, may partly account for these reactions together with some anxiety aroused by the fact that 'home' children were singled out for testing; moreover, it was their first contact with the investigators. Such unfavourable attitudes could be expected to lead to an underestimate of the children's ability. That this was so, is suggested by the findings of the individual test on which higher mean quotients were obtained by each age group.

The marked preponderance of dull children is likely to be due to the effects of both environmental and constitutional factors. The great majority of deprived children come from families where educational and cultural standards are low. The fathers of most of the children were described as unskilled labourers and mothers who worked, followed routine occupations such as domestic service. Thus, it is unlikely that during the preschool years the children were provided with the stimulation and experiences necessary for the full development of their intellectual potentialities. In addition, the low standards and socio-economic difficulties of the homes were in many instances due to mental dullness and the instability of one or both parents; thus one would expect a larger than normal proportion of children to be handicapped by poor mental endowment. It may well be that similar findings would be obtained for children living in their own homes but in equally impoverished circumstances—impoverished culturally, socially and emotionally. As no information was gathered on this point, it is impossible to say to what extent, if any, the higher than normal incidence of dullness was due to the effects of deprivation.

Age and sex differences. The 11-year-olds were relatively superior not only in intelligence but in most of the other aspects studied. It may be that our group of 11-year-olds happened to be more mature for its age than the other two groups. On the other hand, it may be that children are more capable of accepting separation from their parents and of adjusting to a new environment without undue ill effects at this age than when they are younger or at the adolescent stage. However, further investigations with larger numbers would be required to test the validity of this hypothesis.

The fact that the boys received higher mean intelligence quotients than the girls may be due to the girls' sample being a less representative one (for reasons mentioned earlier). This hypothesis is supported by the fact that only the difference between the 14-year-olds was statistically significant and it is in this age group that the discrepancy between the number of boys and girls is greatest. It is worth noting that Wechsler found the reverse: at almost every age level, the mean quotients of girls were superior to those of boys, but again not significantly so.

Differences according to the three criteria of deprivation. There is no evidence in our data for the theory that early maternal deprivation leads to mental subnormality. Our results do, however, support the hypothesis that intellectual backwardness is more marked in children who have been separated from their mothers for the first time at an early age. But it could be argued that the duller and the more unstable the parents, the more likely it is that their child, or children, is removed from home at an early age. Thus the lower ability of our 'early entrants' could be due, partly or entirely, to constitutional inferiority.

It is difficult to see, according to either explanatory theory, why length of institutionalisation has not resulted in differences of ability. It is usually considered that the longer separation lasts, the more harmful its effects; similarly, one would expect that the duller and the more unstable the parents, the more likely it is that their children will remain in care for a long time. Perhaps some pointers may be found in the fact that among the 'late entrants', the 'long stay' children obtained higher mean intelligence quotients than the 'short stays'. This suggests that if institutionalisation takes place after the age of five years, the longer it lasts the higher a child's tested intelligence. It may be that older children have developed sufficient stability and emotional maturity to adjust themselves to a different way of life without undue effect on their testable intelligence; while the inevitable disturbance caused by removal from home, is reflected in the lowered scores of the 'short stays' who have not yet had time to adjust or readjust themselves to the new circumstances.

Rises in I.Q. points after a period of institutionalisation have been reported in studies dealing with the effects of environmental influences upon the constancy of the I.Q. (Lithawer and Klineberg, 1933; Reymert, 1940; Clarke and Clarke, 1954). These findings have been criticised on the grounds that the children had not had time to adjust to the new environment when they were first tested. Thus apparent subsequent gains could have been due mainly to a more adequate test performance resulting from the children's familiarity with and acceptance of their new circumstances, rather than to a real improvement in general intelligence (Woodworth, 1941). On the basis of this argument it may be that if our 'short stay' children had been retested at a later stage, they would have received higher scores; these might have resulted in differential mean quotients for the criterion of length of institutionalisation (with the 'short stays' being the superior group).

Our results support the hypothesis that intellectual backwardness is more marked where the child has had no contact with his family. We found close agreement between different observers: school teachers and the staff of the Children's Homes made more adverse comments regarding the general alertness and responsiveness of those children who, we subsequently discovered, had no contact with their parents or other relatives. Our own observations, made prior to obtaining this information, were along similar lines.

b. *Emotional development*

There was considerable agreement between the findings from Raven's Projection Test, the Bristol Social Adjustment Guides—completed by both teachers and house parents—and the clinical observations, made during the interview. The hypothesis that deprived tend to differ from ordinary children in many of their personal attitudes and reactions, is supported by all these data. Both quantitative and qualitative differences were found. Symptoms of maladjustment were shown by a considerable proportion of the children and the qualitative differences indicate that—at least on the conscious level—maladjustment is to a large extent due to separation from their families rather than to the effects of institutional life.

Raven's Controlled Projection Test. The trend of the 'unique responses' strongly suggests that many of the children's anxieties and worries are due to separation from their parents. Similarly, the idealised picture of the mother is likely to arise from an unresolved, unconscious conflict about her responsibility for the separation. To accept the objective fact of her rejection or desertion may increase a deprived child's sense of insecurity and worthlessness to an intolerable degree; to accept his own misbehaviour as the main cause of her denial of love and of the separation, may increase guilt feelings to an intolerable degree. Thus the phantasy of an ideal, loving mother may be both a safety valve and a wishfulfilling day-dream.

The Bristol Social Adjustment Guides. The majority of children were classed as being either 'unsettled' or 'maladjusted', both by their class teachers and by the Home staff. This confirms the hypothesis that deprived tend to show a more serious degree of emotional disturbance than ordinary children. The extent to which this is due to the effects of separation or to constitutional factors of instability cannot be determined from our data. However, the nature of the symptoms suggests a direct link with separation experiences and with a lack of individual adult attention. Furthermore, they are similar to the syndromes of behaviour disturbance described by other investigators who consider them to be linked with or caused by deprivation, particularly maternal deprivation (Lowrey, 1940; Goldfarb, 1945; Bowlby, 1951; Bourne, 1955).

Clinical observations. Many children showed changes in attitude and emotional control during the administration of the personality test as well as during the informal interview. From the content of their

c

projection responses it appears that, in the majority of cases, unhappiness and conflict regarding their homes and parents are unresolved and near the surface; they can thus be fairly easily aroused and then disturb the children's self-control and poise, which may be more apparent than real. Partly, too, it may be due to the fact that in an institution opportunities for a fairly unstructured, face-to-face relationship with one adult do not often arise. This situation may also be reminiscent of parent-child contacts and thus arouse feelings of anxiety, guilt and ambivalence.

Attitudes towards other people. The three categories of emotional responses which were distinguished on the basis of all the data, are similar to those reported by Bowlby and others (Bowlby and Ainsworth, 1956). It seems that the majority of children in this study have failed to learn 'the art of living with other people; i.e. to enjoy them, to identify with them and to appreciate their friendship and affection' (Spence, 1946). This is perhaps the most difficult problem which deprived children present to those looking after them. Both teachers and house parents made numerous comments to this effect. On the other hand, more than a third of our sample showed no symptoms of maladjustment or deprivation, reacting emotionally in ways very similar to those of ordinary children of their own age.

c. *Social development*

This is the only developmental aspect where the deprived equalled ordinary children. In fact, a large proportion in each age group was accelerated in social as compared with intellectual development. In a study of normal 8-year-olds the incidence of acceleration found was 17·5 per cent, which is considerably lower than that in our 8-year-old group (Pringle, 1951). No comparative data are available for the other two age groups.

While according to Doll (1937) social maturity depends mainly upon native potentiality, there is evidence to suggest that where environmental demands for social independence are very pressing, there is a tendency for children to become rather precocious socially. An apparently satisfactory level of social competence may also be found, and partly be due to the effects of living in an institutional environment (Goldfarb, 1945 and 1947; Dunsdon 1947; Pringle, 1950). While our data showed trends in the expected direction, they were not statistically significant. Whether and to what extent the relatively high level of social competence in our sample was produced by the external control of an institutional routine, cannot be determined from our data. To judge from some observations made by one of the writers while living among the children for several weeks, this may be so: regressive and infantile behaviour was frequently shown, especially at times of crisis. There is also the clinical evidence of such behaviour during the interviews.

Age and sex differences. Doll reports a slight negative correlation between intellectual level and social maturity (Doll, 1935 and 1953). The same pattern was found among our deprived children, the relatively brightest age group (11-year-olds) having the lowest mean S.Q. and the lowest incidence of social acceleration. Similarly, the girls, who are rather duller than the boys, received slightly higher mean scores.

Differences according to the three criteria of deprivation. Neither the age at the first separation, nor the total length of institutionalisation, nor the severity of deprivation seem to have a significant influence on the achievement of social competence as measured by the Vineland Scale. Thus our findings suggest that institutionalisation produces a level of social development similar to that found in impoverished or overdemanding homes. That child-rearing practices and expected standards of behaviour are similar in institutions and in such homes, is highly unlikely. All we can conclude from our data is that the overall effect on social competence is similar. Only further research can determine whether there are any subtle differences, such as differential effects on the various aspects of social development or a difference in the permanency of social precocity.

Summary
This investigation had two main aims: first, to study the development and achievement of deprived children comparing them with those of the ordinary school population. In addition to the aspects reported here, language development and reading attainment were assessed. The second aim was to test three hypotheses regarding the results of deprivation: that its ill-effects are more marked: (1) where the first separation from the mother occurred at an early age; (2) where separation has lasted for a long time; and (3) where deprivation has been complete. Altogether 188 institutionalised children were studied at three age levels, 8, 11 and 14 years of age.

The majority of this sample of deprived children was of average ability. However, the proportion of dull children was considerably higher, and that of bright considerably lower, than among school children generally. The incidence of emotional maladjustment was high, supporting previous research evidence. Both quantitative and qualitative differences were found between the institutionalised and ordinary children. Only with regard to social development did the achievement of the deprived equal that of the children living with their own family. However, there is evidence to suggest that an apparently satisfactory level of social competence may be produced by the very circumstance of living in an institutional environment. Regarding the three criteria of deprivation, it was found that early first separation from the mother resulted in significantly greater ill-effects on the children's development. Similarly, complete deprivation had a significantly deleterious effect. On the other hand, sheer length of institutionalisation did not appear to be of great importance.

References

ALDRICH, C. A., SUNG, C. and KNOP, C. (1945a) 'The crying of newly born babies, I: The community phase', *Journal of Pediatrics*, **26**, 313–26.

ALDRICH, C. A., SUNG, C. and KNOP, C. (1945b) 'The crying of newly born babies, II: The individual phase', *Journal of Pediatrics*, **27**, 89–96.

ALDRICH, C. A., SUNG, C. and KNOP, C. (1945c) 'The crying of newly born babies, III: The early period at home', *Journal of Pediatrics*, **27**, 428–35.

ALDRICH, C. A., NORVAL, M., KNOP, C. and VENEGAS, F. (1946) 'The crying of newly born babies, IV. A follow-up study after additional nursing care had been provided', *Journal of Pediatrics*, **28**, 665–70.

ALLEN, F. H., TIBOUT, N. H. C. and FREUD, A. 'Aggression in relation to emotional development, normal and pathological', in International Congress on Mental Health, 1948, *Proceedings of the International Conference on Child Psychiatry*, **2**, 4–23.

BODMAN, F., MACKINLEY, M. and SYKES, K. (1950) 'The social adaptation of institution children', *Lancet*, **258**, 173–6.

BOURNE, H. (1955) 'Protophrenia; A study of perverted rearing and mental dwarfism', *Lancet*, **269**, 1156–63.

BOWLBY, J. (1946) *Forty-four juvenile thieves; their characters and home life*. London, Baillère, Tindall & Cox.

BOWLBY, J. (1951) 'Maternal care and mental health', *Monograph Series of the World Health Organisation*, No. 2, Geneva.

BOWLBY, J., AINSWORTH, M. D., BOSTON, M. and ROSEN-BLUTH, D. (1956) 'The effects of mother–child separation; a follow-up study', *British Journal of Medical Psychology*, **29**, 211–44.

BOWLEY, A. H. (1947) *The psychology of the unwanted child*. Edinburgh, Livingstone.

BOWLEY, A. H. (1951) *Child care: a handbook on the care of the child deprived of normal home life*. Edinburgh, Livingstone.

BROSSE, T. (1950) *Homeless children; report of the proceedings of the conference of directors of children's communities, Trogen, Switzerland*. Paris, Unesco.

BURLINGHAM, D. and FREUD, A. (1954) *Infants without families; the case for and against residential nurseries*. London, Allen & Unwin.

BURT, SIR C. (1944) *The young delinquent*. 4th edn. London, University of London Press.

BURT, SIR C. (1946) *The backward child*. 2nd edn. London, University of London Press.

CALIFORNIA STATE BOARD OF CONTROL (1918) *Intelligence of orphan children and unwed mothers in Californian charitable institutions*. Sacramento, California.

CAREY-TREFZER, C. J. (1949) 'The results of a clinical study of war-damaged children who attended the Child Guidance Clinic, Hospital for Sick Children, Great Ormond Street, London', *Journal of Mental Science*, **95**, 535–59.

CLARKE, A. D. B. and CLARKE, A. M. (1954) 'Cognitive changes in the feeble-minded', *British Journal of Psychology*, **45**, 173–9.

CRISSEY, O. L. (1937) 'Mental development as related to institutional residence and educational achievement', *University of Iowa Studies*, **13**, No. 1.

DOLL, E. A. (1937) 'The inheritance of social competence', *Journal of Heredity*, **28**, 152–65.

DOLL, E. A. (1935) 'A genetic scale of social maturity', *American Journal of Orthopsychiatry*, **5**, 180–90.

DOLL, E. A. (1953) *The measurement of social competence; a manual for the Vineland Social Maturity Scale*. Minneapolis, Educational Test Bureau.

DUNSDON, M. I. (1947) 'Notes on the intellectual and social capacities of a group of young delinquents', *British Journal of Psychology*, **38**, 62–6.

EDMISTONE, R. W. and BAIRD, F. (1949) 'Adjustment of orphanage children', *Journal of Educational Psychology*, **40**, 482–88.

FERNALD, G. M. (1918) *The mental examination of 75 children at the "Y" House*. Sacramento, California State Board of Control.

FITZGERALD, O. W. S. (1948) 'Love deprivation and hysterical personality', *Journal of Mental Science*, **94**, 701–17.

FORD, D. (1955) *The deprived child and the community*. London, Constable.

GINDL, I. and HETZER, H. (1937) 'Unangemessenheit der Anstalt als Lebensraum für das Kleinkind', *Zeitschrift für Angewandte Psychologie und Psychologische Sammelforschung*, **52**, 310–58. Leipzig.

GOBB, M. (1922) 'The mentality of dependent children', *Journal of Delinquency*, **7**, 132–40.

GOLDFARB, W. (1943) 'Infant rearing and problem behavior', *American Journal of Orthopsychiatry*, **13**, 249–65.

GOLDFARB, W. (1943) 'The effects of early institutional care on adolescent personality (Graphic Rorschach data)', *Child Development*, **14**, 213–23.

GOLDFARB, W. (1945) 'The effect of psychological deprivation in infancy and subsequent stimulation', *American Journal of Psychiatry*, **102**, 18–33.

GOLDFARB, W. (1947) 'Variations in adolescent adjustment in institutionally reared children', *American Journal of Orthopsychiatry*, **17**, 449–57.

HOME OFFICE (1946) *Report of the Care of Children Committee*. Cmd. 6922. London, H.M.S.O. (Curtis report.)

LAWRENCE, E. M. (1929) 'An investigation into the relation between intelligence and inheritance', Ph.D. Thesis, London University.

LEAGUE OF NATIONS. Advisory Committee on Social Questions (1938) *Enquiry into measures of rehabilitation of prostitutes. Part 1. Prostitutes; their early lives*. Geneva.

LEVY, R. J. (1947) 'Effects of institutional versus boarding home care on a group of infants', *Journal of Personality*, **15**, 233–41.

LEWIS, H. (1954) *Deprived children; the Mersham experiment. A social and clinical study*. London, Oxford University Press.

LINDQUIST, E. F. (1940) *Statistical analysis in educational research*. Boston, Mass., Houghton Mifflin.

LITHAUER, D. B. and KLINEBERG, O. (1933) 'A study of the variation in I.Q. of a group of dependent children in institutions and foster-homes', *Journal of Genetic Psychology*, **42**, 236–42.

LOWRY, L. G. (1940) 'Personality distortion and early institutional care', *American Journal of Orthopsychiatry*, **10**, 576–85.

34

PRINGLE, M. L. KELLMER (1951) 'Social maturity and social competence', *Educational Research*, **3**, 183–95.

PRINGLE, M. L. KELLMER (1950) 'A study of Doll's Social Maturity Scale.' Ph.D. Thesis, London University.

REYMERT, M. L. and HINTON, R. T. (1940) 'The effect of a change to a relatively superior environment upon the I.Q.s of one hundred children'. *National Society for the Study of Education;* Yearbook **39**, part II, 255–68. Bloomington, Ind., Public School Publishing Co.

RHEINGOLD, H. L. (1943) 'Mental and social development of infants in relation to the number of other infants in the boarding home', *American Journal of Orthopsychiatry*, **13**, 41–4.

SIMONSEN, K. M. (1947) *Examination of children from children's homes and day-nurseries by the Bühler-Hetzer developmental tests.* Copenhagen, Busck.

SPENCE, J. C. (1946) *The purpose of the family: a guide to the care of children.* (National Children's Home. Convocation lecture.) London, N.C.H.

SPITZ, R. A. (1945) 'Hospitalism; an inquiry into the genesis of psychiatric conditions in early childhood', in *Psycho-analytic study of the child*, **1**, 53–74. London, Imago Publishing Co.

SPITZ, R. A. and WOLF, K. M. (1946) 'Anaclitic depression; an inquiry into the genesis of psychiatric conditions in early childhood', in *Psycho-analytic study of the child*, **2**, 313–42. London, Imago Publishing Co.

STOTT, D. H. (1956) *Unsettled children and their families.* London, University of London Press.

TERMAN, L. M. and WAGNER, D. (1918) 'Intelligence quotients of 68 children in a Californian orphanage', *Journal of Delinquency*, **3**, 115–21.

THEIS, S. VAN SENDEN (1924) *How foster children turn out; a study and critical analysis of children 910 who were placed in foster homes by the State Charities Aid Association and who are now eighteen years of age or over.* (Publication no. 165.) New York, State Charities Aid Association.

UNITED NATIONS: Department of Social Affairs (1952) *Children deprived of a normal home life.* New York.

WOODWORTH, R. S. (1941) *Heredity and environment; a critical survey of recently published material on twins and foster-children.* Social Science Research Council Bulletin, no. 47.

3. Language development and reading attainment of deprived children*

with Victoria Bossio

Previous studies

Some challenging results have been reported in recent studies of language development in children brought up in hospitals and institutions. How early the effects of environmental deprivation are manifested is shown in an investigation of newborn infants (Gatewood and Weiss, 1930). Given various stimuli such as light, sound, smells and temperature, neonates vocalised much more than in situations where they were 'allowed to lie naturally without any external stimulation'.

Brodbeck and Irwin (1946) compared the frequency and variety of phonemes uttered by a group of orphanage children with those heard among a group living with their own families. Statistically significant differences were found in favour of the latter. Differences were evident as early as the first two months, and the discrepancies between the two groups became more marked by the fourth to sixth months of life. The orphanage groups were markedly below children from the homes of unskilled labourers, even in the first six months, although feeble-minded children were excluded from the institutionalised groups. Goldfarb, in a comparative study of institutionalised and fostered children, investigated speech sounds, intelligibility of speech and level of language organisation at three age levels: in early infancy, at 6 to 8 years and in adolescence (Goldfarb, 1943a, 1943b and 1945). At each age level the institution children showed marked language deficiency in all the areas measured. Freud and Burlingham reported retardation in language development during the second year of life (Burlingham and Freud, 1954).

Confirming the finding that infants brought up in institutional environments showed severe developmental retardation, particularly

* First published in *Vita Humana*, 1958, 1, 3/4, 142–170.

in linguistic ability, Roudinesco and Appell (1950) introduced a change of regime; this was designed to provide the children with more individual attention from the nurses and other attendants. A retest after a period of 18 months showed considerable gains in motor, social and adaptive behaviour, but the least improvement was brought about in language development. Williams and McFarland applied a vocabulary test to sixty-four orphanage children and compared them with a large group of children living in their own homes (Williams and McFarland, 1937). The latter were markedly superior in vocabulary scores, much more so than could be accounted for on the basis of I.Q. or socio-economic level. Moore, using the same vocabulary test, analysed two-minute samples of oral language of orphanage and non-orphanage children (Moore, 1947). Again, the former group was markedly retarded. Holding C.A. and M.A. constant, analysis of variance showed a statistically significant difference attributable to environmental influences. Gesell and Amatruda, describing the dynamics of environmental deprivation, stress that it operates by 'attrition' as well as by 'impoverishment' and that the results tend to be cumulative (Gesell and Amatruda, 1947). The monotony and impersonal character of an institutional environment appear to reduce early vocalization in contrast to the stimulation provided by the variety and warmth of normal family life.

Milner (1951) selected contrasting groups of 6- to 7-year-old Negro children on the basis of their 'Language I.Q.' obtained with the California Test of Mental Maturity. Patterns of parent–child interaction were studied for children who received high and low scores respectively on a number of language criteria. The samples were drawn from widely divergent socio-economic levels and marked differences were found in the patterns of family life between those receiving high and low scores. In the homes of the high-scoring children there was much more conversation at meal times, in which the children participated actively; similarly, they received more overt expressions of affection from significant adults in the home than those who scored low on the language tests. These factors tended to be concomitant with variations in socio-economic status which has frequently been shown to be related to language development. Milner suggests that it is parental attitudes towards children and patterns of family life which are the really significant factors for language development and that these happen to vary also with socio-economic class.

That children in orphanages and institutions are seriously retarded in vocabulary and language development has been shown in a number of other investigations (Little and Williams, 1937; Skeels, Updegraff, Wellman and Williams, 1938; Flemming, 1942). Although such children undoubtedly come from lower socio-economic levels, are somewhat below average ability and probably have restricted environmental experiences, their retardation appears to be so marked that it is necessary to look for additional causative factors. Even when matched with ordinary children for mental age, the deprived are much more retarded in vocabulary (Little and Williams, 1937). If association with adults is a factor facilitating language development (McCarthy, 1930; Smith, 1935), it is understandable why institutionalised children show marked retardation; they associate much more with other children, especially contemporaries, and have far fewer individual contacts with, and attention from, adults.

Dawe (1942) planned a training scheme with a group of orphanage children aiming at increasing their understanding and use of language symbols. Matching eleven pairs of children for age, sex, school group, M.A., I.Q., and score on the Smith–Williams vocabulary test, one member of each pair received the training and the other served as a control. About fifty hours of individual and small-group teaching was given, providing the kind of enriching experiences children receive as a matter of course in good, educated homes. The experimental group showed significant gains (at the 1 per cent level of confidence) in most language measures; moreover, these language gains were reflected in an increase in average I.Q. from 80·6 to 94·8 as a result of the fifty hour training which was spread over a period of three months. During the same period the control group decreased slightly from a mean I.Q. of 81·5 to a mean of 79·5. The implications of these findings could be quite far-reaching not only for deprived children, but for education generally, if they can be substantiated with larger groups.

There are comparatively few investigations dealing with the educational attainments of institutionalised children. Feinberg (1954) studied 138 children aged 9 to 15 years who lived in Homes and compared their scholastic levels on the Stanford Achievement Test with those of a control group of foster home children. The former were found to be 0·1 to 0·8 grades below the controls and were even more behind in class placement in each of the subjects tested except

38

in literature. The relative superiority in literature was interpreted as possibly being due to the deprived child's tendency to immerse himself in books, perhaps to compensate for his emotionally and socially rather restricted life. There was less variability in achievement among the deprived compared with the controls. The investigator considered that these differences were due to environmental stimulation since the two groups had been carefully matched for age, socioeconomic background and mental age. In a foster home the child is motivated by factors similar to those operating in a normal family, namely a desire to please and in return to be valued by the foster parents. Though the child who grows up in an institution also desires to win adult approval, prevailing staffing conditions tend to render nugatory the force of this motivating power. Similar results were reported in another study (Smith *et al.*, 1935) which also employed the Stanford Achievement Test for the assessment of educational levels. A group of orphanage children were found to be seriously retarded in all school subjects when compared with ordinary pupils. Length of institutionalisation did not seem to result in significantly different levels of scholastic attainment.

Lewis (1954) in her study of 500 cases found an extremely high incidence of educational retardation; in reading 80 per cent and in arithmetic 90 per cent of the children received scores below their mental ages in these subjects. This she ascribed to the culturally unfavourable home backgrounds and to the high incidence of emotional disturbance in her sample. However, as noted previously*, Lewis's cases cannot be considered representative of deprived children. A rather different conclusion was reached by Castle (1954) who argues that the deprived children studied by her failed to adjust satisfactorily at school and to make adequate educational progress, for three main reasons: first, feeling different from other children, they 'ganged together' thus becoming an 'out-group'; secondly, tensions and strains in the Homes, particularly on the part of the house-mothers, had an adverse effect on them; thirdly, being more difficult and educationally retarded than ordinary children, they tended to receive less sympathetic and understanding treatment at school.

There have been some investigations into the relationship between linguistic maturity and reading attainment. Though not directly concerned with deprived children, they are of some relevance to our own findings. Shire (1945) considered that several measures of lan-

* Chapter One, p. 9.

guage development, when combined, were helpful in predicting success in first-grade reading (6-year-olds). Children who did not make satisfactory progress also showed various linguistic immaturities. Yedinack (1949) concludes from a study of 7- to 8-year-old poor readers that there is a tendency for such children to have also an inferior speaking vocabulary. It seems that by the time school age is reached language disabilities begin to exert a more widespread influence because by then the child is expected to acquire the secondary forms of language, namely reading and writing.

Adjustment to school life represents a further stage in the emotional weaning of the child from the mother. McCarthy, when treating fifty cases of language disorder, identified two behaviour syndromes usually found among poor readers (McCarthy, 1947, 1952a and b). One group manifested an aggressive personality syndrome, the other a submissive syndrome of infantile behaviour. In tracing the aggressive syndrome, McCarthy found that it was actually associated with marked parental rejection of the child, harsh disciplinary methods and unfavourable comparisons with siblings. It is difficult, she considered, to make an aggressive child sufficiently secure so that learning can progress satisfactorily, since often there is no basic parental love on which to build. Sobel reports that work with children having educational difficulties invariably reveals 'related if not causative emotional factors', the educational difficulties being often secondary to early warping experiences with significant adults (Sobel, 1948). This ties in well with the study by Milner (1951) on the effect of the environment.

With regard to sex differences, the majority of the numerous studies into backwardness in language development and reading attainment have shown a greater incidence among boys than girls (Monroe, 1932; Little and Williams, 1937; MacMeeken, 1939; Moore, 1939; Durrell, 1940; Stalnaker, 1941; Schonell, 1942; Stroud and Lindquist, 1942; Fernald, 1943; Samuels, 1943; Hallgren, 1950; Min. of Education, 1950; City of Leeds Educ. Committee, 1953 and Middlesbrough Head Teachers' Association 1953). However, McCarthy (1953) and Vernon (1957) consider that in the light of present evidence there is little ground for postulating inherent differences between the sexes in their ability to acquire language skills. They consider that there are various environmental influences in the home and at school, as well as differences in temperament, which result in this differential incidence of backwardness among boys and girls.

Test and other Measuring Devices Used

Because of the different ages, certain tests could not be used with all the children. Where this was the case, the age group is indicated in brackets after the test. The results from the following tests and assessments will be discussed:

a. *Group test*
Schonell Silent Reading Test, Form B.

b. *Individual tests and assessments*
1. Mill Hill Vocabulary Scale, Oral Definition Form.
2. Watts English Scale and Vocabulary Test for Young Children (8-year-olds).
3. Wechsler Intelligence Scale for Children.
4. Schonell Graded Reading Vocabulary Test (8- and 11-year-olds).

Results

a. *Language development*
1. *Mill Hill Vocabulary Scale, Oral Definition Form.* The mean Language Quotient* of each age group was well below the average range and

Table 3.1. Distribution of Language Quotients and incidence of backwardness

	Mean	Sigma	L.Q. below 85 N	%
8-year-olds N = 50	67·08	12·14	41	82
11-year-olds N = 50	79·19	19·19	32	64
14-year-olds N = 42	79·12	11·82	28	67
Total N = 142	74·88	15·91	101	71

in fact more than two-thirds of the total sample had Language Quotients below 85 (table 3.1).

In some cases the children's already limited capacity for self-

* The term Language Quotient has been used instead of Verbal Quotient to avoid confusion with the WISC Verbal Quotient.

expression may have been further interfered with by anxieties and preoccupations regarding their parents. The following examples may serve as illustrations: an 11-year-old boy replied to item 6, set A (What does the word 'unhappy' mean?): 'Worry.' (Q.)* 'About my mother and father.' (Q.) 'They are getting a divorce.' A 7½-year-old girl replied to item 4, set B (What does 'afraid' mean?): 'That my mother will not come on Saturday.' (Q.) 'She promised she would come.' A 10½-year-old girl answered the same item by saying: 'As when I was crying in bed last night.' (Q.) 'Because Mummy said she cannot take me home with her and she had promised she would.' Such emotionally charged, free-association type of responses occurred frequently, especially among the two younger age groups. In some cases the child's emotional reaction was so intense that further prompting might have led to increased upset and possibly tears; thus, even when permitted, prompting could not always be used. In other cases the child became so engrossed in his own thoughts that prompting proved ineffective.

Age and sex differences. The 8-year-olds were relatively speaking the most backward group (table 3.1). The differences between this group and the other two age groups were both significant at the 1 per cent level. While the means of the 11- and 14-year-olds were almost identical, a greater dispersion of scores was found among the 11-year-olds, who contained the relatively largest number of average and bright children.

Girls obtained a lower Language Quotient than boys at each age level, and for the total sample this trend was significant at the 5 per cent level of confidence (table 3.2).

Differences according to the three criteria of deprivation. Regarding the age at the first separation, the 'early-entrants' received consistently lower mean scores in all three age groups (table 3.3).

All the differences—except for the 14-year-olds—were significant at the 5 per cent level. On the other hand, when the children were regrouped according to the length of institutional residence no significant differences were found.

When both these variables were considered simultaneously, the mean quotients for the sub-categories 'early entrants'/'short stay' and 'early entrants'/'long stay' were lower than the mean quotients for the 'late entrants'/'short stay' and the 'late entrants'/'long stay'.

* (Q.) is used as an abbreviation for: The examiner asked a question to elicit a further response.

Table 3.2. Sex differences in Language Quotients

	Boys	Girls	t and F ratios
8-year-olds			
Mean	68·87	65·42	t = 1·00
Sigma	13·86	10·30	d.f. = 48
11-year-olds			
Mean	81·07	76·83	t = 0·77
Sigma	19·01	19·57	d.f. = 48
14-year-olds			
Mean	80·03	77·08	t = 0·74
Sigma	15·07	8·47	d.f. = 40
Total			
Mean	77·04	72·40	F = 92·51 *
Sigma	16·30	15·11	d.f. = 1 and 2

* Statistically significant beyond the 5 per cent level.

Table 3.3. Differences in Language Quotients according to the age at first separation

	Early entrants	Late entrants	t and F ratios
8-year-olds			
Mean	63·97	72·61	t = 2·61 *
Sigma	9·85	14·05	d.f. = 48
11-year-olds			
Mean	73·04	83·89	t = 2·06 *
Sigma	19·36	17·98	d.f. = 48
14-year-olds			
Mean	74·86	81·25	t = 1·69
Sigma	10·28	12·13	d.f. = 40
Total			
Mean	69·15	80·15	F = 45·17 *
Sigma	14·40	15·48	d.f. = 1 and 2

* Statistically significant beyond the 5 per cent level.

For the total sample these differences proved to be significant at the 5 per cent and 1 per cent level respectively (table 3.4).

Lastly, regarding the severity of deprivation, the mean quotients of the 'severely deprived' were lower than those of the 'deprived', which in turn were below those of the 'mildly deprived' children in each age group. For the total sample the difference between the means of the 'severely deprived' and 'deprived' and between the 'severely deprived' and 'mildly deprived' proved significant beyond the 1 per cent level; for the 8-year-olds these differences were significant at the 5 per cent level (table 3.5).

Table 3.4. Differences in Language Quotients according to the age of first separation and the length of institutional residence

	Early-long	Early-short	Late-long	Late-short	F ratio
8-year-olds					
Mean	63·20	65·25	73·11	72·11	2·17
Sigma	9·19	11·18	15·30	13·59	d.f. = 3 and 46
11-year-olds					
Mean	74·36	70·75	83·63	84·06	1·40
Sigma	21·67	15·58	21·13	16·32	d.f. = 3 and 46
14-year-olds					
Mean	71·67	77·25	82·29	79·64	1·30
Sigma	5·67	12·56	12·92	11·20	d.f. = 3 and 38
Total					
Mean	68·37 †	70·25 *	80·46†	79·84 *	13·14
Sigma	15·16	13·43	16·38	14·75	d.f. = 3 and 6

* Statistically significant beyond the 5 per cent level.
† Statistically significant beyond the 1 per cent level.

Table 3.5. Differences in Language Quotient according to the severity of deprivation

	Severely deprived	Deprived	Mildly deprived	F ratio
8-year-olds				
Mean	59·75	67·25	71·78	3·96 *
Sigma	4·86	13·20	12·39	d.f. = 2 and 47
11-year-olds				
Mean	69·64	78·06	84·39	2·35
Sigma	19·23	15·77	20·19	d.f. = 2 and 47
14-year-olds				
Mean	74·00	77·29	84·60	3·02
Sigma	7·34	12·50	11·89	d.f. = 2 and 39
Total				
Mean	67·36	73·73	80·39	50·93†
Sigma	13·26	14·48	16·80	d.f. = 2 and 4

* Statistically significant beyond the 5 per cent level.
† Statistically significant beyond the 1 per cent level.

2. *Watts English Language Scale and Vocabulary Test for Young Children.* Since both these tests were suitable only for the 8-year-olds the data were not analysed for sex differences or for the three criteria of deprivation. However, a brief summary of the results is presented. The English Scale, consisting of thirty-six pictures, was designed to measure 'the progress of young children in mastering the basic varieties of the English sentence' (Watts, 1950). It covers the age range from 4 to 10 years. The mean language quotient obtained on

D

this test by our sample of 8-year-olds was 82·54 (sigma 10·0) showing them to be backward in this aspect of language development.

The Vocabulary Test consists of 100 questions, the replies to all of which, according to Watts (1950), 'should be known by an average child of 8½ years. The words required as answers occur among the 6,000 commonest English words.' Our group of 8-year-olds obtained a mean Language Quotient of 75·50 (sigma 12·63), again considerably below the average. The test is divided into twenty subcategories and failures occurred most frequently among the following: household articles, face and features, shopkeepers and cooking the dinner. For example, many children did not know the answer to the question: what do we call the man who brings the letters round or who sells sugar and tea, or the correct names for various articles of men's clothing. Many did not know the name for their nostrils, eyebrows and lashes or the name for a safety pin, a razor blade or the pavement.

3. *Wechsler Intelligence Scale for Children.* It was thought that further light might be shed on our sample's facility to use language by comparing their results on the verbal and performance scale of this test. As can be seen from table 3.6 each age group obtained higher mean quotients on the Performance Scale of the WISC. All the differences between the mean verbal and the performance quotients were statistically significant at the 5 per cent or 1 per cent levels.

Age and sex differences. The highest mean quotients on both parts of the WISC were received by the 11-year-olds (table 3.6). However, only the differences in mean V.I.Q.s between this group and each of the other two age groups were significant at the 5 per cent level.

Girls tended to obtain lower mean quotients on the verbal and on the performance scale. None of the differences proved significant except that between the mean performance quotients of the 14-year-old boys and girls (significant beyond the 1 per cent level).

Differences according to the three criteria of deprivation. Regarding the age at the first separation, the 'early entrants' received consistently lower mean quotients on the verbal scale in all three age groups. All the differences—except for the 14-year-olds—were significant (table 3.7).

There were no significant differences or even consistent trends between the 'early' and 'late entrants' mean performance scale quotients. When the children were regrouped according to the

Table 3.6.   Distribution of intelligence quotients on the WISC Verbal and Performance Scales

	Verbal I.Q.		Perform. I.Q.		
	Mean	Sigma	Mean	Sigma	t ratios
8-year-olds N = 50	82·40	9·74	93·24	13·72	t = 4·55† d.f. = 98
11-year-olds N = 50	91·42	14·37	98·20	13·75	t = 2·42* d.f. = 98
14-year-olds N = 42	85·43	13·36	95·31	17·26	t = 2·98† d.f. = 82
Total N = 142	86·47	13·09	95·60	14·90	t = 4·40* d.f. = 182

* Statistically significant at the 5 per cent level.
† Statistically significant at the 1 per cent level.

Table 3.7.   Differences in WISC Verbal Scale Quotients according to the age of first separation

	Early entrants	Late entrants	t and F ratios
8-year-olds			
Mean	79·31	87·89	t = 3·28†
Sigma	6·63	11·97	d.f. = 48
11-year-olds			
Mean	87·00	94·89	t = 2·00*
Sigma	13·03	14·62	d.f. = 48
14-year-olds			
Mean	80·28	88·00	t = 1·82
Sigma	9·80	14·29	d.f. = 40
Total			
Mean	82·00	90·58	F = 10·26
Sigma	10·22	14·13	d.f. = 1 and 2

* Statistically significant beyond the 5 per cent level.
† Statistically significant beyond the 1 per cent level.

length of institutional residence, again no significant differences were found on either of the scales.

Considering age at first separation and length of institutional residence simultaneously, no significant differences were found on the performance scale. On the verbal scale however, the mean quotients for the subcategories 'early entrants'/'short stay' and 'early entrants'/'long stay' were lower than the mean quotients for

46

the 'late entrants'/'short stay' and the 'late entrants'/'long stay'. The differences proved to be significant for the total sample and for the 8-year-olds (table 3.8).

Table 3.8. Differences in WISC verbal quotients according to the age at first separation and the length of institutional residence

	Early-long	Early-short	Late-long	Late-short	F ratio
8-year-olds					
Mean	78·40	80·83	88·11	87·67	3·64*
Sigma	4·87	8·89	10·76	13·73	d.f. = 3 and 46
11-year-olds					
Mean	86·57	87·75	96·64	93·76	1·36
Sigma	12·77	14·33	18·12	12·37	d.f. = 3 and 46
14-year-olds					
Mean	79·17	81·13	86·29	90·64	1·33
Sigma	10·30	10·03	13·52	15·68	d.f. = 3 and 38
Total					
Mean	81·37	82·89	89·81	91·35	20·72†
Sigma	9·72	11·01	14·80	13·58	d.f. = 3 and 6

* Statistically significant beyond the 5 per cent level.
† Statistically significant beyond the 1 per cent level.

Lastly, regarding severity of deprivation, the mean verbal quotients of the 'severely deprived' were lower than those of the 'deprived' which in turn were below those of the 'mildly deprived'. For the total sample both these differences were significant at the 1 per cent level (table 3.9). Again no significant differences were found on the performance scale.

Table 3.9. Differences in WISC Verbal Scale Quotients according to the severity of deprivation

	Severely deprived	Deprived	Mildly deprived	F ratio
8-year-olds				
Mean	79·67	81·55	85·17	1·29
Sigma	5·77	11·54	9·42	d.f. = 2 and 47
11-year-olds				
Mean	86·18	92·44	93·22	0·94
Sigma	11·44	9·27	17·99	d.f. = 2 and 47
14-year-olds				
Mean	79·20	86·65	88·20	1·51
Sigma	9·90	14·04	14·01	d.f. = 2 and 39
Total				
Mean	81·70	86·47	89·28	18·03*
Sigma	9·51	12·42	14·80	d.f. = 2 and 4

* Statistically significant at the 1 per cent level.

b. *Reading attainment*

1. *Schonell Silent Reading Test, Form B.* The mean Reading Quotients of the total sample and of the 8- and 14-year-olds were well below the average range (table 3.10). For comparative purposes the

Table 3.10. Mean Reading Quotients, incidence of intellectual and reading backwardness (Quotients 85 and below) and of reading retardation (Ratios 85 and below)

Age group	R.Q. Mean	R.Q. Sigma	Intellectual backwardness N	Intellectual backwardness %	Reading backwardness N	Reading backwardness %	Reading retardation N	Reading retardation %
8-year-olds N = 50	78·06	14·52	18	36	36	72	22	44
11-year-olds N = 50	85·86	15·93	12	24	21	42	13	26
14-year-olds N = 42	75·78	14·50	15	36	31	74	22	52
Total N = 142	80·13	15·54	45	32	88	62	57	40

incidence of intellectual backwardness as well as backwardness and retardation in reading are shown on the same table. In each case the number and percentage of children with quotients below 85 is given. Thus there are approximately twice as many children backward in reading as in tested intelligence (WISC Full Scale).

Age and sex differences. The 11-year-olds had, relatively speaking, the highest attainment level in reading, their mean quotient falling just within the average range. The differences between this group and the other two age groups were both statistically significant beyond the 1 per cent level. Similarly, the incidence of educational backwardness and of retardation is much lower among the 11-year-olds.

In each age group girls obtained slightly higher mean reading quotients than the boys but none of the differences was statistically significant.

Differences according to the three criteria of deprivation. Regarding the age at the first separation, the 'early-entrants' received consistently lower mean scores in all three age groups; however, none of the differences was statistically significant. No significant differences or even consistent trends were found with regard to the length of institutional residence.

Regarding severity of deprivation, the mean quotients of the 'severely deprived' were lower than those of the 'deprived', which in turn were below those of the 'mildly deprived' children. For the total sample the differences between the means of the 'severely deprived'/'mildly deprived' and the means of the 'deprived'/'mildly deprived' were statistically significant beyond the 5 per cent level.

Reading backwardness and emotional adjustment. It was decided to investigate the incidence of unsettled and maladjusted behaviour

Table 3.11. Incidence of stable and unsettled or maladjusted behaviour among backward readers

Age group	Backward readers N	Stable N	%	Unsettled or maladjusted N	%
8-year-olds	36	7	19	29	81
11-year-olds	21	3	14	18	86
14-year-olds	31	7	23	24	77
Total	88	17	19	71	81

among the backward readers. Only those children were included who were thus classified on the Bristol Social Adjustment Guides by both school-teachers and house-parents. Analysis showed that the proportion of stable children among the backward readers was considerably lower than among the deprived sample as a whole; this was also the case for each age group. Thus about 80 per cent of backward readers were unsettled or maladjusted as against approximately 60 per cent in the total sample (table 3.11).

Table 3.12. Mean Reading Quotients

	Mean	Sigma
8-year-olds N = 50	83·72	14·11
11-year-olds N = 50	87·42	15·00

2. *Schonell Graded Reading Vocabulary Test.* Unfortunately it did not prove possible to give this test to the 14-year-olds and in view of the incompleteness of the data, it was decided not to analyse them for the three criteria of deprivation. Though still below the mean for the ordinary school population, the means for the 8- and 11-year-olds in this test are somewhat higher than on the comprehension reading test (table 3.12). Again, the 11-year-olds received a rather

higher score than the 8-year-olds and girls did slightly (but not significantly) better than the boys in each age group.

Discussion of the findings

a. *Language development*

Our findings support the hypothesis that deprived children are backward in language development. It seems very likely that this is, at least to some extent, functional and due to adverse environmental factors. Prior to separation the majority of children live in homes where verbal stimulation is minimal: overworked and underprivileged mothers, often burdened with too many pregnancies or forced by economic necessity to go out to work, have little time and energy available to encourage the baby in his early experiments with sound and to elicit continued trial and effort by taking delight in his prespeech vocalisations; similarly, once the child is beginning to speak, there is likely to be less verbal stimulation in the form of nursery rhymes, stories, songs and general conversation. When the child enters an institution, the staff-child ratio as well as the training of the staff are of paramount importance: too low a staffing ratio, frequent staff changes and over-emphasis on child training as against child development, are all likely to have a retarding effect on the growth of language. Our results suggest that young children deprived of normal family life tend to have very limited knowledge of everyday activities which take place in the home and that they are not even sure of the name for the various parts of their own bodies. The all-too-common absence of father figures, especially in Homes for preschool children, is also reflected in their ignorance of male personal effects and apparels. Probably the older children can more readily widen their experience as their growing independence increases the opportunity for outside contacts.

The extent of backwardness in language development was considerably larger than that in intelligence or reading attainment; similarly, it was greater than the incidence of unsettledness and maladjustment, shown both at the day school and at the residential home. These results support Gesell's (Gesell and Amatruda, 1947) and Goldfarb's (Goldfarb, 1945) assertion that the effects of deprivation tend to be more detrimental to a child's language development than to any other aspect of his developing personality. If that is so, it is likely that assessing the intelligence of deprived children by predominantly verbal tests inevitably results in an underestimate. This view is supported by our findings on the WISC where all three age groups obtained significantly higher scores on the Performance Scale. Moreover, another investigator, working with deprived children, also reports consistently higher quotients on the Performance Scale.* There are a number of possible hypotheses, which are not mutually exclusive, to account for the differential results on the Verbal and Performance Scale of the WISC. First, as a group, our sample of deprived children was of low average intelligence and Wechsler states 'that subjects of superior intelligence generally do better on the verbal, and subjects of inferior intelligence do better on the performance part'.

Secondly, the abilities measured by the verbal subtests (especially information, arithmetic and vocabulary) depend to some extent on opportunities and stimulation given at home and at school. The majority of children-in-care come from homes with a culturally and educationally low level; their schooling is often irregular, including frequent changes. Thirdly, when in care and living in a residential home, opportunities for outside contact tend to be rather limited and the staff ratio of one adult to ten or more children further reduces opportunities for discussion and verbal stimulation. Fourthly, once a child is able to read he can increase his vocabulary and enlarge his knowledge by the use of books. Since the incidence of backwardness and retardation in this subject was quite considerable in our sample, this avenue, too is closed to many. Lastly, the severe degree of backwardness in language development found in our sample may well be the most important single factor.

Age and sex differences. Though the 11-year-olds achieved the highest mean Language Quotient, it was only slightly above the mean of the 14-year-olds, whereas the youngest group received a significantly low score. To some extent this may be a reflection of differences in intelligence. Ability to read may also play a part, since 8-year-olds, even if progressing satisfactorily in this subject, are unlikely to have reached a level where through their reading they are able to enlarge their vocabulary.

The fact that the boys received higher mean Language Quotients than the girls may seem rather unexpected since girls usually perform on language tests as well as, if not better than, boys. However, this is likely to be due to the fact that the girl's sample was less representative (for reasons mentioned earlier) than the boys. Thus,

* Private communication from Mrs J. M. Williams at Guy's Hospital, London.

the sex differences found may largely reflect differences in intelligence.

Differences according to the three criteria of deprivation. Our results support the hypothesis that backwardness in language development is more marked in children who have been separated from their mothers for the first time at an early age. To some extent, however, this may also be linked with the fact that the 'early entrants' were found to be intellectually more backward than children whose separation took place at a later age.

As was argued with regard to intelligence (p. 26), it is difficult to account for the fact that length of institutional residence has not resulted in differences of language development. It may be that for language development it is the preschool period (i.e. before the age of 5 years) which is of greatest importance; moreover, if children enter an institution after that age and without seriously impaired language development, it is likely that they will be able to acquire reading skills more readily and thus enlarge their vocabulary through reading even though they may remain in a Home; the results obtained from the reading test would seem to lend some support to this hypothesis.

Continued contact with the family seemed to be related to the children's language development since backwardness in this aspect of growth was most marked where no contact had been maintained. Thus, considering the evidence from the three criteria of deprivation together, it would seem that the important factors are the time when the mother-child relationship is first severed and the nature of the contact maintained subsequently; maybe what matters most is the opportunity to develop early a close personal relationship with the mother or mother-substitute and for this relationship to continue even though the child cannot live in his own home. For example, McCarthy (1952) strongly supports the view that language development depends to a considerable extent upon the child's identification with his mother. If contact with her or a mother-substitute is maintained, then the child continues to strive to communicate his thought and experiences; thus continued personal interest and contact seem to provide the requisite motivational forces which stimulate this learning process.

b. *Reading attainment*
Educational attainments show the responses a child is making in a

more formal and structural learning situation. To obtain a comprehensive picture of a child's scholastic level it might seem desirable to give a full range of attainment tests covering the basic subjects. Practical considerations of time, however, precluded the use of more than one or two attainment tests. Reading was chosen since it is the most fundamental skill and the basis of all academic learning. Backwardness in this subject almost inevitably leads to difficulties with most other aspects of school work.

A very serious degree of backwardness in comprehension reading was found in our sample of deprived children. Though completely comparable statistics are not available, it seems that the incidence of backwardness and retardation in this subject is at least twice as high among our sample as in the ordinary school population. Results from a national survey of normal children, carried out in 1948 (Ministry of Education, 1950), showed that reading backwardness among 11-year-olds amounted to 23 per cent and among 15-year-olds to 30 per cent; while a retest in 1956 (Ministry of Education, 1957) indicated that the incidence had decreased to 21 per cent and 25 per cent respectively. Thus our two comparable age groups of deprived children contain at least twice the proportion of backward readers. No national surveys have been carried out to ascertain the incidence of retardation in reading. However, regional investigations (Kellmer Pringle, 1956) indicate that among 7- to 9-year-old children it ranges from 11 per cent to 23 per cent; while among children aged 9 to 12 years the incidence of reading retardation ranges from zero to 12 per cent (City of Leeds Education Committee, 1953). Thus, again the incidence is twice as high in our samples.

There are a number of possible hypotheses, which are not mutually exclusive, to explain the deprived child's inferior attainment. Retarded speech development and a limited vocabulary inevitably handicap him in learning to read. Moreover, in the deprived child's home little interest is usually taken in books and in education generally. Because of these circumstances, he is less ready for school when he starts at the age of 5 years, than are his more fortunate contemporaries. Thus right from the beginning, the methods and materials used for the majority are unsuited to his needs. (Just as success begets further success, so failure begets further failure.) Soon he will be labelled backward. (In any case, he is aware of the fact that others are doing much better than he, which results in a loss of confidence and diminished effort, which in turn lead to further educational difficulties.) Frequent absences and changes of school are also likely to hinder progress in reading. The deprived child tends to come from families where there are frequent minor ailments, where he is kept at home to look after younger siblings or to run errands, or where he himself may play truant. Removal from home usually means a change of school and all that this involves, such as developing new loyalties, adjusting to a different school atmosphere and possibly also to different teaching methods. Lastly, there is research evidence to show that children who have emotional difficulties tend to do badly at school, partly because of preoccupation with their problems (Monroe, 1932; Gates, 1941; Schonell, 1942; Burt, 1946; Vernon, 1957).

Age and sex differences. Once again, the 11-year-olds achieved significantly higher mean scores than the other two age groups. Their superior achievement in reading may in part, if not wholly, be due to their superiority in most other aspects which were measured. It will be remembered that this group was relatively superior in intelligence, language development and emotional adjustment.

Since the boys achieved higher mean intelligence and higher mean language quotients than the girls, one would have expected the latter to have also lower attainments in reading. However, this was not the case. Girls consistently scored higher than boys though this difference did not reach a statistically significant level; deprived boys, despite their relative superiority, tended to be more backward in reading than girls. Thus the same sex difference, though to a less severe degree, seems to exist among the deprived as among ordinary pupils.

Differences according to the three criteria of deprivation. Our findings lend some support to the hypothesis that early first separation has an adverse influence on later reading achievement. However, the link here is likely to be indirect: early first separation appears to have an adverse effect on intellectual and language development and this in turn exercises a detrimental influence on reading ability. A similar indirect influence is likely to be responsible for the fact that severity of deprivation was also associated with poorer attainments in reading. On the other hand, length of institutional residence did not seem to affect the level of attainment in this subject.

Reading backwardness and emotional adjustment. Since learning to read depends to a considerable extent upon intellectual and language development, one would expect deprived children to be more backward in reading attainment. Once allowance has been made for these limitations or disabilities, one would not necessarily expect to find a more serious degree of retardation than among the ordinary school population. However, this was the case (table 3.10, p. 47). Thus it seems that additional adverse factors were influencing the learning process, such as a lack of motivation, a poor relationship with the teacher and emotional maladjustment. We were only able to assess the extent of the last mentioned factor. Nor can we judge from our findings whether the high incidence of unsettledness and maladjustment among the poor readers was due to their learning difficulty or whether the learning difficulty was causing the maladjustment. There is a great deal of evidence (Monroe, 1932; Gates, 1941; Schonell, 1942; Fernald, 1943; Burt, 1946; Vernon, 1957; Kellmer Pringle, 1958) to support both these explanatory hypotheses. If one accepts the close interrelationship between educational and emotional difficulties, it becomes apparent that deprived children are caught in a vicious circle: the very circumstances preceding and eventually leading to separation are likely also to lead to a high incidence of maladjustment; maladjustment militates against successful learning; unsuccessful learning results in a sense of failure and frustration, thus further increasing the likelihood, and possibly also the degree, of maladjustment.

Summary and conclusions

The results of the individual intelligence testing showed that the majority of our sample of deprived children fell within the average range of ability, although the mean I.Q. was considerably below 100. Moreover, the proportion of educationally subnormal and dull children was considerably higher, and that of bright and very able children considerably lower than among the ordinary school population. In language development and reading attainment the deprived children were also markedly backward. In addition, they tended to differ from ordinary children in many of their personal attitudes and reactions and a considerable proportion showed symptoms of maladjustment, both in the residential home and at school. Social competence was the only developmental aspect in which the deprived equalled ordinary children.

Regarding the three criteria of deprivation it was found that early first separation from the mother resulted in significantly greater ill-effects on the various developmental aspects which were measured;

similarly, complete deprivation, i.e. no contact whatever with the family or relatives, had a significantly deleterious effect. Sheer length of institutional residence, on the other hand, did not result in any significant differences.

The 11-year-olds were superior to the two other age groups in all respects except social competence. It may be that at this age children are better able to accept separation from their parents and to adjust to institutional life than when they are younger or during adolescence. This hypothesis receives some support from developmental psychology since for normal children the latency period is considered to be a time of relative calm and settledness. However, our sample is too small to draw this inference with any certainty.

Lastly, boys tended to be superior in general ability and language development, while girls were relatively better readers and socially more competent. These trends, however, were not statistically significant.

Hitherto the various aspects studied have largely and necessarily been analysed and discussed separately. Yet it is likely that our findings are the end product of a chain of adverse conditions which interact and reinforce one another and which affect the lives of deprived children long before they come into care. Among these conditions the following are probably of considerable importance: poor intellectual and possibly poor emotional endowment; unstimulating and impoverished cultural conditions; a lack of educational standards and ambitions; a family which may be broken in spirit if not in reality; poverty, ill-health and unemployment. Thus a vicious circle is produced: impoverished and often unhappy home conditions, leading to backwardness in intellectual and language development as well as to emotional maladjustment, which in turn result in unsatisfactory school adjustment.

Since at home the child's early learning efforts are often met with little interest and encouragement, he is likely to be discouraged and to accept low standards of achievement. When he starts school, these attitudes are transferred to class room learning; moreover, possessing only a limited speaking vocabulary, educational difficulties are likely to follow. The teacher, very understandably, is disappointed at the child's lack of responsiveness and progress and yet this disappointment is likely to make the child feel even more hopeless and insecure; hence further lack of progress and apathy follow. Removal to a children's Home means usually also a change of school, so that the child has to make new adjustments all round. Except perhaps in a few cases, institutional life can hardly be expected to have beneficial effects on a backward, discouraged and insecure child; on the contrary, existing difficulties may be still further aggravated.

Incidentally, our findings shed some light on the reasons why teachers and houseparents commonly believe that most deprived children are very dull: children's ability is judged by what they say and by what they are able to do. Since deprived children tend to suffer from a severe degree of language and educational retardation, they give the impression of lacking ability, when in many cases they have lacked mainly appropriate stimulation and opportunity.

Practical implications

These can be conveniently discussed under two headings, prevention and treatment. Prevention in the widest sense—i.e. how to bring about a decrease in the number of children coming into care—is outside the scope of our investigation.

Prevention

There seems little doubt that deprived children's retardation in language skills and in reading attainment is in large measure due to environmental deprivation, often operative before removal from home. Thus perhaps the most fruitful time for the prevention of language and educational difficulties is in the preschool years. More liberal provision of nursery schools (catering for 2- to 5-year-olds) for children from overcrowded, broken, poverty-stricken or otherwise 'problem homes' would ensure more favourable conditions for all-round development. For those already in care, residential nurseries should provide conditions closely akin to those available in the best nursery schools. In many cases this would mean a more liberal child–staff ratio than exists at present as well as the provision of fully trained nursery school teachers, at least in key positions and for part of the day.

Similarly, once the children attend school, a strong case could be made for the provision of much smaller classes with specially skilled teachers in charge of those children who come from problem homes and slum areas. At present the opposite is often the case since it is difficult in a time of teacher shortage to attract teachers to schools in districts where the work is less rewarding due to poor buildings, over-crowded classes and less teachable children. Smaller classes, extra equipment and apparatus, and possibly a special responsibility allowance might be used as incentives. In the long run, these are cheaper to the community than the burden of illiterate, delinquent or neurotic adolescents and adults.

Once in care, the houseparents of older children could also give a good deal of help. As much time as possible should be devoted to talking with the children, reading and telling stories to them, encouraging them to relate any small happenings that have taken place during the day—in short, using every device to encourage and develop the children's desire and ability to express their ideas, thoughts and feelings. This kind of help needs to be given longer to deprived than to ordinary children because so often they have missed these experiences at the right time. For a number of reasons, chief among them a shortage of suitable staff, this extra stimulation is at present not forthcoming in the majority of children's homes.

The system of family units (where children of various ages and both sexes are housed together in one cottage instead of in a single sex, narrow ageband grouping) which is being increasingly introduced into Homes, is also likely to foster language development: younger children are able to learn from older children and the latter can be encouraged to read and talk to the little ones, ostensibly to help the houseparents, but in fact improving their own power and wish for self-expression.

To prevent emotional maladjustment, it seems of paramount importance to ensure that contact is maintained, or established, with a loved and loving adult, where possible of course with one or both parents. For long-term cases, especially those without any close and dependable ties, the present policy of early and permanent boarding-out needs to be intensified; this applies particularly to boys, who seem less acceptable to fosterparents.

Lastly, all-age family units may serve to modify institutional routine and thus lead to less pressure on the children to become socially competent as early as possible.

Treatment

Many children of school age are seriously retarded in language development and in English subjects generally by the time they come into care. Thus they become doubly handicapped, being now deprived of home life as well as unable to keep pace in school alongside ordinary children. Not only prevention but curative work could be done if classes were smaller and teachers perhaps a little more aware of the very special needs and difficulties of this group. In a few schools special help of one kind or another is available but at present facilities for remedial teaching are on a quite inadequate scale.

Remedial education is based on a total approach to the failing child, and includes various creative and therapeutic activities, such as painting, modelling, puppetry and drama. When successful, it results in considerable acceleration in the rate of educational progress. Perhaps even more important, attitudes to learning, and relationships with children and adults become happier and more constructive. Often too, a remission of symptoms follows. That this is also the case with deprived children has already been demonstrated by some recent pioneering work. As a result of our research, three remedial treatment units have been set up in different parts of the country, each one being organised and financed in a different way.*

A different approach is probably needed for short-term and long-term cases. For the former, it might be argued that having to adjust to life in a Children's Home and to a new school during a brief period of time, is making things doubly difficult for a child who may already have been an educational problem in his previous school. The period away from home could be made profitable in at least one respect by providing intensive remedial treatment within the Home for seriously retarded children instead of their attending local schools. Long-term cases could receive either full-time or part-time remedial help as well as, or instead of, ordinary schooling depending on the nature and severity of their difficulties and on the provision available in the locality.

It might be argued that since the incidence of emotional maladjustment is high among the deprived, psychotherapy ought to take precedence over educational help. While this may be desirable on theoretical grounds, in practice most child guidance clinics are,

---

* 1. The Birmingham Children's Officer created a precedent by setting up remedial reading groups within Children's Homes outside school hours; these are tutored by part-time teachers who are paid by the Children's Committee. 2. A remedial group has been established through the initiative of the Superintendent of the Residential Home from which our main sample was drawn; children who proved too difficult or retarded for the ordinary school, attend this group instead, for a limited period of time. 3. A remedial unit, financed by a grant from the Nuffield Foundation, has been started at the Caldecott Community in Kent, which caters for maladjusted and deprived children.

for a variety of reasons, reluctant to treat children in care. Thus such children are at present further handicapped by lack of appropriate facilities; educationally they are more seriously retarded and psychotherapy is less readily available to them than to the ordinary school population. Since remedial treatment has a stabilizing influence and enables pupils to fit in more happily at school, it seems even more urgent that facilities be created for deprived children than for those living in their own homes.

Clearly our enquiry has raised many more questions than it has answered. To mention just a few: the family unit scheme where small groups of children live in adapted council houses on ordinary housing estates and the boarding-out of deprived children, have been practised in recent years on a large enough scale to permit a comparative study to determine to what extent such schemes eliminate or minimise the ill-effects of institutional life. It would be of considerable interest to study various developmental aspects of children who are living with their own parents but whose social, cultural, economic and emotional background is closely similar to that of children who come into care. Such an investigation would make it possible to assess more specifically the effects of maternal deprivation and of separation from the family. The present findings largely demonstrate the detrimental effects resulting from environmental deprivation and institutional life. The conclusions regarding the children's emotional adjustment and the effects of early first separation give, however, some pointers to the consequences of maternal deprivation. In addition, more systematic studies are needed regarding the adequacy of substitute relationships at different ages. Lastly the short- and long-term effects of different types of remedial treatment with deprived children need to be studied, once provisions have been made in a sufficient number of Children's Homes.

Summary

The hypothesis that deprived children are markedly backward in language development, is supported by our findings. Moreover, the extent of this backwardness was larger than that found in any other aspect of development and achievement. Thus it seems that the effect of deprivation tends to be most detrimental to a child's language development. It is likely, therefore, that assessing the intelligence of deprived children by predominantly verbal tests inevitably

E

results in an underestimate. This view is supported by our findings on the WISC on which all three age groups obtained significantly higher scores on the Performance Scale. With regard to the three criteria of deprivation, early first separation and subsequent complete deprivation had a significantly deleterious effect. Sheer length of institutional residence did not result in differences of language development.

A serious degree of backwardness in comprehension reading was also found. The incidence of backwardness and retardation in this subject was at least twice as high among our sample as in the ordinary school population. Once again, early first separation and lack of continued contact with the family appeared to have an adverse (though probably indirect) influence on later achievement in reading.

In the discussion of all the results, two aspects are stressed: the multiplicity of adverse interacting circumstances which affect the lives of children who eventually come into care; and the vicious circle in which they seem caught as a result of this fact: thus impoverished and often unhappy home conditions lead to backwardness in language development and to emotional maladjustment which in turn result in unsatisfactory school adjustment, discouragement and hence further lack of progress.

Finally, the practical implication of our findings is considered together with some suggestions for both prevention and treatment.

References

BRODBECK, A. J. and IRWIN, O. C. (1946) 'The speech behaviour of infants without families', *Child Development*, **17**, 145–56.

BURLINGHAM, D. and FREUD, A. (1954) *Infants without families; the case for and against residential nurseries*. London, Allen & Unwin.

BURT, SIR C. (1946) *The backward child*. 2nd edn. London, University of London Press.

CASTLE, M. (1954) 'Institution and non-institution children at school', *Human Relations*, **7**, 349–66.

DAWE, H. C. (1942) 'A study of the effect of an educational programme upon language development and retarded mental functions in young children', *Journal of Experimental Education*, **11**, 200–9.

DURRELL, D. D. (1940) *Improvement of basic reading abilities*. Yonkerson-Hudson, New York, World Book Co.

EDUCATION, MINISTRY OF (1950) *Reading ability; some suggestions for helping the backward* (Pamphlet No. 18). London, H.M.S.O.

EDUCATION, MINISTRY OF (1957) *Standards of reading, 1948–1956* (Pamphlet No. 32). London, H.M.S.O.

FEINBERG, H. (1954) 'Achievement of children in orphan homes as revealed by the Stanford Achievement Test', *Journal of Genetic Psychology*, **85**, 217–29.

FERNALD, G. M. (1943) *Remedial techniques in basic school subjects*. New York, McGraw-Hill.

FLEMMING, V. V. (1942) 'A study of Stanford-Binet vocabulary attainment and growth in children in the city of Childhood, Mooseheart, Illinois, as compared with children living in their own homes', *Journal of Genetic Psychology*, **60**, 359–73.

GATES, A. I. (1941) 'The role of personality maladjustment in reading disability', *Journal of Genetic Psychology*, **59**, 77–83.

GATEWOOD, M. C. and WEISS, A. P. (1930) 'Race and sex differences in newborn infants,' *Journal of Genetic Psychology*, **38**, 31–49.

GESELL, A. and AMATRUDA, C. S. (1947) *Developmental diagnosis; normal and abnormal child development; clinical methods and pediatric applications.* 2nd edn. New York, Hoeber.

GOLDFARB, W. (1943) 'Infant rearing and problem behavior', *American Journal of Orthopsychiatry*, **13**, 249–65.

GOLDFARB, W. (1943) 'The effects of early institutional care on adolescent personality', *Child Development*, **14**, 213–23.

GOLDFARB, W. (1945) 'The effect of psychological deprivation in infancy and subsequent stimulation', *American Journal of Psychiatry*, **102**, 18–33.

HALLGREN, B. (1950) 'Specific dyslexia ("congenital word-blindness"); a clinical and genetic study', *Acta Psychiatrica et Neurologica*, supplementum 65. Copenhagen.

LEEDS: Education Committee (1953) *Report on a survey of reading ability.* Leeds, Education Department.

LEWIS, H. (1954) *Deprived children; the Mersham experiment. A social and clinical study.* London, Oxford University Press.

LITTLE, M. F. and WILLIAMS, H. M. (1937) 'An analytical scale of language achievement', *University of Iowa Studies in Child Welfare*, **13**, 47–78, 88–94.

MCCARTHY, D. A. (1930) *The language development of the pre-school child.* Institute of Child Welfare Monographs, No. 4. Minneapolis, University of Minnesota Press.

MCCARTHY, D. A. (1947) 'The psychologist looks at the teaching of English', *Independent Schools Bulletin*, **5**, 3–11.

MCCARTHY, D. A. (1952) 'Language and personality development', *Reading Teacher*, **6**, 28–36.

MCCARTHY, D. A. (1952) 'Organismic interpretation of infant vocalisations', *Child Development*, **23**, 273–80.

MCCARTHY, D. A. (1953) 'Some possible explanations of sex differences in language development and disorders', *Journal of Psychology*, **35**, 155–60.

MACMEEKEN, M. (1939) *Ocular dominance in relation to developmental aphasia; certain facts and interpretations arising out of an investigation into incidence of reading disability and the nature of the difficulties involved in such disability.* London, University of London Press.

MIDDLESBROUGH: Education Committee (1953) *Report of a survey of reading ability carried out in the schools of the authority during 1951 and 1952 by the Middlesbrough Head Teachers' Association in co-operation with the officers of the Authority.*

MILNER, E. (1951) 'A study of the relationship between reading readiness in grade one school children and patterns of parent-child interaction', *Child Development*, **22**, 95–112.

MONROE, M. (1932) *Children who cannot read; the analysis of reading disabilities and the use of diagnostic tests in the instruction of retarded readers.* Chicago, University of Chicago Press.

MOORE, J. E. (1939) 'Sex differences in spread of reading', *Journal of Experimental Education*, **8**, 110–14.

MOORE, J. K. (1947) 'Speech content of selected groups of orphanage and non-orphanage pre-school children', *Journal of Experimental Education*, **16**, 122–33.

PRINGLE, M. L. KELLMER (1956) 'The backward child, Part I', *The Times Educational Supplement*, 12 October 1956.

PRINGLE, M. L. KELLMER (1958) 'Learning and emotion', *Educational Review*, **10**, 146–68.

ROUDINESCO, J. and APPELL, G. (1950) 'Les répercussions de la stabulation hospitalière sur le développement psychomoteur des jeunes enfants', *Semaine des Hôpitaux de Paris*, **26**, 2271–3.

SAMUELS, F. (1943) 'Sex differences in reading achievement', *Journal of Educational Research*, **36**, 594–603.

SCHONELL, F. J. (1942) *Backwardness in the basic subjects.* Edinburgh, Oliver and Boyd.

SHIRE, SISTER M. L. (1945) 'The relation of certain linguistic factors to reading achievement in first grade children.' Ph.D. Thesis, Fordham University.

SKEELS, H. M., UPDEGRAFF, R., WELLMAN, B. L. and WILLIAMS, H. M. (1938) 'A study of environmental stimulation; an orphanage pre-school project', *University of Iowa Studies in Child Welfare*, **15**.

SOBEL, F. S. (1948) 'Remedial teaching as therapy', *American Journal of Psychotherapy*, **2**, 615–23.

SMITH, H. P. and HIXON, L. (1935) 'A comparative study of orphanage and non-orphanage children', *Elementary School Journal*, **36**, 110–15.

SMITH, M. E. (1935) 'A study of some factors influencing the development of the sentence in pre-school children', *Journal of Genetic Psychology*, **46**, 182–212.

STALNAKER, J. M. (1941) 'Sex differences in the ability to write', *School and Society*, **54**, 532–5.

STROUD, J. B. and LINDQUIST, E. F. (1942) 'Sex differences in achievement in the elementary and secondary schools', *Journal of Educational Psychology*, **33**, pp. 657–67.

VERNON, M. D. (1957) *Backwardness in reading; a study of its nature and origin*. Cambridge, Cambridge University Press.

WATTS, A. F. (1944) *The language and mental development of children*. London, Harrap.

WILLIAMS, H. M. and McFARLAND, M. L. (1937) 'Development of language and vocabulary in young children', *University of Iowa Studies in Child Welfare*, **13**.

YEDINACK, J. G. (1949) 'A study of the linguistic functioning of children with articulation and reading disabilities', *Journal of Genetic Psychology*, **74**, 23–59.

4. Early, prolonged separation and emotional maladjustment*

with Victoria Bossio

Introduction

In the current literature, the term 'deprived' is used to describe a child who, for one reason or another, is unable to live with his own family but is being brought up in an institution (Home Office, 1946; United Nations, 1952; Ford, 1955). The term is also used for children who, although now living in their own homes, have early in life been separated from their parents, particularly the mother, or who are unloved and rejected by her. Like institutionalisation, early separation and 'maternal deprivation' are considered to be detrimental to children's development (Bowley, 1947; Fitzgerald, 1948; Bowlby, 1951). In recent years considerable research has been devoted to these topics, yet there have been comparatively few systematic investigations of unselected groups of deprived children. There has been a tendency for special categories such as pre-school, hospitalised or delinquent children, or for certain aspects, such as emotional adjustment or social maturity to be studied (Goldfarb, 1943; Rheingold, 1943; Spitz, 1945; Bowlby, 1946; Bodman *et al.*, 1950). Our investigation aimed at a comprehensive enquiry into the development and achievement of some unselected samples of deprived children, to examine the interrelationship between their abilities and attainments and to make comparisons with ordinary children wherever possible. In addition, three hypotheses were tested regarding the results of deprivation: that its ill-effects are more marked (*a*) where the first separation from the mother occurred at an early age; (*b*) where deprivation has been severe; and (*c*) where there has been a prolonged period of institutionalisation.

When studied, all the children (N = 188) were in care and living in large children's homes. The main results of this study have been

* First published in *Child Psychology and Psychiatry*, 1960, 1, 37–48.

reported elsewhere (Pringle and Bossio, 1958). Though a considerable proportion of children showed symptoms of maladjustment, some 30 per cent were considered to be stable by their teachers and the house staff, when rated on the Bristol Social Adjustment Guides. Thus our findings suggested that previous views had been incorrect, or at least overstated, and that separation and institutionalisation do not necessarily result in children becoming affectionless or psychopathic personalities. In a subsequent study, Bowlby and Ainsworth (1956) came to the same conclusion. To gain further insight into the dynamics of deprivation and personality reactions, it was decided to make an intensive, clinical study of two groups of children selected from our main sample of 142 cases according to the following criteria:

a. That the first removal from home had occurred before the age of 5 years.
b. That the child had continued to live apart from his parents for more than half of his life.
c. That he had been rated either 'notably stable' or 'severely maladjusted' on all the following measures:
  i. The Bristol Social Adjustment Guides completed by the house staff.
  ii. The same Guides completed by the class teachers.
  iii. The results from a Personality Test (Raven's Controlled Projection Test).
  iv. The clinical observations made by the investigators throughout the individual testing and interviewing of each child.
d. That he should be of average ability (i.e. I.Q. range on the full WISC between 85 and 114).

In that way the most severely deprived children were chosen and the possibly complicating factor of low or high intelligence was excluded. Applying these criteria, we found eleven 'severely maladjusted' and five 'notably stable' children, some from each of the age groups of the main sample, namely 8-, 11- and 14-year-olds. A detailed case study was made of each of the sixteen children, eleven boys and five girls, and this is the subject of the present chapter.

Summary of the case studies
The results of the individual tests and assessments used with the main sample and two intensively studied groups are shown on table 4.1.

Table 4.1. Test results obtained for the main experimental sample and for the intensively studied groups

Tests	Main experimental sample N = 142		Severely maladjusted group N = 11		Notably stable group N = 5	
	Mean quotient	Range	Mean quotient	Range	Mean quotient	Range
WISC Full Scale	89·84	62–128	91·72	86–100	99·00	90–107
WISC Verbal Scale	86·47	58–130	84·72	77–96	89·80	77–99
WISC Performance Scale	95·60	55–136	100·36	86–100	108·80	100–114
Mill Hill Vocabulary Scale (Oral Definitions)	74·88	45–120	72·90	59–97	93·60	85–109
Schonell Silent Reading Test B	80·13	51–124	75·18	63–92	98·20	90–112
Vineland Social Maturity Scale	104·67	70–138	102·63	80–116	112·00	106–117
Raven's Controlled Projection Test (Coefficient of Conformity)	51·36	17–85	42·36	30–50	78·00	70–85

The main sample and the maladjusted group are markedly backward in language development which was assessed by the Mill Hill Vocabulary Scale, and in comprehension reading, tested on Schonell's Silent Reading Test B. The stable group achieved average mean scores on both these measures.

Similarly, the mean coefficient of conformity on Raven's Controlled Projection Test is considerably below the expected mean of 100 both for the main sample and the maladjusted group. A qualitative analysis of the responses given by the latter shows many answers indicative of aggression, a feeling of hopelessness or anxiety about parents and general insecurity, as well as ambivalent and guilt feelings. The drawings made while answering the test questions are rather poor in content, detail, colour and movement, suggesting a paucity of ideas, general immaturity and restricted powers of self-expression. On the other hand, the answers given by the stable group to the personality test contain fewer 'unique responses' and the mean 'coefficient of conformity' is consequently higher. The drawings made while answering the test items are quite pleasing and lively, showing a free use of colour, variety in content and an eye for detail.

Though both groups receive an average score for social competence on the Vineland Scale, the children in the maladjusted group were reported to show from time to time regressive tendencies in social behaviour, both in the home and at school.

The main test results for each child in the two groups are shown on tables 4.2 and 4.3. The close correspondence of all the results obtained by the identical twins, Roger and Allan, are noteworthy. The descriptions of the children's outstanding personality traits are a summary arrived at by combining the assessments made both by the school and home staffs on the Bristol Social Adjustment Guides. Perhaps the most outstanding feature is the inability of the maladjusted children to make relationships with adults or children or both, while being over-anxious for adult approval and over-attentive to any newcomers. This attachment is, however, only temporary and soon gives way to indifference or uncertainty. In contrast, the stable group are all reported to have established good relationships, both with adults and contemporaries.

The life history and family background of each child are summarised on tables 4.4 and 4.5. The severely deprived group came into care rather younger than the stable children, all but two having been separated from their mothers for the first time by 1 year of age or before. Most of the maladjusted children had been deserted by their mothers or abandoned near children's homes, police stations or in churches. Both groups have experienced a number of placements. Fostering had been tried for five children in the maladjusted group, but their difficult behaviour led to a breakdown in the arrangements and a return to a children's home. This was not done for the stable children, as they had dependable ties with a parent or other adult even though they could not live with them. Most of the children had been in hospital but only one boy had been seriously ill (No. 9 Leonard with rheumatic fever). John had numerous periods in hospital for observation of an eye defect which was soon to be operated upon; otherwise his health was good, except that he had gastro-enteritis at the age of 10 months. It is worth noting that in the case of eight of the maladjusted children their first stay in hospital occurred near the time of the first separation from their mothers.

The records relating to the children's parentage were found to be rather scanty. This may well have been because there had been several placements and because the children have been in care for a long time. A little more is known about the parents of the stable group, but there is insufficient information for a comparison between the two groups. It is evident, however, that the rate of illegitimacy is much higher among the maladjusted children.

The most marked difference between the two groups is in the amount of contact maintained with parents or parent substitutes. 'Regular' means that contact has consistently been maintained by the same people, in the form of letters, parcels, visits, outings and holidays for the children; 'occasional' means that for some years there has not been continuous and regular contact and even that has only been forthcoming at the repeated requests of the Children's Officer; 'none at all' means that the child has never known a continuing relationship with any adult outside the children's home, whether relative or friend. All the stable children have experienced a dependable, lasting relationship with a parent or parent substitute, whereas only one child in the maladjusted group has had such a contact.

Discussion and conclusion
Although the number of cases upon which this study is based is small, they were chosen from a fairly large and unselected sample of deprived children in institutional care. The criteria governing their selection ensured that they had been separated from their mothers at

Table 4.2. Test results and personality assessments for the severely maladjusted group

Name	Wisc V.Q.	Wisc P.Q.	Wisc F.Q.	L.Q.	R.Q.	S.Q.	C. of C.	P.Q. V.Q. discrep.	S.Q. I.Q. discrep.	Outstanding personality traits
1. John	81	103	91	63	71	108	41	22	+1·29 D.S.	Craves affection and attention, moody, resents correction; lacks interests and persistence; severe nail biting and body scratching
*2. Roger	80	104	91	65	67	108	30	24	+1·36 D.S.	Apathetic but shows aggressive resentment if corrected; careless and destructive with property and toys; solitary and unpopular among children, detached, secretive and has formed no close relations with anyone but his twin brother
*3. Allan	77	106	90	66	81	109	42	29	+1·46 D.S.	Is described in almost identical terms to those used for his twin brother Roger
4. Charlotte	81	110	94	69	80	102	45	29	+0·59 D.S.	Craves adult attention to the point of making herself a constant nuisance to teachers and house staff; aggressive to other children; moody, destructive; severe bedwetting, nail biting and thumb sucking
5. Paul	90	86	88	71	83	116	41	—	+2·32 D.S.	Timid and cries easily; has no friends at school; neat worker but often day dreams; in the home he is often depressed, 'wrapped up in himself'; a deeply unhappy, lonely boy who has never apparently accepted separation from mother and sister

Name	WISC V.Q.	WISC P.Q.	WISC F.Q.	L.Q.	R.Q.	S.Q.	C. of C.	P.Q. V.Q. dis-crep.	S.Q. I.Q. discrep.	Outstanding personality traits
6. Sandra	96	100	98	97	86	103	46	4	+0·41 D.S.	Moody, restless, temper outbursts; over-anxious for adult approval and jealous of other children; lies and steals food and money; distrusts adults
7. Kathleen	96	104	100	76	92	107	45	8	+0·67 D.S.	Stammers, bites nails and has temper tantrums; gets fond of children and adults but attachments do not last; many fears and very restless
8. Colin	85	93	88	59	63	84	40	8	−0·72 D.S.	Very backward at school, moody, violent if corrected; nail biting, body scratching and enuresis are among his many symptoms; craves adult approval yet hostile to them
9. Leonard	79	94	86	88	64	80	41	15	−0·90 D.S.	Moody, temper outbursts and full of infantile fears; steals from and spiteful to other children; extremely attached to his mother, lives for her infrequent letters and visits; has made no lasting relationship to any other adult
10. Nicholas	85	107	95	74	77	112	45	22	+1·47 D.S.	Stammers, moody; defiant to adults and distrustful; boasts, craves attention and is restlessly and aimlessly 'on the go'
11. Terry	82	97	88	74	63	100	50	15	+0·80 D.S.	'Wrapped up in himself', hostile to women and rather solitary; lies, boasts and rebuffs kindness from adults as if mistrusting them

* Identical twins.

WISC V.Q. = WISC Verbal Quotient
WISC P.Q. = WISC Performance Quotient
WISC F.Q. = WISC Full Scale Quotient
L.Q.   = Language Quotient

R.Q.   = Reading Quotient
S.Q.   = Social Quotient
C. of C. = Coefficient of Conformity
D.S.   = Difference between standard score in terms of I.Q. mean and standard deviation

Table 4.3. Test results and personality assessment for the notably stable children

Name	WISC V.Q.	WISC P.Q.	WISC F.Q.	L.Q.	R.Q.	S.Q.	C. of C.	P.Q. V.Q. dis- crep.	S.Q. I.Q. discrep.	Outstanding personality traits
1. Elizabeth	81	111	95	85	98	110	75	30	+1·28 D.S.	Friendly, responsive and well-behaved; popular with contemporaries; works well at school and takes care of her belongings; very attached to younger brother, house mother, 'official aunt' and her teachers
2. Jacqueline	77	106	90	86	90	113	70	29	+1·90 D.S.	Affectionate, responsive and liked by children and adults; very attached to her mother and siblings but has warm relationships with house staff
3. Peter	99	114	107	109	92	117	80	15	+1·08 D.S.	Helpful, friendly and well-behaved; does well in school; gets on well with contemporaries; very good relation- ships with his mother, 'aunt', teachers and house parents
4. Dennis	95	113	104	89	112	106	85	18	+0·31 D.S.	Well-behaved, responsive and hard working in school where he is doing very well; mixes well; fond of his father and sisters and good relations with most adults
5. Roy	97	100	99	99	99	114	80	3	+1·39 D.S.	Cheerful, good natured and well liked by children and adults; very fond of his foster-mother

WISC V.Q. = WISC Verbal Quotient
WISC P.Q. = WISC Performance Quotient
WISC F.Q. = WISC Full Scale Quotient
L.Q. = Language Quotient

R.Q. = Reading Quotient
S.Q. = Social Quotient
C. of C. = Coefficient of Conformity
D.S. Difference between standard score in terms of I.Q. mean and standard deviation

an early age and had continued to live apart from them for considerable periods. In fact most of the sixteen children had spent virtually all their lives in children's homes only interrupted by unsuccessful periods in foster homes. How then can we account for the difference in emotional adjustment found between them? Constitutional inferiority and thus greater susceptibility to emotional instability in the face of environmental stresses might be one hypothesis. Though only meagre evidence was available on the children's parentage, the very high incidence of illegitimacy among the maladjusted group together with subsequent parental rejection could be interpreted as indicating greater parental instability than was operative in the stable group. Alternatively, however, one could argue that parents whose children come into care almost permanently are likely to be themselves unstable and too disorganised to provide, and cope successfully with, normal family life. The loss of contact and rejection among the many illegitimate children in the maladjusted group could be due largely to the social stigma and other practical difficulties encountered in our society by the unmarried mother. The very young age at which the illegitimate children first came into care also supports this view. Moreover, some of these women were known to have married subsequently and to be providing a home for their legitimate offspring. Thus we must conclude that we have insufficient evidence regarding the influence of hereditary or constitutional factors.

More factual information is available on environmental influences. The first mother–child separation occurred before the first year for nine of the maladjusted children. In Bowlby's terminology (Ainsworth and Bowlby, 1954) they suffered from complete 'privation of a mother–child relationship, implying that one has never existed'. Complete privation is defined as separation in very early infancy before a stable and secure dependency relationship has been established, and subsequent rearing of the child in an institution were he is cared for in a more or less impersonal way by a variety of adult figures. Secondly, for the maladjusted children separation was accompanied by lasting parental rejection. Lastly—and this may be equally if not more important—none of the maladjusted group had had the opportunity or the ability to build up and consolidate stable relationships with parent figures.

In contrast, all but one child in the stable group remained with its mother until well after the first year of life, by which time a stable relationship is likely to have been established. Separation appears to

Table 4.4. Summary of the life history and family background of the severely maladjusted group

Name	C.A. at time of study Yrs. Mths.	Age at first separation Months	Reasons for coming into care	No. of placements	No. of hospitalisations	Legit./illegit.	Family background		Contact with parent or parent-substitutes
							Father's occupat. status	Mother's reported status or mentality	
1. John	7 6	8	Unsuitable living conditions	4	5	Illegit.	Unknown	Illiterate	Occasional
2. Roger	7 7	7	Mother deserted	3	None	Illegit.	Taxi driver	Mental Hosp.	Occasional
3. Allan	7 7	7	Mother deserted	3	None	Illegit.	Taxi driver	Mental Hosp.	Occasional
4. Charlotte	8 4	1	Abandoned by mother	5	1	Illegit.	Unknown (Negro)	Unstable	Not at all
5. Paul	8 8	11	No home	3	1	Illegit.	Unknown	Dom. servant	Occasional
6. Sandra	10 0	11	Parents divorced; children to father	3+	1	Legit.	No job for 6 yr.; died 1 yr. ago	In prison	Not at all
7. Kathleen	10 3	5	Mother deserted	6	2	Illegit.	Labourer (Maltese)	Dom. servant	Not at all
8. Colin	11 1	19	Abandoned by mother	4	2	Illegit.	Unknown	Very dull	Occasional
9. Leonard	11 6	2	Unsettled home	5	3	Illegit.	Labourer	Unknown	Regular
10. Nicholas	14 6	18	Ill-treated and abandoned	5	2	Illegit.	Unknown (Cypriot)	Illiterate	Not at all
11. Terry	14 8	12	Mother dead; father no home	3	1	Legit. mother dead	Labourer	Dead	Not at all

Table 4.5. Summary of the life history and family background of the notably stable group

Name	C.A. at time of study Yrs. Mths.		Age at first separation Months	Reasons for coming into care	No. of placements	No. of hospitalisations	Legit./illegit.	Family background		
								Father's occupat. status	Mother's reported status of mentality	Contact with parent or parent-substitutes
1. Elizabeth	8	6	36	Evicted, no home since	2	3	Legit.	Labourer	Unknown	Regularly till recently (both parents)
2. Jacqueline	8	7	46	Mother deserted; father abroad	3	1	Legit.	Regular army	Unstable	Regular (with mother)
3. Peter	10	1	25	Mother chronic T.B.; father neglectful	5	1	Legit.	Coal-loader	Chronic T.B. in sanatorium	Regular (with 'nurse')
4. Dennis	10	8	36	Mother's death leaving four children	2	None	Legit.	Gas-meter reader	Dead	Regular (with father)
5. Roy	13	11	12	Evacuation, then beyond control	3	2	Illegit.	Unknown	Responsible	Regular (with 'aunt')

have been caused by unfortunate circumstances rather than by the rejection of the child. Even the mother who deserted her family (table 4.5, case No. 2) continued to keep in touch with the child. Three children never experienced a complete severance of family relations but a prolonged physical separation; the other two children in this group (table 4.5, Nos. 3 and 5) formed a stable and lasting relationship with a mother-substitute. It is worth noting that they never lived permanently in the homes of their mother-substitutes but visited regularly and spent holidays there. Our maladjusted group may be described as being psychologically deprived, while the stable group was deprived of family life and physically separated but nevertheless loved and cherished by adults who were important to them.

The fact that the maladjusted group was found to be markedly backward in language development and reading attainment, supports the view that emotion and learning are inseparably linked (Pringle, 1957, 1958). Similarly, people working with young deprived children have noted that separation from the mother is often followed by indifferent physical health, in some cases necessitating entry into hospital. This was found to be so for the majority of children in our maladjusted group.

Thus our evidence supports the hypothesis that the child who is rejected very early in life and remains unwanted is likely to become insecure, maladjusted and educationally backward. Never having experienced lasting love and loyalty from any adult, the child becomes unable to develop these qualities in his human relationships. Some of the children in our maladjusted group were beginning to show the characteristics of the so-called 'affectionless character', although many seemed still to be searching for and attempting to form affective ties.

It almost seems as if children in our society need to feel they matter and are valued as individuals by someone outside the children's home where the adults are paid for the job of looking after them. Physical separation and prolonged institutionalisation by themselves do not necessarily lead to emotional difficulties or character defects. Susceptibility to maladjustment and resilience to the shock of separation and deprivation appear to be determined by the quality of human relationships available to the child during critical periods of growth. Further research is needed to verify this hypothesis and to investigate whether and when this process becomes irreversible.

The main practical implication of our evidence lies in the need to ensure that every child in institutional care has the opportunity to make a stable relationship with an adult in the outside world. At present the emphasis in Child Care is firstly on the prevention of the break-up of the family and secondly on its reunification at the earliest possible moment. There is perhaps some doubt about the wisdom of this policy in every case of separation. If it is accepted that a child can suffer deprivation of emotional needs without physical separation from his mother and family, a return to a home where he is rejected is not necessarily a desirable solution. Rather there should be increased practical recognition of a child's need to feel valued by a dependable adult and increased emphasis to such adults (whether parents, relatives or friends) on the fact that it is essential to maintain their contacts with the child regularly and reliably over a period of years.

Summary

A comparative study was made of two groups of children, one considered to be 'notably stable' and the other 'severely maladjusted'. Both groups had been separated from their mothers at an early age and had remained in institutional care for a large part of their lives. They were selected from a larger group of deprived children studied previously. Our evidence suggests that the child who is rejected and remains unwanted is likely to become insecure, maladjusted and educationally backward. On the other hand, early physical separation and prolonged institutionalisation do not necessarily lead to emotional difficulties or character defects.

References

AINSWORTH, M. D. and BOWLBY, J. (1954) 'Research strategy in the study of mother–child separation', *Courrier du Centre International de l'Enfance*, **4**, 105–31.

BODMAN, F., MACKINLAY, M. and SYKES, K. (1950) 'The social adaptation of institution children', *Lancet*, **258**, 173–6.

BOWLBY, J. (1946) *Forty-four juvenile thieves, their characters and home life*. London, Baillière, Tindall & Cox.

BOWLBY, J. (1951) 'Maternal care and mental health', *Monograph Series of the World Health Organisation*, No. 2, Geneva.

BOWLBY, J., AINSWORTH, M. D., BOSTON, M. and ROSENBLUTH, D. (1956) 'The effects of mother–child separation; a follow-up study', *British Journal of Medical Psychology*, **29**, 211–244.

BOWLEY, A. H. (1947) *The psychology of the unwanted child*. Edinburgh, Livingstone.

FITZGERALD, O. W. S. (1948) 'Love deprivation and hysterical personality', *Journal of Mental Science*, **94**, 701–17.

FORD, D. (1955) *The deprived child and the community*. London, Constable.

GOLDFARB, W. (1943) 'Infant rearing and problem behaviour', *American Journal of Orthopsychiatry*, **13**, 249–65.

HOME OFFICE (1946) *Report of the Care of Children Committee*. Cmd. 6922. London, H.M.S.O. (Curtis Report).

PRINGLE, M. L. KELLMER (1957) 'Differences between schools for the maladjusted and ordinary boarding schools', *British Journal of Educational Psychology*, **27**, 29–36.

PRINGLE, M. L. KELLMER (1958) 'Learning and emotion', *Educational Review*, **10**, 146–68.

PRINGLE, M. L. KELLMER and BOSSIO, V. (1958) 'A study of deprived children. Part 2. Language development and reading attainment', *Vita Humana*, **1**, 142–70.

RHEINGOLD, H. L. (1943) 'Mental and social development of infants in relation to the number of other infants in the boarding home', *American Journal of Orthopsychiatry*, **13**, 41–4.

SPITZ, R. A. (1945) 'Hospitalism; an inquiry into the genesis of psychiatric conditions in early childhood', in *Psychoanalytic Study of the Child*, **1**, 53–74. London, Imago Publishing Co.

STOTT, D. H. (1956) 'The effects of separation from the mother in early life', *Lancet*, 624–8.

UNITED NATIONS. Department of Social Affairs (1952) *Children deprived of a normal home life*. New York.

Supplementary bibliography

DOLL, E. A. (1953) *The measurement of social competence; a manual for the Vineland Social Maturity Scale*. Educational Test Bureau, Minneapolis, U.S.A.

RAVEN, J. C. (1948) *Mill Hill Vocabulary Scale*. London, H. K. Lewis.

RAVEN, J. C. (1951) *Controlled projection for children*. 2nd edn. London, H. K. Lewis.

SCHONELL, F. J. and SCHONELL, F. E. (1956) *Diagnostic and attainment testing*. (*Silent Reading Test B.*) 3rd Edn. London, Oliver & Boyd.

STOTT, D. H. (1958) *The social adjustment of children; manual to the Bristol Social Adjustment Guides*. London, University of London Press.

WECHSLER, D. (1949) *Wechsler Intelligence Scale for Children*. New York, Psychological Corporation.

5. Conditions associated with emotional maladjustment among children in care*

with L. Clifford

Introduction

In a previous study (Pringle and Bossio, 1960) it was found that early separation from the mother or mother-substitute and prolonged institutionalisation did not necessarily lead to emotional difficulties or character defects in children. The experience of a stable, dependable and long-term relationship with an adult in the outside world seemed to be of paramount importance in the achievement of emotional adjustment while living in residential care. Our evidence supported the view that the child who is rejected early and remains unwanted, is likely to become insecure and maladjusted; while the child who remains loved and cherished by adults important to him, maintains emotional stability even though he continues to be deprived of normal family life.

The study to be described here was undertaken to verify or disprove the hypothesis that among the most stable children in residential care, a significantly higher proportion would be found to have regular and frequent contact with parents or parent substitutes than among those considered to be the most maladjusted.

Perhaps it should be mentioned that this study was carried out in a different part of the country from the earlier one. At the time when the fieldwork was being done, the results of the former had not yet been published and so could not have influenced the replies of those who cooperated.

The present investigation

The house mothers in a Local Authority Cottage Home, each of whom is responsible for a group of eight to fourteen children, were asked to complete a questionnaire which aimed at ascertaining

* First published in *Educational Review*, February 1962, 14, 2, 112–123.

whether or not a child had contact with adults outside the Home. The questionnaire was designed to give information on the frequency, regularity and nature of this contact. Only factual replies were required. A weighted score was then given to each possible answer; thus a child who received weekly letters and visits, and who spent week-ends away from the Home, would receive the maximum score possible (namely 18 points). The questionnaire, with the weightings written beside each category, is shown in the Appendix. The study was limited to those aged 6 to 12 years, and children who had been in care less than a year were excluded. This part of the investigation was concerned with sixty-six children.

Several weeks later, the house mothers were asked to rank the same children in their group from the most stable and adjusted to the most difficult problem child. To ensure that these terms would be interpreted by the eleven house mothers in as similar a way as possible (some guidance was given regarding the term 'maladjustment'), it was suggested that most children show difficult, unacceptable behaviour occasionally and temporarily; that a child should be considered maladjusted only if his behaviour was difficult or deviant more or less consistently and over a considerable period of time; and that over-timidity and withdrawn behaviour may be as much a symptom of emotional disturbance as aggression and hostility. Of course, despite this precaution, such factors as personal incompatibility between some children and their house mothers, or their relative skill in handling them, were bound to influence not only the adult's judgments regarding the children's adjustment, but also the very way in which the children did in fact adjust. However, the seriousness of this difficulty was lessened to some extent, since only a rank order and not absolute judgments were obtained. In addition the house mothers' judgments were checked by the Superintendent of the Home.

The children from each house were then divided into three groups, the most maladjusted, those neither markedly stable nor maladjusted, and the most stable. As far as possible, the numbers in these groups were maintained in the ratio 1 to 2 to 1. The mean scores obtained on the 'visits' questionnaire for these three groups were 4·14, 5·00 and 7·07 respectively. (It will be remembered that a high score indicates regular and frequent contacts.) An analysis of variance showed that these means differed significantly at the 10 per cent level; our figures correspond to a correlation coefficient eta (η) of

0·28. Considering the small numbers involved and the fact that a heterogeneous sample of house mothers were making the assessments of relative adjustments, these results can be taken as positive evidence in favour of the hypothesis that there exists a relationship between emotional adjustment and the regularity and frequency of contact a child is experiencing with adults in the outside world.

To corroborate further the reliability of the judgments made by the house mothers, and to gain some insight into some other aspects which might distinguish the stable from the maladjusted child in care, it was decided to study the 25 per cent most stable and the 25 per cent most maladjusted children (the criterion being the ranking made by the house mothers); each group comprised seventeen children, of which twenty-one were boys and thirteen girls. The proportion of the sexes is very similar to that in the Cottage Home population of that age. However, there were twice as many boys in the maladjusted as compared with the stable group (table 5.1).

Table 5.1. **Proportion of 6- to 12-year-old boys and girls in the Home and in the selected groups**

	In the Home		Selected groups		Stable		Maladjusted	
	N	%	N	%	N	%	N	%
B	39	59	21	62	7	41	14	82
G	27	41	13	38	10	59	3	18

To obtain some information on the children's background and to check the reliability of the answers given by the house mothers on the 'visits' questionnaire, the case files kept for each child by the Children's Department were consulted. Regarding the latter point, a very close correspondence was found between these two sources of information (table 5.2). Of the two stable children with little or no contact with adults outside, one had a younger brother living in the same Home with whom she had a very close and warm relationship. The other child was described by the house mother as warm-hearted and spontaneous; she had always been very popular among children and adults and tended to 'mother' those younger than herself.

The personal and family background of the children was very similar. A majority in both groups had been separated from their mother for the first time before the age of 2 years, and had been in

Table 5.2. Frequency and regularity of contact with outside adults

		Regular and frequent	Irregular and infrequent	Very little or no contact
Stable	files*	12	1	2
N = 17	house mother	13	2	2
Maladjusted	files	2	3	12
N = 17	house mother	2	3	12

* For two of the stable children there was no information in the files regarding this point.

care for five years or more (tables 5.3 and 5.4). Nearly half the children in each group were illegitimate, but the number of mothers in mental deficiency hospitals was rather larger in the maladjusted group (table 5.5). For the latter, the most frequent reason for coming into care was being abandoned or deserted, while for the stable children there was no single outstanding reason (table 5.6).

Table 5.3. Age at first separation (in months)

	0–12	13–24	25–60	61 or more
Stable	5	4	2	6
Maladjusted	6	3	5	3

Table 5.4. Total time in care (in months)

	12–24	25–60	61 or more
Stable	1	4	12
Maladjusted	2	1	14

Table 5.5. Family background

	Father's status				
	Illegitimate	Skilled	Unskilled	Unknown	Prison
Stable	7	2	5	8	2
Maladjusted	8	3	4	9	1

	Mother's status			
	Unskilled	Unknown	Prison	Mental deficiency hospital
Stable	3	11	2	1
Maladjusted	2	9	1	5

Table 5.6. Main reasons for coming into care *

	Deserted or abandoned	Cruelty	Neglect	Unsuitable housing	Mother a mental defective
Stable	4	2	6	5	1
Maladjusted	8	2	3	3	5

* More than one reason was given for some children.

About a month after the house mothers had ranked all the children in order of adjustment, they were asked to complete the Bristol Social Adjustment Guides (Stott, 1958) for the seventeen most stable and the seventeen most maladjusted children. Perhaps it should be mentioned that not until all the field-work was completed was the purpose of the investigation and the method of selecting the children for further individual study discussed with any of the staff in the Home or in the Children's Department. The results obtained from the Guides show that this more objective assessment of emotional adjustment distinguished quite clearly the stable from the maladjusted group, thus fully supporting the more subjective ranking made by the house mothers earlier on (table 5.7).

Table 5.7. Bristol social adjustment guides

	Mean	Range
Stable N = 17	14·0	1–38
Maladjusted N = 17	33·7	7–68

It will be remembered that a high score on the Guides denotes maladjustment. The section called 'Relatives' on the Guides was also compared with the replies given by the house mothers to the 'Visits Questionnaire'. Almost complete correspondence was found, proving again the reliability of this information.

Each child in the stable and maladjusted groups was also interviewed individually to explore emotional attitudes and to obtain some indication of formal attainments. A simple interview schedule was devised to ensure that each child was asked the same questions in the same order. The questions were designed to elicit information on the children's spare-time activities and interests; on their attitudes to school and their friendships; and on their personal ambitions and wishes. There were no different patterns of answers or specially noteworthy replies received from the two groups, with two exceptions which are described below. First, regarding vocational ambition, more than half of the stable group chose jobs which can broadly be classified as 'helping people': nursing, looking after children, being a house mother, etc.; none of the maladjusted group made such a choice, but more than half gave what might be termed childish stereotypes: becoming a cowboy, soldier or policeman; none of the stable but four of the maladjusted refused to commit themselves (table 5.8).

Table 5.8. Vocational ambition

	Childish stereotype	Same job as parent(s)	'Helping people'	Don't know
Stable	6	1	10	—
Maladjusted	10	3	0	4

Secondly, when invited to give three wishes, the greatest number of wishes in both groups were for personal possessions such as toys, pets and sweets, but the total number of such wishes was higher in the maladjusted group. Thirteen of the stable children expressed the wish to live with one or both parents or with parent substitutes, but only three maladjusted children gave voice to this desire. In each group the same number mentioned some future ambition, such as 'to play football for Aston Villa', or 'to be the boss of a big firm', or 'to work on a farm'. Four children, two in each group, were quite unable or unwilling to answer this question (table 5.9).

Table 5.9. Children's 'three wishes'

	Possessions	Return home	Future ambition
Stable	25	15	7
Maladjusted	35	3	7

A drawing of a man was also obtained from each child. There were unusual and rather bizarre features in seven drawings of the maladjusted group, but in only one of the stable group. Bizarre features included a huge nose in profile; a very elongated neck; a face with huge eyes and long lashes but no nose; and one drawing which consisted of very detailed and well executed eyes, nose and mouth to which, however, the child would add nothing else despite repeated instructions to draw the whole man.

Lastly, there was also a marked difference in the attitude of the two groups of children during the interview and towards the examiner. A friendly, relaxed manner, and a willingness to talk readily and spontaneously, characterised the behaviour of the majority in the stable group. Many of the maladjusted children, on the other hand, appeared to be rather tense and lacking in confidence, often confining their answers to a minimum and being unwilling to volunteer any observations. The information supplied by the house mothers on the Bristol Social Adjustment Guides also brings out the apparent inability of many of the maladjusted group to make easy relationships. Over-anxiety for approval on the one hand, and 'unforthcomingness' on the other, figured quite prominently in the descriptions.

To assess achievements, the Vocabulary Test from the WISC (Wechsler, 1949) and the Neale Reading Test (Neale, 1958) were administered. The results show that whereas about half of the children in the maladjusted group scored below average, more than two-thirds of the stable group received an average or above average scaled score (table 5.10).

Table 5.10. WISC vocabulary test means and scaled scores

		0–6	7–13	14–20
	Mean	below average	average	above average
Stable	8·2	5	11	1
Maladjusted	6·9	9	8	—

There was one outstanding, qualitative difference between the two groups concerning the response given to the word 'knife'. A definition implying aggression or violence was given by seven of the maladjusted children, compared with only two of the stable group. For example, three of the maladjusted children said 'you stick it into people', and two said 'for killing'.

In reading, the stable group was also superior in attainment. The pattern of differences is very similar for all the three aspects of reading which were tested, with more than twice as many maladjusted as stable children falling into the illiterate category (table 5.11).

Table 5.11. Level of literacy reached on the Neale Test

	Comprehension			Accuracy			Speed		
	Illiterate	Semi-literate	Literate	Illiterate	Semi-literate	Literate	Illiterate	Semi-literate	Literate
Stable	5	10	2	4	8	5	3	8	6
Maladjusted	11	4	2	9	6	2	8	7	2

The categories adopted for levels of literacy are those suggested by the Ministry of Education (1950), namely:
illiterate = reading age below 6 years 11 months
semi-literate = reading ages between 7 and 8 years 11 months
literate = reading age 9 years and above

Discussion and conclusion

The results of this investigation confirm the hypothesis advanced previously that one of the conditions which distinguishes the stable from the maladjusted child in care is the regularity and frequency of contact with parents or persons outside the Home. Where a dependable relationship exists with an adult outside the Children's Home, a child stands a significantly better chance of remaining emotionally adjusted despite being deprived of normal family life.

It may be asked whether a dependable relationship with a house mother or the Superintendent of a Home may not become a source of stability and security to a child. This question was not examined in this investigation. But theoretical considerations lead one to think that such a relationship may not be easily achieved: first, however well the staff look after a child, he is aware of the fact that in a residential establishment the people who care for him are paid to do so; secondly, the shortage and rate of turnover of staff militate against the building up of a long-term relationship; thirdly, the child knows that he is different from those children who live with their own parents or whose family at least keep in touch with them, yet he does not, indeed cannot, understand why this should be so; thus it may well be that it is the child who has no dependable adult in the outside world (who cares for him for his own sake) who rejects whatever friendship and affection is offered to him by members of the Home staff.

It may well be that if unconditional loyalty and affection from an adult outside the Home is not experienced, a child can become eventually unable to develop these qualities in his human relationships. The child who failed to learn in early childhood the responses appropriate and expected in such a relationship, remains immature, like a very young infant who takes love for granted and demands unceasing devotion. Thus the emotionally deprived child tends to alienate and often to lose any affection and goodwill offered subsequently, because he seems selfish, greedy and ungrateful. This deprives him of the opportunity to learn the very skills needed in making close human relationships; instead he learns to mistrust affection when offered. And so the vicious circle develops of the unloved and friendless child, in turn becoming unloving and hostile towards others. In our study this tendency was reflected in the assessments made by the house mothers and by the reactions of the maladjusted children during the psychological interview.

There was little difference in the family background of the two groups, except that more maladjusted children came into care because they had been deserted or abandoned. This again supports the view that it is the element of definite parental rejection which has the most adverse effect (Bowlby 1951; Bevan and Jones 1961). It is in the same group that the number of mentally defective mothers was greater, which may indicate a higher degree of inherent weakness among the maladjusted children.

During the psychological interview, three main differences emerged between the two groups. The first was in the children's general attitude to the situation and to the examiner. The second was in the choice of vocational ambition, which suggests that many of the stable children had made some identification with the various professional workers who were taking care of them. Thirdly, when asked to give three wishes, a high proportion of the stable group voiced the desire to be reunited with their family; the fact that only a few maladjusted children mentioned the same wish suggests that they were denying the reality of a loss that had become unbearable. A similar phenomenon was found among pre-school children living in a residential nursery, who rarely used the word 'mummy' in comparison with children of the same age living with their own families (Pringle and Tanner, 1958).

Lastly, with regard to achievements, the performance of the stable group was superior on both the vocabulary and the reading tests which were administered. Again, similar findings were obtained in earlier studies (Pringle and Bossio, 1958 and 1960) supporting the view that emotion and learning are closely interlinked.

The main practical implication of our evidence lies in the need for preventive action. Recent work tends to show that many of the ill-effects of deprivation are preventable (Gray and Parr, 1957; Clarke and Clarke, 1960; Trasler, 1960). That rehabilitation and recovery can also take place even during late adolescence and adulthood has been convincingly demonstrated in recent years, notably by the work of Clarke and Clarke (1954, 1958 and 1959). But an early enrichment of experience—emotional, experiential and educational—seems preferable both from a humanitarian and an economic point of view. There is little doubt that the public care of children is still very inadequate despite the tremendous improvements which have taken place during the past twelve years, and despite all the efforts of child care workers. As a community we are as yet unwilling to spend sufficient money not only on preventing the break-up of families but also on providing an adequate child care service. Perhaps the chief stumbling block is the shortage of staff, especially house staff. Is it realistic to expect children to form close and dependable ties with house mothers when the national rate of turnover for such staff is about 30 per cent annually? The shortage of really suitable people for this highly skilled and exacting work is also chronic. At present the duties are too arduous, the hours too long and the salary too low to attract a sufficient number of candidates even to existing training courses. It is beyond the scope of this paper to make detailed suggestions for preventive measures, but this has been done elsewhere (Pringle and Sutcliffe, 1960; Pringle, 1961). Suffice it to say that the present shortcomings will be perpetuated until it becomes possible for child care staff to be selected in such a way that in each Children's Home an enriched environment can be provided to enable the children to recover from past deprivations and to have experiences which compensate for the lack of 'normal' family life.

Summary

Further evidence has been obtained to support the hypothesis that among the most stable children in care, a significantly higher proportion have regular and frequent contact with parents or parent-substitutes than those considered to be most maladjusted. A long-term, dependable relationship with an adult in the outside world seems to make an important contribution to the achievement of emotional stability of children placed in residential care. Some other differences between a stable and a maladjusted group of children were also explored in this study. The need is stressed for early preventive action and for provision of enriching experiences to compensate for some of the shortcomings of residential life.

QUESTIONNAIRE-VISITS*

Name of child................ Resident at.................

Please underline what applies

1. Does the child receive cards, letters and parcels
   almost every week (6)/about once a month (4)/only birthdays and Christmas (2)/very rarely (1)/ never (0)
2. Is the child visited
   almost every week (6)/about once a month (4)/only at special occasions (2)/ very rarely (1)/never (0)

   * The scoring used is indicated in brackets after the appropriate items.

3. From whom does he receive mail and visits?
   members of his family/other relatives/friends
4. Does the child spend a holiday away from the Home
   every week-end (6)/about once a month (6)/only at Christmas or
   birthday (2)/only rarely (1)/never (0)
5. If he does have such holidays does he spend them
   with different people each time/with his own family/with other
   relatives.

Maximum score possible = 18 points.

Signed ....

Date   ....

References

BEVAN, R. T. and JONES, B. (1961) 'Signs occurring in childhood which indicate a poor social prognosis', *Case Conference*, **7**, 206–211.

BOWLBY, J. (1951) 'Maternal care and mental health', *Monograph Series of the World Health Organisation*, No. 2, Geneva.

CLARKE, A. D. B. and CLARKE, A. M. (1954) 'Cognitive changes in the feeble-minded', *British Journal of Psychology*, **45**, 173–9.

CLARKE, A. D. B. and CLARKE, A. M. (1959) 'Recovery from the effects of deprivation', *Acta Psychologica*, **16**, 137–44. Amsterdam.

CLARKE, A. D. B. and CLARKE, A. M. (1960) 'Some recent advances in the study of early deprivation', *Journal of Child Psychology and Psychiatry*, **1**, 26–36.

CLARKE, A. D. B., CLARKE, A. M. and REIMAN, S. (1958) 'Cognitive and social changes in the feeble-minded; three further studies', *British Journal of Psychology*, **49**, 144–57.

EDUCATION, MINISTRY OF (1950) *Reading ability; some suggestions for helping the backward.* (Pamphlet no. 18.) London, H.M.S.O.

GRAY, P. G. and PARR, E. A. (1957) *Children in care and the recruitment of foster parents; an enquiry made for the Home Office.* London. Social Survey.

NEALE, M. D. (1958) *Neale analysis of reading ability. Manual of directions and norms.* Test booklet. London, Macmillan.

PRINGLE, M. L. KELLMER (1961) 'Emotional adjustment among children in care. Part 2. Practical implications', *Child Care*, **15**, 54–8.

PRINGLE, M. L. KELLMER and BOSSIO, V. (1958) 'A study of deprived children. Part 2. Language development and reading attainment', *Vita Humana*, **1**, 142–70.

G

92

PRINGLE, M. L. KELLMER and BOSSIO, V. (1960) 'Early, prolonged separation and emotional maladjustment', *Journal of Child Psychology and Psychiatry*, 1, 37–48.

PRINGLE, M. L. KELLMER and SUTCLIFFE, B. (1960) *Remedial education; an experiment. An account of two years' work by a remedial unit for maladjusted and deprived children at the Caldecott Community.* University of Birmingham and Caldecott Community.

PRINGLE, M. L. KELLMER and TANNER, M. (1958) 'The effects of early deprivation on speech development', *Language and Speech*, 1, 269–87.

STOTT, D. H. (1958) *The social adjustment of children; manual to the Bristol social adjustment guides.* London, University of London Press.

TRASLER, G. (1960) *In place of parents; a study of foster care.* London, Routledge & Kegan Paul.

WECHSLER, DAVID (1949) *Wechsler Intelligence Scale for Children.* Manual. New York, Psychological Corporation.

6. Remedial education—an experiment*

with B. Sutcliffe

Foreword

A history of the Caldecott Community is shortly to be published. For those unacquainted with its work a short description of its aim may be of value. The Caldecott Community undertakes the care of deprived or homeless and disturbed children; as a Community we recognise that the mental health and wellbeing of the children depend largely on our ability to discover any factors likely to contribute to their harmonious development.

Most of the children in the Community are of high average or superior intelligence, but recently we became aware of the great discrepancy between their educational attainments and potential ability. This appears to be due largely to the emotional disturbances in their home background during early childhood and partly to the fact that they had frequent changes of schools at an age when continuous, uninterrupted teaching in the basic subjects of number and reading is essential.

Caldecott children remain in our own primary school until eleven. They then attend daily the secondary schools of the neighbourhood. We found that comparatively few were placed in classes in the A stream; far too many of our intelligent children found themselves in the C or D streams of a large school. Here their confidence in themselves was sapped and they appeared incapable of 'catching up' in basic subjects or facing their failure. Such children obviously require individual therapeutic teaching and help, which should be available if required as soon as they enter the Community.

We were fortunate in coming in contact with Dr Pringle from the Department of Child Study of Birmingham University and, owing to the generosity of the Trustees of the Nuffield Foundation, we were

* First published by the Caldecott Community, 1960.

able to appoint one of Dr Pringle's experienced students, Miss Sutcliffe, to establish a small remedial unit at the Community. Dr Pringle herself kindly undertook to supervise this Unit and to conduct conferences every term on the children attending it. These conferences, combined with the daily work of Miss Sutcliffe, proved invaluable to the staff of the Community as well as to the children themselves; for not only did we hear of the actual results of the remedial teaching, but the conferences (in which we all could take part) added greatly to our understanding of individual children through discussion and interchange of observations. We all gained increased insight into the problems of each child under review.

The Remedial Unit has been invaluable to the whole Community and the necessity of remedial teaching in a Community of maladjusted children has proved itself beyond dispute.

Leila Rendel,
The Caldecott Community,
Mersham le Hatch,
Ashford, Kent.   1 February 1960.

Introduction

Comments made by teachers about deprived children would lead one to conclude that they have greater educational difficulties than the pupil who lives with his own family. Since intellectual ability is often judged by a child's educational achievements, it is not surprising that deprived children living in children's homes of one kind or another, are thought to be mentally dull on the whole. However, a recent study of the incidence of dullness among deprived children refutes this opinion (Pringle and Bossio, 1958). It was found that the majority of the deprived children were of average intelligence, the proportion being very similar to that among ordinary children (79 per cent and 82 per cent, respectively). With regard to educational attainment the picture is very different. Recent investigations have shown that the proportion of educationally backward and retarded children is considerably greater among the deprived than among ordinary pupils of comparable age (Lewis, 1954; Pringle, 1957; Pringle and Bossio, 1958). Similarly, a serious degree of backwardness in language development was found among the deprived children, corroborating previous research results (Gesell and Amatruda, 1947; Moore, 1947; Burlingham and Freud, 1954; Pringle and Tanner, 1958). There is clearly a link between language development and success in learning to read, since retarded speech and a limited vocabulary inevitably handicap a child in mastering the printed word.

Coming into care is usually the end product of a chain of adverse circumstances which interact and reinforce one another and which affect the lives of deprived children long before they are taken into care. Among these, the following are likely to be of importance: unstimulating and impoverished cultural conditions; a lack of educational standards and ambitions; poverty, illhealth and unemployment; a family broken in spirit if not in reality.

If one accepts that there is a close interrelationship between educational and emotional difficulties, it becomes apparent that deprived children are caught in a vicious circle; the very circumstances preceding and eventually leading to their removal from home, are also likely to lead to a high incidence of language retardation and maladjustment; these militate against successful learning; unsuccessful learning results in a sense of failure and frustration, thus further increasing the likelihood of maladjustment and learning difficulties.

The aim of the experimental unit

At the instigation of Miss Leila Rendel a remedial unit was established at the Caldecott Community to study the effectiveness of remedial treatment with deprived and maladjusted children. Help with reading was considered to be most important, with help in arithmetic taking second place. The work was to last for two years and a full-time teacher, possessing special training and experience, was appointed. Two groups of educationally backward children were eligible for help; first, those living in the Community and attending its own school: secondly, children in the care of the Kent Children's Committee and living either in a children's home or in foster homes. It is worth commenting that although the former were taught in relatively small classes (about twenty children), their learning difficulties had persisted. The latter group of children attended local primary schools where classes were large.

If the remedial work proved of help to one or both groups of children, it was hoped that local authorities and other bodies might become interested in providing similar facilities for the children in their care who were having serious educational difficulties.

The selection procedure

It was decided to concentrate on children of junior school age who were of average intelligence (defined as an I.Q. of 85 and above on the Terman–Merrill Intelligence Scale). The main criterion for selection was backwardness or retardation in reading, in arithmetic, or in both. For the purpose of this investigation retardation was defined as a discrepancy of two years or more between mental age and attainment level on individually administered tests. In fact, many of the children were not only retarded but also backward, showing a discrepancy of two years or more between their chronological and attainment age. Altogether, twenty-seven children attended the unit, of which twenty-one lived in the Caldecott Community. The remaining six were in the care of the local authority, five of them staying in a children's home and one living with a foster family. All but three attended junior schools.

For the Caldecott children the method of selection was as follows: the class teachers put forward a list of children who, in their opinion, were likely to benefit from remedial treatment. Then a case conference was held, attended by all concerned with the children's life in the Community. After a full consideration of the history of each child, and of his progress since being admitted to the Caldecott, a final selection was made. Referral of local authority children was made by the Children's Officer after discussion with the schools and homes. Again, the final selection of cases to be accepted for treatment was made at a case conference.

For each child a school report was obtained as well as information from the housemothers, both before and after treatment; the remedial teacher similarly rated the children for various personality traits. However, in this report, the response to remedial treatment is evaluated mainly in terms of improvement measured by the following objective tests: (a) Schonell's Graded Reading Vocabulary test; (b) Schonell's Silent Reading test A; (c) Schonell's Mechanical Arithmetic test A. The maximum possible period of remedial treatment was twenty-one months while the shortest time for which a child attended was four months.

The children
Of the twenty-seven children only five were girls. In fifteen cases the main problem was reading, in thirteen cases arithmetic; only one boy received help in both subjects (No. 27, pp. 104 and 110). Eleven out of fifteen children were both backward and retarded in reading, while in arithmetic five out of thirteen were both backward and retarded.

Details of the children's age, intelligence and level of attainment before remedial treatment began, are shown on tables 6.1, 6.3, 6.5, 6.7 and 6.10 (pp. 102, 104, 106, 108 and 110). In one case (No. 26, table 6.10) the child's level of attainment did not justify his receiving remedial help, but his attitude to school work was very hostile and negative, and he was a severe behaviour problem both in school and in the Community. It was therefore decided to try this approach.

All the children who were selected for attendance at the remedial unit had not only severe educational problems but also showed a wide variety of symptoms of emotional maladjustment. These ranged from temper tantrums, sullenness and stealing, to apathy, lack of concentration and an inability to mix with their fellows. A brief description of each child may give some indication of the home background, the range of problems encountered and of the children's responses to remedial treatment. These accounts will be found in the Appendix (p. 118). Summarising, it may be said that in almost every case the preschool years had been a very unsettled or unhappy time and family life had remained seriously disrupted or otherwise unsatisfactory. Thus, twenty-one children came from broken homes, where one or both parents had abandoned the child or left the family, or where because of circumstances such as divorce, desertion, a prison sentence or death, the child could no longer remain in his home. Since being separated from their families most children had experienced a number of different placements, such as residential nurseries, children's homes, foster families and temporary returns to their homes or to relatives. In addition, ten of the children were illegitimate. It was, therefore, not unexpected that the incidence of emotional maladjustment and of educational difficulty was very high among this group of children.

Throughout the two-year period, remedial treatment was given during school terms. Each child was taken individually for at least one hour per week, this being divided into two weekly sessions in some cases. Where necessary, a child attended more frequently for a period of time. Group work was tried but was found to be unsatisfactory in most cases. Partly because of their emotional disturbance and partly because of differential rates of educational progress, individual attention remained essential for most children. Flexibility and regular consultations with the schools were deliberate features of the remedial unit.

Shortly after its inception, the remedial teacher kept the unit, which consisted of a classroom and a play room, open on four evenings a week in answer to requests made by the children. The opportunity to spend additional periods in the unit could not be offered to the children in the care of the local authority since they lived a considerable distance away from the Caldecott. In other respects, too, the children living in the Caldecott Community were more favourably placed than the children cared for in the local authority children's homes: in the former there is a small turnover of staff since people remain working there for many years; the staff–child ratio is more favourable; the same applies to the provision of toys, books and spare time activities, including sports and games; the Community is housed in a gracious building situated in beautiful grounds; lastly, and probably most important, the directors of the Community have built up over the years a secure and therapeutic atmosphere which permeates everything done for and with the children and which has become a way of life. On the other hand, it must be remembered that more than half of the children are ascertained as being maladjusted; but once they have been accepted into the Community, they usually remain there without further changes unless it becomes possible for them to return to a settled home with their parents or some relatives.

Since there were these considerable differences between the lives and circumstances of the local authority and the Caldecott children, different responses to remedial treatment might be expected from the two groups. For this reason, they are discussed separately.

The nature and aim of remedial education

Before describing the results achieved, we might briefly discuss what we mean by remedial education.

Not all children who have fallen behind in their school work need a special educational approach. Where a pupil remains willing and able to learn, systematic coaching may well meet the case. Remedial education is required by children whose educational underfunctioning is accompanied by emotional difficulties. These may range from apathy, lack of concentration and overtimidity to aggressiveness and antisocial behaviour. In some cases, these may be caused by the learning difficulties, while in others the position may well be reversed. In practice, it is often difficult, if not impossible, to disentangle cause and effect. Perhaps the main reason for this is the inevitable and continuing interaction between emotional and intellectual processes; for instance, readiness to learn, be it in the narrower sense of the three Rs or in the wider one of learning to control feelings, depends not merely on age, physical maturation and intellectual ability, but as much on interpersonal relationships, social expectations and adequate motivation.

In practice, it is not always possible or, indeed, essential, to determine whether the emotional difficulties have caused the educational problems or vice versa. In the present state of knowledge, where so much remains to be learned about emotional and educational difficulties in childhood, it must suffice to know that remedial education often leads to improved adjustment in both spheres. It aims at modifying the child's often hostile or defeatist attitude to learning, and at restoring self-confidence and a sense of curiosity. Motivation is usually the key problem. To bring about changes in attitude and feelings, creative and therapeutic activities such as acting, miming, painting and modelling play an essential part. Remedial teaching is, as far as possible, linked to these activities, so as to ensure the child's active participation and interest. No generalisations can be made regarding the most suitable teaching methods or techniques. Their choice depends entirely on the nature of the child's learning difficulties, the stage he has reached and the methods which have been employed previously. Similarly, one cannot generalise on the type of therapeutic play which is most effective or on the proportion of time which should be devoted to 'play' and to 'work'. This will vary not only from one child to another, but also for the same child from one remedial session to another. For this reason, the remedial teacher needs to have available a wide range of play and creative materials as well as a wide range of books and other teaching aids.

When successful, remedial treatment results in considerable acceleration in the rate of educational progress. Equally important, attitudes to learning, to difficulties and to challenge improve, and relationships with adults and other children become happier. Often too, a remission of symptoms follows. How to assess these improvements is a difficult problem. As yet, there are no reliable measures available to evaluate changes of attitude and personality, though retests of attainment cover one important aspect. Of course, it can always be argued that improved emotional and social adjustment may be due to causes other than remedial education. This assertion is unanswerable but it applies equally to most other kinds of treatment. For the time being then, acceleration in the rate of learning and

improved behaviour reported by teachers and house parents, have
to be accepted as criteria of improvement.

The results

1. *The test results and their interpretation*

The level of tested intelligence and attainment for each child before
and after treatment is shown on Tables 6.1, 6.3, 6.5, 6.7 and 6.10
(pp. 102, 104, 106, 108, 110). The amount of backwardness and retardation is indicated only where either exceeded two years. Every
child made considerably more progress during remedial treatment
than he had done previously; however, eighteen children remained
backward or retarded although to a less serious degree. This is due to
the fact that for some years past these children had made less than
twelve months progress during each year. If as a result of remedial
treatment eighteen months' progress is made during a twelve-month
period—i.e., a considerable increase in the rate of progress—the
discrepancy between chronological and attainment age will only be
narrowed by six months. For this reason, increase in attainment age
does not reflect adequately the acceleration of the learning process
resulting from remedial teaching. A comparison between the rate of
progress before and during treatment was, therefore, made. When
referred to the unit, all children were reported by their teachers to be
making very slow progress or to have come to a standstill altogether.
In most cases it was impossible to determine whether present attainments had been reached within the first year or two of schooling, or
whether these had been acquired slowly over the years. It was
certain, however, that in no case accepted for treatment, had there
been a recent sudden spurt of improvement. This was evident both
from school reports and test results available for the majority over a
period of at least twelve months prior to the children's referral to the
remedial unit.

To enable a comparison to be made, it was decided to calculate
progress made in reading and arithmetic prior to remedial treatment
on the assumption that it had proceeded at a constant rate during the
preceding years. Present attainment (expressed in months) was
therefore divided by the total time (also expressed in months) which
a child had spent in school since he started at the age of 5 years. Then
the rate of progress made during remedial treatment was calculated
by dividing the progress made (i.e., increase in attainment age) by
the number of months during which treatment was given. Pupils of

normal intelligence who have no learning difficulties make one month's educational progress during each calendar month. Backward children fail to do so and remedial treatment aims at bringing about an acceleration in their rate of learning. In order 'to catch up' and to hold their own with their contemporaries, it is not sufficient if backward children begin to make normal progress; if they are to reach the level of attainment commensurate with their age and ability, they need to make more than one month's progress during each month of remedial teaching.

The assessment of any measurable improvement resulting from remedial treatment is beset by a problem for which it is difficult to make allowance. It is not infrequently found that test results are somewhat unreliable with children who have experienced severe learning difficulties. Even when good progress has been made and unfavourable attitudes have been changed, testing procedures seem to revive the feelings of apprehension and lack of confidence previously shown. When this happens, the tests are likely to give an underestimate of the child's actual level of attainment. From the type of book the pupil is reading, the remedial teacher knows what level of achievement has been reached, yet the test results may indicate a considerably lower level of reading ability (see for example cases Nos. 6 and 10, pp. 120 and 122).

One last point needs to be made regarding the results obtained in this experimental study. Ideally a child should receive remedial treatment until he has made sufficient progress to be able to hold his own with his peers. The period of time needed for this would vary from one case to another. Alternatively, it would make a 'tidier' experiment if each child received special help for the same period of time. Practical considerations, however, prevented the adoption of either of these procedures and the length of treatment varied from a minimum period of four months to a possible maximum of twenty-one months. A detailed analysis of the length of treatment given to the reading and arithmetic cases, respectively, is shown in table 6.15 (p. 113). It might well be that more satisfactory results would have been achieved if every child had at least received treatment for the whole period of the experiment.

2. Improvement in reading
a. *Caldecott children.* The level of attainment reached by each child in mechanical and comprehension reading before and after remedial

Table 6.1. Mechanical reading level before and after treatment

Caldecott Children. N = 8

	Before remedial treatment						After remedial treatment						
Name	C.A. Yrs. Mths.	M.A. Yrs. Mths.	I.Q.	G.R.V. Yrs. Mths.	Back. Yrs. Mths.	Ret. Yrs. Mths.	C.A. Yrs. Mths.	M.A. Yrs. Mths.	G.W.R. Yrs. Mths.	Back. Yrs. Mths.	Ret. Yrs. Mths.	Progress Months	Total period of treatment months
1. Edward*	11 8	10 0	86	6 7	5 1	3 5	13 6	11 7	8 10	4 8	2 9	27	17
2. Paula	11 6	10 4	90	7 6	4 0	2 10	11 10	10 7	8 5	3 5	2 2	11	4
3. Gertrude	10 6	11 7	111	8 1	2 5	3 6	12 2	13 6	10 1	2 1	3 5	24	20
4. George	10 0	8 9	88	5 1	4 11	3 8	11 5	10 0	6 8	4 9	3 4	19	17
5. Charles	9 2	12 3	133	7 5	—	4 10	9 10	13 0	9 0	—	4 0	19	8
6. Donald	9 0	9 10	110	5 10	3 2	4 0	10 9	11 9	7 10	2 11	3 11	24	21
7. Keith	7 7	7 11	105	Below 5 0	2 7	2 11	9 1	9 6	7 1	2 0	2 5	25	18
8. Betty	8 6	10 2	120	7 1	—	3 1	8 11	10 8	8 2	—	2 6	13	5

* This child went abroad with his family for 5 months and during this time did not receive any remedial treatment. Therefore, 5 months has been subtracted from the total period of treatment (i.e., date of commencement of remedial treatment and date of discharge).

Abbreviations:

C.A.—Chronological age at the start of remedial treatment.
M.A.} Mental Age and Intelligence Quotient measured by the Terman–
I.Q. } Merrill Intelligence Scale.
G.W.R.—Schonell's Graded Reading Vocabulary Test.
Back.—Backwardness, i.e., discrepancy between tested reading age and chronological age.
Ret.—Retardation, i.e., discrepancy between tested reading age and mental age.

treatment is shown in tables 6.1 and 6.3 (pp. 102 and 104). Two children (cases No. 4 and 7, table 6.1) were non-readers. All except two children (Nos. 5 and 8) were both backward and retarded. With regard to comprehension reading, several children were unable, at the beginning of remedial treatment, to obtain a score on Schonell's Silent Reading test, the norms of which commence at 6 years 9 months (cases 1, 4, 6 and 7, table 6.3). Thus one cannot readily calculate the degree of backwardness and retardation, except to state that it was severe in every case. Progress made in comprehension reading was calculated from a base line of 6 years 7 months.

As can be seen from tables 6.2 and 6.4 column IV (pp. 103 and

Table 6.2. Rate of progress in mechanical reading before and during remedial treatment

Caldecott children. N = 8

I	II	III	IV	V	VI	VII
Name	Time in school * Months	Progress in reading Months	Rate of progress per month in school Months	Period of remedial treat- ment Months	Progress during remedial treat- ment Months	Rate of progress per month of treat- ment Months
1. Edward	80	19	0·2	17	27	1·6
2. Paula	78	30	0·4	4	11	2·7
3. Gertrude	66	37	0·6	20	24	1·2
4. George	60	1	0·0	17	19	1·1
5. Charles	50	29	0·6	8	8	1·0
6. Donald	48	10	0·2	21	24	1·1
7. Keith	31	0	0·0	18	25	1·4
8. Betty	42	25	0·6	5	13	2·7

* Present age minus age at start of school (5 years).

105) no child had made normal progress in school before remedial treatment (i.e., one month's progress per month in school). During the period of remedial treatment, the majority were making more than a month's educational progress during each month (column VII). The rate of progress accelerated on an average five to six times in mechanical reading and seven times in comprehension reading (see columns IV and VII, pp. 103 and 105). Thus in over half the cases, the rate of learning had become considerably faster than normal. Most of the other children made about one month's progress during each month of remedial treatment but even this meant progress for children (such as George, No. 4, table 6.2 above) who had virtually been at a standstill educationally for several years.

Table 6.3. Comprehension reading level before and after treatment

Caldecott children. N = 9

	Before remedial treatment						After remedial treatment						
Name	C.A. Yrs. Mths.	M.A. Yrs. Mths.	I.Q.	Sil.A. Yrs. Mths.	Back. Yrs. Mths.	Ret. Yrs. Mths.	C.A. Yrs. Mths.	M.A. Yrs. Mths.	Sil.A. Yrs. Mths.	Back. Yrs. Mths.	Ret. Yrs. Mths.	Progress Months	Total period of treatment Months
1. Edward	11 8	10 0	86	Below norms	—	Severe	13 6	11 7	7 11	5 7	3 8	16	17
2. Paula	11 6	10 4	90	7 11	3 7	2 5	11 10	10 7	10 10	—	—	35	4
3. Gertrude	10 6	11 7	111	8 2	1 4	3 5	12 2	13 6	10 10	—	2 8	32	20
4. George	10 0	8 9	88	Below norms	—	Severe	11 5	10 0	6 9	4 8	3 3	2	17
5. Charles	9 2	12 3	133	7 11	—	4 4	9 10	13 0	11 4	—	—	41	8
6. Donald	9 0	9 10	110	Below norms	—	Severe	10 9	11 9	7 11	2 10	3 10	16	21
7. Keith	7 7	7 11	105	Below norms	—	Severe	9 1	9 6	7 2	—	2 4	7	18
8. Betty	8 6	10 2	120	7 3	—	2 11	8 11	10 8	9 11	—	—	32	5
27. Paul	8 11	11 4	128	8 7	—	2 9	10 1	12 10	10 10	—	2 0	27	14

Abbreviations:

C.A.   Chronological age at the start of remedial treatment.
M.A.⎱ Mental age and intelligence quotient measured by the Terman–Merrill.
I.Q. ⎰ Intelligence scale.
Sil.A.   Schonell's Silent Reading Test 'A'.
Back.   Backwardness, i.e. discrepancy between tested reading age and chronological age.
Ret.   Retardation, i.e. discrepancy between tested reading age and mental age.

Table 6.4. Rate of progress in comprehension reading before and during remedial treatment

Caldecott children. N = 9

I	II	III	IV	V	VI	VII
			Rate of progress per month	Period	Progress	Rate of progress per month
	Time in	Progress in	in	of treat-	during treat-	treat-
Name	school *	reading	school	ment	ment	ment
	Months	Months	Months	Months	Months	Months
1. Edward	80	0	0·0	17	16	0·9
2. Paula	78	35	0·4	4	35	8·7
3. Gertrude	66	38	0·6	20	32	1·6
4. George	60	0	0·0	17	2	0·1
5. Charles	50	35	0·7	8	41	5·1
6. Donald	48	0	0·0	21	16	0·8
7. Keith	31	0	0·0	18	7	0·4
8. Betty	42	27	0·6	5	32	6·4
27. Paul	47	43	0·9	14	27	2·0

* Present age minus age at start of school (5 years).

b. *Local authority children*. The level of attainment reached by each child in mechanical and comprehension reading before and after remedial treatment is shown on table 6.5 and 6.7 (pp. 106 and 108). Two children were virtually non-readers (cases 10 and 12, table 6.5). All but one (No. 14) were backward and retarded. With regard to comprehension reading, again all but one (No. 9) were unable, at the beginning of remedial treatment, to obtain a score on Schonell's Silent Reading test. For the reason stated above, progress was, therefore, calculated from a base line of 6 years 7 months.

As can be seen from tables 6.6 and 6.8 (column IV, pp. 107 and 109) no child had made normal progress in school before remedial treatment. During the period of remedial treatment, the majority were making more than a month's educational progress during each month (column VII). The rate of progress accelerated on an average seven times in mechanical reading and fourteen times in comprehension reading. Thus, in over half the cases, the rate of learning had become considerably faster than normal. Most of the other children made about one month's progress during each month of remedial treatment but even this meant progress for children (such as Stephen, table 6.6, No. 11) who had virtually been at a standstill educationally for several years.

The progress made by the two groups of children can be shown in

Table 6.5. Mechanical reading level before and after treatment

Local authority children.   N = 6

	Before remedial treatment						After remedial treatment						
Name	C.A. Yrs. Mths.	M.A. Yrs. Mths.	I.Q.	G.R.V. Yrs. Mths.	Back. Yrs. Mths.	Ret. Yrs. Mths.	C.A. Yrs. Mths.	M.A. Yrs. Mths.	G.W.R. Yrs. Mths.	Back. Yrs. Mths.	Ret. Yrs. Mths.	Progress Months	Total period of treatment Months
9. John	12 2	12 10	106	7 10	4 4	5 0	13 3	14 0	9 5	3 10	4 7	19	13
10. Cyril	9 2	9 3	101	5 4	3 10	3 11	10 9	10 10	7 0	3 9	3 10	20	19
11. Stephen	9 1	8 0	89	5 8	3 5	2 4	10 3	9 1	6 10	3 5	2 3	14	14
12. David	9 0	8 8	97	Below 5 0	4 0	3 8	10 9	10 5	7 11	2 10	2 6	35	21
13. Alan	9 1	8 5	93	6 1	3 0	2 4	9 10	9 1	7 6	2 4	—	17	9
14. Sandy	8 5	7 1	84	5 10	2 7	—	9 5	7 10	8 2	—	—	28	12

Abbreviations:

C.A.   Chronological age at the start of remedial treatment.
M.A. } Mental age and intelligence quotient measured by the Terman-Merrill
I.Q. }   Intelligence Scale.
G.W.R. Schonell's Graded Reading Vocabulary Test.
Back.   Backwardness, i.e. discrepancy between tested reading age and chronological age.
Ret.   Retardation, i.e. discrepancy between tested reading age and mental age.

another way. It has been suggested (Ministry of Education, 1950) that backward readers may be classified as follows:

'illiterate' if reading ages are below 7 years;

'semi-literate' if reading ages are between 7 and 9 years;

'literate' if reading ages are above the 9-year level.

Using these dividing lines, the majority of the reading cases were illiterate at the start of remedial treatment, whereas afterwards only two children remained in this category either for mechanical or for

Table 6.6.   Rate of progress in mechanical reading before and during remedial treatment

Local authority children.   N = 6

	I	II	III	IV	V	VI	VII
		Time in school Months	Progress in reading Months	Rate of progress per month in school Months	period of remedial treat-ment Months	Progress during remedial treat-ment Months	Rate of progress per month of treat-ment Months
9. John		86	34	0·4	13	19	1·4
10. Cyril		50	4	0·1	19	20	1·0
11. Stephen		49	8	0·2	14	14	1·0
12. David		48	0	0·0	21	35	1·7
13. Alan		49	13	0·3	9	17	1·7
14. Sandy		42	10	0·2	12	28	2·3

comprehension reading (table 6.9, p. 109). Similarly, at the beginning of remedial treatment, none fell into the literate group for mechanical reading and only one for comprehension reading; as a result of treatment, three cases could be classed as literate in the former and seven in the latter aspect of reading.

A comparison between the children from the Caldecott and from the local authority, shows that the latter were on the average somewhat younger, rather less intelligent, and more backward in reading. Yet the rate of learning accelerated more steeply among the local authority children. There was also a marked difference in the nature and quality of the play shown by the two groups. The children from the local authority homes sampled all the available materials, apparatus and toys at every session, so that they never settled to a sustained activity. The Caldecott children, on the other hand, tended to choose one activity and to pursue it for two or three weeks before devoting their interest to something else.

H

Table 6.7. Comprehension reading level before and after treatment

Local authority children. N = 6

Name	Before remedial treatment						After remedial treatment						
	C.A. Yrs. Mths.	M.A. Yrs. Mths.	I.Q.	Sil.A. Yrs. Mths.	Back. Yrs. Mths.	Ret. Yrs. Mths.	C.A. Yrs. Mths.	M.A. Yrs. Mths.	Sil.A. Yrs. Mths.	Back. Yrs. Mths.	Ret. Yrs. Mths.	Progress Months	Total period of treatment Months
9. John	12 2	12 10	106	10 3	—	2 7	13 3	14 0	12 4	—	—	25	13
10. Cyril	9 2	9 3	101	Below norms	All severely backward		10 9	10 10	6 11	3 10	3 11	4	19
11. Stephen	9 1	8 0	89	Below norms			10 3	9 1	7 9	2 6	—	14	14
12. David	9 0	8 8	97	Below norms			10 9	10 5	9 9	—	—	38	21
13. Alan	9 1	8 5	93	Below norms			9 10	9 1	7 6	2 4	—	11	9
14. Sandy	8 5	7 1	84	Below norms	—		9 5	7 10	8 11	—	—	28	12

Abbreviations:

C.A. Chronological age at the start of remedial treatment.
M.A. ⎱ Mental age and intelligence quotient measured by the Terman–Merrill Intelligence Scale.
I.Q. ⎰
Sil.A. Schonell's Silent Reading Test 'A'.
Back. Backwardness, i.e. discrepancy between tested reading age and chronological age.
Ret. Retardation, i.e. discrepancy between tested reading age and mental age.

Table 6.8. Rate of progress in comprehension reading before and during remedial treatment

Local authority children. N = 6

I	II	III	IV	V	VI	VII
			Rate of Progress per month	Period of	Progress during	Rate of progress per month of
	Time in school *	Progress in reading	in school	remedial treat-ment	remedial treat-ment	treat-ment
Name	Months	Months	Months	Months	Months	Months
9. John	86	63	0·7	13	25	1·9
10. Cyril	50	0	0·0	19	4	0·2
11. Stephen	49	0	0·0	14	14	1·0
12. David	48	0	0·0	21	38	1·8
13. Alan	49	0	0·0	9	11	1·2
14. Sandy	42	0	0·0	12	28	2·3

* Present age minus age at start of school (5 years).

Table 6.9. Level of literacy before and after treatment

		Illiterate R.A. below 7 yrs. N	Semiliterate R.A. 7–9 yrs. N	Literate R.A. 9 years + N
Mechanical reading N = 14	Before treatment	10	4	0
	After treatment	2	9	3
Compre-hension Reading N = 15	Before treatment	9	5	1
	After treatment	2	6	7

3. *Improvement in arithmetic*

Caldecott children. The level of attainment reached by each child in mechanical arithmetic before and after remedial treatment is shown on table 6.10 (p. 110). At the beginning of treatment three children (Nos. 18, 19 and 27) succeeded on only one item of the test. Five of the children were both backward and retarded (Nos. 15 to 19); the rest were retarded only. One boy (No. 26) though neither backward nor retarded, was accepted for treatment because of his poor attitude to work and general lack of confidence.

As can be seen from table 6.11 (p. 111) only two children had made normal progress in school before remedial treatment (Nos. 25 and 26). Following treatment, all were making more than a month's

Table 6.10. Mechanical arithmetic level before and after treatment

Caldecott children. N = 13

Name	Before remedial treatment											After remedial treatment													
	C.A. Yrs.	Mths.	M.A. Yrs.	Mths.	I.Q.	Arith.A. Yrs.	Mths.	Back. Yrs.	Mths.	Ret. Yrs.	Mths.	C.A. Yrs.	Mths.	M.A. Yrs.	Mths.	Arith.A. Yrs.	Mths.	Back. Yrs.	Mths.	Ret. Yrs.	Mths.	Progress Months	Total period treatment Months
15. Anne	12	8	14	2	112	9	0	3	8	5	2	13	10	15	2	10	4	3	6	4	10	16	14
16. Andrew	10	6	11	4	108	8	1	2	5	3	3	11	3	12	1	10	4	—		—		27	9
17. Jimmy	10	6	14	2	133	8	6	2	0	5	8	11	7	15	5	11	2	2	7	4	3	32	13
18. Derek	10	4	11	6	112	7	0	3	4	4	6	11	1	12	4	8	6	—		3	10	18	9
19. Martin	9	4	9	10	106	7	0	2	4	2	10	10	1	10	7	8	10	—		—		22	9
20. Peter	13	0	17	3	133	11	6	—		5	0	14	2	19	8	13	2	—		6	6	20	14
21. Frank	11	7	15	0	130	10	0	—		5	0	13	1	17	0	12	11	—		4	1	35	18
22. Dan	10	8	16	0	150	9	8	—		6	4	11	5	17	1	10	8	—		6	5	12	9
23. Brian	10	5	13	11	134	8	8	—		5	3	11	7	15	6	11	4	—		4	2	32	14
24. Gwen	10	2	12	11	129	9	2	—		3	9	11	2	14	4	11	0	—		3	4	22	12
25. Roger	9	11	12	11	131	10	0	—		2	11	11	3	14	9	13	4	—		—		40	16
26. Nigel	9	10	11	6	117	9	10	—		—		10	7	12	4	11	0	—		—		14	9
27. Paul	8	11	11	4	128	7	0	—		4	4	10	1	12	11	9	2	—		3	9	26	14

Abbreviations:

C.A.   Chronological age at the start of remedial treatment.

M.A. } Mental age and intelligence quotient measured by the Terman-Merrill

I.Q. }   Intelligence Scale.

Arith.A. Schonell's Mechanical Arithmetic Test 'A'.

Back.   Backwardness, i.e. discrepancy between tested arithmetic age and chronological age.

Ret.   Retardation, i.e. discrepancy between tested arithmetic age and mental age.

Table 6.11. Rate of progress in mechanical arithmetic before and during remedial treatment

Caldecott children. N = 13

I	II	III	IV	V	VI	VII
Name	Time in school Months	Progress in arith. Months	Rate of progress per month in school Months	Period of remedial treatment Months	Progress during remedial treatment Months	Rate of progress per month of treatment Months
15. Anne	92	48	0·5	14	16	1·1
16. Andrew	66	37	0·6	9	27	3·0
17. Jimmy	66	42	0·6	13	32	2·4
18. Derek	64	24	0·4	9	18	2·0
19. Martin	52	24	0·5	9	22	2·4
20. Peter	96	78	0·8	14	20	1·4
21. Frank	79	60	0·8	18	35	1·9
22. Dan	68	56	0·8	9	12	1·3
23. Brian	65	44	0·7	14	32	2·3
24. Gwen	62	50	0·8	12	22	1·8
25. Roger	59	60	1·0	16	40	2·5
26. Nigel	58	58	1·0	9	14	1·5
27. Paul	47	24	0·5	14	26	1·9

Table 6.12. Retest results for mechanical reading

Caldecott and L.E.A. children. N = 8

Name	Rate of progress before treatment Months	Rate of progress during treatment Months	Rate of progress after treatment Months	Period since discharge Months
1. Edward	0·2	1·6	0·3	11
2. Paula	0·4	2·7	2·0	11
3. Gertrude	0·6	1·2	2·0	11
5. Charles	0·6	1·0	2·0	7
6. Donald	0·2	1·1	1·5	11
8. Betty	0·6	2·7	1·0	5
9. John	0·4	1·4	2·0	6
13. Alan	0·3	1·7	1·0	7

educational progress during each month. The mean rate of progress was doubled.

Comparing the children who received help in reading with those who had difficulties in arithmetic, the latter group showed a less severe degree of underfunctioning, only five out of thirteen children being both backward and retarded. The comparable figures for reading were eleven out of fifteen cases. As a group, the arithmetic cases were more intelligent, but they contained a greater number of severe behaviour problems. Their attitude to the subject seemed much more unfavourable than that of the reading failures. The average length of attendance at the remedial unit was similar for the two groups, namely fourteen months for the reading and twelve months for the arithmetic cases. It will be remembered that the maximum possible period was twenty-one months. The rate of progress increased more steeply for the reading cases.

Table 6.13. Retest results for arithmetic

Caldecott children. N = 8

Name	Rate of progress before treatment Months	Rate of progress during treatment Months	Rate of progress after treatment Months	Period since discharge Months
15. Anne	0·5	1·1	0·0	17
12. Jimmy	0·6	2·4	0·7	17
18. Derek	0·4	2·0	1·7	7
19. Martin	0·5	2·4	0·7	17
20. Peter	0·8	1·4	0·5	7
24. Gwen	0·8	1·8	0·0	7
26. Nigel	1·0	1·5	0·0	7
27. Paul	0·5	1·9	0·0	7

4. *Changes in attitude to school work*

a. *Reading.* With one exception (case No. 3, p. 119), there was considerable improvement in the children's attitude to the subject. Dislike or even fear were replaced by acceptance of, and in some cases by a liking for reading. Greater persistence was shown in the face of difficulties; from the pleasure of successful learning, many children progressed to enjoying the activity for its own sake. Books were borrowed more readily and read for interest and information.

b. *Arithmetic.* In only three cases was there a real change in attitude to the subject. However, eight out of the thirteen children showed greater confidence and increased persistence in tackling difficulties.

5. *Improvement in behaviour and adjustment*

As mentioned earlier, detailed personality assessments were obtained for all children both at the beginning and at the end of remedial treatment. These assessments were made independently by the Caldecott and local authority home staffs, by the head teachers and by the remedial teacher. Here we shall confine ourselves to the answers given to one very general question, namely: 'Has there been any improvement in the child's behaviour and adjustment during remedial treatment?' The replies given are shown on table 6.14 (below). In summary, it can be said that for the majority of reading cases the answer was in the affirmative. For the arithmetic cases the position was rather less favourable and improvement was reported for under half the number of children.

Table 6.14. Improvement in behaviour and adjustment

	Numbers showing improvement as assessed by		
	Caldecott and L.E.A. staff	Head teachers	Remedial teachers
Caldecott: Reading Cases N = 9	6	7	6
L.E.A.: Reading Cases N = 6	3	6	4
Caldecott: Arithmetic Cases N = 13	5	7	5

Table 6.15. Length of treatment

	0–5 months	6–10 months	11–15 months	16–21 months
Reading Cases N = 15	2	2	4	7
Arithmetic Cases N = 13	—	5	6	2

6. *Retest results*
In theory one would expect some slowing down in the rate of progress when special individual help is no longer being given. However, progress should continue at a greater rate than that shown before treatment and progress could be regarded as satisfactory if it were at the normal rate, i.e., one month's educational progress in one month.
a. *Reading.* It proved possible to arrange a retest for eight children several months after they had been discharged. In the light of the above considerations, the results can be regarded as very satisfactory (table 6.12, p. 111). Four children had not only maintained the rate of learning achieved during the treatment but were progressing at an even faster pace; three children showed some slowing down but their rate of learning remained much greater than before treatment, being at an average rate for two cases and considerably better than average for one; only one child had relapsed so that his rate of learning was again as slow as it had been prior to receiving remedial treatment.
b. *Arithmetic.* Here retest results revealed a disappointing picture (table 6.13, p. 112). Only for one child did the rate of learning remain

faster than before treatment, even though there was some slowing down; three children's rate of progress had become as slow as it had been before treatment; four children had grown rather worse, since they had come to a complete standstill.

7. *Discussion and conclusions*

A comparison between the children from the Caldecott and from the local authority Homes shows rather interesting, and to some extent unexpected, differences. Although the latter were on the average rather less intelligent and at the same time more backward in reading, their rate of learning during remedial treatment accelerated more steeply than that of the Caldecott children. One might have expected the reverse since the children living in the Caldecott were more favourably placed in many ways such as, for example, a better staff–child ratio, a smaller turnover of staff and smaller classes. Perhaps the greater progress of the local authority children is due to this very fact. For them individual attention, work and play in very small groups, and the provision of a wealth of books, toys and creative activities, was a completely new experience. For the Caldecott children, on the other hand, it was merely an improvement in the circumstances of their everyday lives. Moreover, since the remedial unit was situated within the Community, it soon became part of it, in the same way as other activities such as music lessons or country dancing. This hypothesis would also account for the differences in the nature and quality of the play shown by the two groups. Being used to a wide variety of play materials, the Caldecott children were able to make a definite choice and pursue one activity over a period of time. The local authority children behaved as if they were not used to such a wide variety and therefore had to sample all the available material and activities during each visit to the unit.

Bearing in mind that all the children who attended during the two year experimental period were deprived, maladjusted or both, the results achieved by remedial treatment can be considered quite satisfactory. In the great majority of cases a considerable increase took place in the rate of learning; attitudes to the subject in which the child was doing badly became more favourable; and for about half the children, improvement in general adjustment was reported by the people in daily contact with them. Thus our results with deprived and maladjusted children confirm the findings reported for ordinary children that remedial education in reading leads to considerable acceleration in the rate of learning of backward and retarded pupils (Schonell, 1942; Fernald, 1943; Birch, 1949; Friedman, 1958).

The long-term effects of remedial education for reading difficulties can also be considered very satisfactory. All but one of the children for whom retest results were available, had maintained or increased their rate of progress.

For the arithmetic cases, however, the position was somewhat different. All the children showed an increase in their rate of learning during remedial treatment. On being retested, all but one were doing either as badly as or worse than before treatment. Why this should be so cannot be answered at present, though the following points may be relevant. Firstly, and possibly most important, serious criticism has recently been expressed concerning the teaching of arithmetic throughout the country. 'Indifference to learning mathematics by pupils of adequate ability is not uncommon and is a difficult attitude to combat. It may occur among really intelligent pupils who react against the learning of mathematical procedures which appear to have little connection with their lives or current interests. . . . It also arises from instruction which offers too little challenge, practical or theoretical, to able and active minds.' (The Mathematical Association, 1959.) Progress in reading brings its own reward since a whole new world is opened to the child who learns to master the printed word. This is not necessarily so with regard to arithmetic. Secondly, the mean increase in the rate of progress during remedial treatment had been much lower for arithmetic. Thirdly, in only a few cases had there been a real change in attitude towards the subject. Lastly, perhaps the remedial techniques used in arithmetic were less suitable than those employed for reading. However, it is only through further research that we can find out whether children with difficulties in arithmetic tend to respond less favourably to remedial treatment; and if this is the case, why it should be so.

At the conclusion of the experiment the teachers and house staff were unanimous in their opinion that the unit had been of great value and that it should continue to be an integral part of the Caldecott Community. Similarly, the staff of the local authority homes and the schools expressed approval of the work done with their children. Some head teachers spontaneously coupled this view with the hope that the facilities of the unit might be extended so as to provide help also to 'ordinary children with a normal home background'.

The functions of a remedial unit in a children's home

It seems that such a unit could serve two main functions. Firstly, it would provide special educational treatment for seriously under-functioning pupils. It is worth noting that at the Caldecott Community some 20 per cent of the eligible children were considered to be in need of this help. Since only children of average intelligence are admitted to the Caldecott, and since classes are much smaller there than in local authority schools, the proportion of children needing remedial treatment is likely to be considerably higher in local authority children's homes. That this is so has been confirmed by recent research (Pringle and Bossio, 1958).

Secondly, in a remedial unit opportunities for creative activities and therapeutic play can be provided. In the Caldecott unit it was found that children attending for treatment spontaneously asked for permission to come also in the evenings. Once the unit was available in the evenings, the house staff suggested that a number of children not receiving remedial treatment would benefit from attending. Among them was a 12-year-old boy who had made little contact with his contemporaries and was given to aggressive temper outbursts and a 7-year-old girl who had only recently come into care and seemed not to know how to play. An art club began to develop where the older children painted, sketched, modelled and made lino prints. Although there are a sufficient number of play rooms and a variety of recreational activities available within the Caldecott, it seems that in a unit a more intimate environment could be provided: individual interests and needs could be catered for; the immature could play at a younger level without fear of ridicule; the apathetic or isolated child, unable to respond in a larger group, could find stimulation in the more sheltered environment of a small group; the aggressive could be provided with acceptable outlets without causing harm to people or to property.

If in an environment as favourable as the Caldecott Community, a remedial unit proved to be of value, it is highly likely that in less well provided and less well staffed children's homes such a unit could contribute much to the children's educational and emotional well-being.*

* This view is supported by the results of the pioneering work which is being carried out by Mr E. J. Holmes, Children's Officer, on behalf of the Birmingham Children's Committee. In the two large Homes of the authority, several peripatetic remedial teachers have been employed for the past three years. The results achieved are reported to be very satisfactory.

Summary and recommendations

1. Remedial treatment succeeded in helping all the children to increase their rate of progress in reading or in arithmetic. The most rapid progress was made by children from local authority Homes whose environment was less favourable than that of the Caldecott children.

2. In more than half the cases there was some alleviation of emotional maladjustment and in a few of them improvement was marked. Such improvement was more frequently associated with progress in reading.

3. Retests several months after discharge showed that good progress was being maintained in reading but not in arithmetic.

4. The remedial unit also provided opportunities for creative and therapeutic activities in the evenings, not only for children who already attended for remedial treatment but for others who were experiencing some emotional or social difficulties.

5. A remedial unit seems to offer one way of helping children in care who have serious educational difficulties which may be accompanied by emotional maladjustment. The possibility of establishing such units on a full- or part-time basis in children's Homes merits serious attention.

6. The relationship between difficulties in arithmetic, emotional maladjustment and special teaching methods needs further study.

Case studies

For each child a brief outline is given firstly of his early background, secondly, of his behaviour in the Home and at school at the commencement of remedial treatment and lastly, of his response to remedial treatment.

Reading cases
a. *Caldecott children*
1. EDWARD was abandoned by his mother when 20 months old and until 6 years of age lived in an institution. His father was killed in the war. Then he was fostered with a professional family with a view to permanent placement, but this broke down after eighteen months. Rejected because of behaviour difficulties and educational backwardness, he was placed at the Caldecott, aged $7\frac{1}{2}$ years. However, he was allowed to return to his foster family for holidays. Unfavourable comparisons continued to be made between him and the parents' two natural daughters.

At the start of the treatment Edward was emotionally unstable, liable to have aggressive outbursts followed by sullenness and depression. His sense of inadequacy often led to boasting which brought ridicule from others for his implausible stories.

Response to remedial treatment was hampered by the fact that after two terms he went abroad with his foster parents. During that time he came again more directly under the influence of their over-ambitious and highly critical attitude. Coaching by his foster mother led to increasing tension and blocking and on his return he seemed to have 'forgotten' what he had mastered previously. Though progress remained very slow, on discharge he was able to extract meaning from reading material and was willing to persevere in all his school work. He had gained considerably in self-confidence.

2. PAULA was illegitimate and from 11 months onwards lived in a succession of foster homes and children's homes. When aged 3 years, she contracted poliomyelitis and was in hospital for 9 months. When she entered the Caldecott, aged $11\frac{1}{2}$ years, she had had fourteen different placements, the longest period having been spent at a residential school for severely maladjusted children.

At the start of treatment she exhibited extreme and rapid mood swings and showed her insecurity by jealousy and overpossessiveness. Probably her educational difficulties were aggravated by the fact that during her four years at the school for maladjusted children, treatment took precedence over academic work.

Response to remedial treatment was favourable. Though still insecure, she seemed to have gained in confidence both in the remedial unit and outside.

3. GERTRUDE was first placed in a foster home at the age of 3 years and shortly afterwards in a private residential school, because her mother had contracted T.B. She died two years later. Father was in the R.A.F. and remarried, but the stepmother refused to take any interest in Gertrude. When her behaviour became difficult she was transferred to a reception home and from there admitted to the Caldecott, aged $9\frac{1}{2}$ years.

At the start of treatment Gertrude was very slipshod in everything she did, avoided making an effort, easily became upset and then grew resentful and defiant. She had many nervous mannerisms and at times regressed completely in her behaviour, lying on the floor and screaming.

Response to remedial treatment was rather limited; her attitude to reading never seemed to alter fundamentally nor did her general behaviour show any improvement.

4. GEORGE came to the Caldecott at the age of 9 years, because of the effects of an unhappy, strained home. Both parents were artists, the father being an alcoholic asthmatic and the mother a cold, rejecting woman. George also suffered from asthma and had come to a complete standstill educationally. At the age of 7 years, after two different schools had been tried, he was given a private tutor for two years, but continued to be an extremely anxious boy, severely blocked with regard to all social or school learning.

At the start of treatment George was markedly lacking in self-confidence, slow in all his reactions, and full of fears.

Response to remedial treatment was very slow but steady. As emotional tension gradually decreased, he became able to respond to teaching. However, each holiday provided a setback, as his mother insisted on coaching him which again increased his anxiety. Yet, from being a complete non-reader and terrified of the subject, he became able to face his difficulties and persevere despite them.

5. CHARLES was the illegitimate child of a very neurotic mother and he had lived in a succession of furnished rooms, residential and foster homes. Taken to court by his mother as being beyond control, he was first placed in a foster home and then came to the Caldecott, aged 8½ years. Holidays are still spent with his mother.

At the beginning of treatment Charles had a courteous manner, conversed readily in a rather adult manner, but showed no persistence in work or play. He tended to get easily upset and to be somewhat light-fingered.

Response to remedial treatment was slow at first but improved when he began to attend the unit also in the evenings for creative activities. Most improvement was shown in silent reading for comprehension, but he remained unable to develop depth of interest and concentration.

6. DONALD was the second of three illegitimate children of a morally unstable mother, an ex-approved school girl, who served a four-year prison sentence for larceny. Father was unknown. In care since the age of 4½ years, Donald was first placed in a residential nursery, then boarded out and when this proved unsuccessful because of his difficult behaviour, he went to a reception centre and then to the Caldecott. By that time he was 6 years old. Another foster home was found for the holidays and some contact with his mother was also established.

At the beginning of treatment he was described as a friendly boy, who reacted with destructiveness and boasting to any discouragement and difficulty, including his educational failure.

Response to remedial treatment was somewhat erratic because of his moodiness and defeatist attitude to reading. Even by the time of his discharge, he would become so tense when given a reading test, that it was not possible to obtain a reliable measure of his progress. Thus, he could read with interest and understanding books requiring a reading age of 9½ to 10 years, yet only scored a reading age of 7 years 11 months on a comprehension test. His progress and improvement was confirmed, however, by the view of his teachers and the house staff.

7. KEITH was left in the care of a great-aunt when aged 4 months. His parents' whereabouts have been unknown ever since. The conditions in the home of the relatives were very undesirable and all the members were known to the police and probation officers. Keith had had numerous illnesses and accidents during his preschool years. When aged 6 years, Keith was excluded from school because of unmanageable aggressiveness, temper tantrums and stealing. Diagnosed as an aggressive psychopath, he was placed at the Caldecott.

At the beginning of treatment he was an overactive, restless child with no interests or hobbies. His physical coordination was very poor. Immune to reprimand, he reacted to frustration by violence and infantile behaviour. Very minor incidents precipitated severe scenes.

Response to remedial treatment was slow and erratic; work sessions tended to be disrupted by emotional outbursts. However, he stole very little from the unit, even when most active in this respect elsewhere. Final testing revealed more progress than had been expected, but his span of attention remained extremely short.

8. BETTY was brought up by her grandmother until the latter's death. When Betty was 18 months old, her parents had been divorced on the grounds of her father's violence and drinking, said to be due to wartime head injuries. After the grandmother's death, the mother, a depressed, neurotic woman, who was out working all day, became unable to control Betty, then aged 6½ years. She was showing temper tantrums, insolence and spiteful aggressiveness with other children. Out of school hours she roamed the streets and obtained her meals from stall-keepers in a neighbouring market. At school, too, she was becoming a behaviour and educational problem. She was admitted to the Caldecott, aged 8 years, but went home to her mother for holidays.

At the start of treatment Betty was reported to have many creative interests and to be quite affectionate and responsive. But her desire for attention and her over-sensitivity to reprimand often led to bouts of screaming and crying.

Response to remedial treatment was quite favourable. She became more self-controlled and able to tolerate sharing attention with others. Though still readily frustrated in the school situation, there, too, she was becoming more amenable to discipline.

b *Local authority children*

9. JOHN was taken into care when his mother was sent to prison for neglecting him and his brother. Nothing was known about the father. After a time, John was put in a foster home but this placement broke down after three years and he returned to a children's home. His own mother took no interest in him nor did she maintain any contact; his brother had been adopted. Fostering was tried once more, and again he soon returned to the home.

At the beginning of treatment John was described as an active, impetuous boy, popular with other children, but not easy to manage by adults.

Response to remedial treatment was quite satisfactory. The school also reported that his reading was greatly improved. On the other hand, John remained a behaviour problem in the Home. It was recommended that he should be allowed to make contact with his mother, which he had wished to do for some time.

10. CYRIL was one of ten children all of whom were in care. His father, a shiftless gambler, seemed unwilling to provide a home, but the mother was anxious for her children to be returned to her. Strong family ties existed between the siblings.

At the start of treatment Cyril, an independent and resourceful boy, had many interests, especially in animals and carpentry. In the Home he was reported to be given to aggressive outbursts.

Response to remedial treatment during seven months was more satisfactory than shown by tests results; he could, in fact, cope with material suitable for $8\frac{1}{2}$ year-olds though he had begun as a virtual non-reader. Yet, he would not read for pleasure and regarded the subject from a purely utilitarian point of view. At the same time the school reported that his attitude to work and his general standard of behaviour were considerably improved.

11. STEPHEN was the illegitimate child of a 16 year-old mentally defective girl. The father was unknown. Taken into care at 6 months of age, Stephen had no further contact with his mother. First, he went into a residential nursery for four months, then he lived with elderly foster parents for two and a half years and from there was removed to a reception centre when the foster home was judged to be unsuitable. He was placed in a second foster home, but this arrangement broke down. Finally, he went to a third foster home and so far seemed settled and happy there. The present foster parents are farmers and all Stephen's interests now centre round country life.

At the beginning of treatment the school reported him to be disobedient, backward and a bully. He himself very much disliked teachers and school work.

Response to remedial treatment was slow, partly because of his marked lack of confidence and partly because he seemed to have some difficulty in auditory discrimination. However, he became much more relaxed in his approach to the subject as well as to school. Both his foster mother and his headmistress wrote to the remedial teacher spontaneously, saying how much Stephen had been helped.

12. DAVID was an illegitimate child whose mother kept moving from one residential job to another. His father was unknown. Though often promising to provide a home for him, the mother never succeeded in doing so.

At the beginning of treatment David was apathetic and poorly motivated in everything connected with school work. In the Home he was said to be lacking in affection and appreciation, to be stubborn and a liar. Though a solitary boy and full of fears, he was good at many physical activities.

Response to remedial treatment was unexpectedly good after a slow start. His attitude to work became more positive and once he could himself see some improvement, he began to take a pride in his achievement. From being a complete non-reader, he reached a sufficiently high level in comprehension reading to be able to tackle most books. Emotionally, he remained unsettled, partly because he continued to long to be with his mother though she let him down again and again.

13. ALAN had been in care for a year but his mother had throughout maintained some contact with him and his brother.

At the start of treatment the Home described him as friendly, cooperative, very active and popular with other children.

Response to remedial treatment was rapid since he showed no resistance to learning. Though he was still backward on discharge, his school considered that there was no need for continued attendance as he was working well and progressing satisfactorily.

14. SANDY had come into care aged 3 months when his father went to prison and his mother into a mental deficiency hospital. For a short period he returned home but soon went back to the residential nursery for a further year. Fostering was tried at the age of $3\frac{1}{2}$ years, but his foster mother returned him to the nursery because of his general backwardness. He remained there for another year and then

was thought to be sufficiently developed to be fostered again. He stayed in his second home for a year and again was returned to a children's home with the same complaint. By now his own father had disappeared while his mother remained in the mental deficiency hospital; each Christmas, she sent him a parcel which Sandy treasured although the garments she gave him were impossible to wear.

At the beginning of treatment Sandy was very immature in every way probably because of his very disturbed background. He was shy, seldom smiled or looked at the person to whom he was talking, and his play activities were those of a preschool child. It was felt that before he would be ready to begin a remedial reading programme his language and emotional development needed to be encouraged through a great variety of creative and therapeutic play activities. To these he responded well and it was decided to discharge him in the hope that he would now be able to benefit from the special help he was receiving at school. Soon after discharge he began to regress, stopped conversing freely and eventually he himself asked whether he could resume attendance. There was one more crisis when Sandy ran away from the children's Home in the middle of the night to a school friend's house 'because I want to live there'. Eventually a third foster home was found for him where he seemed to settle happily.

Response to remedial treatment was very good. From being practically a non-reader, he made over two years' progress in twelve months. There was also a marked improvement in his general level of maturity and linguistic development and he became a happy and confident child. Clearly, his last foster home placement contributed a great deal to this improvement.

Arithmetic cases
Caldecott children
15. ANNE lived a very unsettled life from the age of 2 years onwards, moving through a number of residential nurseries to a foster home and finally stayed for three years with her grandmother. Her mother was a nurse and her father a singer. Their marriage had never been successful and they eventually separated. Anne entered the Caldecott aged 7½ years. Later her parents made their home together again and Anne was spending her holidays with them.

At the beginning of treatment Anne's behaviour was causing as much concern as her arithmetic difficulties. She was described as being absentminded, irresponsible, immature and unable to persevere with any one activity, be it at school or in her leisure time.

Response to remedial treatment was most favourable on the personality side. Both the school and house staff reported increasing self-control and persistence. In arithmetic she also made some measurable improvement.

16. ANDREW came to the Caldecott aged 8 years. His mother was an excitable woman and his father a sadistic alcoholic. There were constant quarrels and violent scenes between the parents. Andrew spent his holidays at home although conditions were in no way improved.

At the beginning of treatment he was reported to be a well-adjusted boy who had many interests, especially outdoor activities. However, his difficulties in arithmetic often resulted in anger or tears, followed by a complete refusal to accept his teacher's help.

Response to remedial treatment was very satisfactory. He worked hard and conscientiously and both his attitude to arithmetic and his level of attainment showed a marked improvement.

17. JIMMY, whose parents were unknown, was adopted when 10 months old. Two years later his adoptive mother died and he was cared for by his grandmother. When the adoptive father remarried, Jimmy, then aged $6\frac{1}{2}$ years, went to live with him. Though well-meaning, the second wife seemed to have little understanding of children. Jimmy became increasingly difficult, lying, stealing and being a member of an antisocial gang. Eventually, he was sent to the Caldecott, aged $9\frac{1}{2}$ years.

At the beginning of treatment Jimmy always wanted to be the centre of attention, was boastful, moody and impatient. He disliked correction and shirked difficulties.

Response to remedial treatment was disappointing as there was no change in his attitude to arithmetic though his level of attainment improved. He remained unwilling to apply himself to thinking through a problem but would deal adequately with routine arithmetical processes.

18. DEREK's parents (both artists) never provided a stable home for him and his two younger sisters. Eventually they obtained a divorce. From a reception centre, Derek went to the Caldecott at the age of 6 years, but after two years was transferred to a school for severely maladjusted children. Since his return to the Caldecott, he had failed to make progress in arithmetic.

At the beginning of treatment his behaviour still tended to be very unpredictable and he showed rapid changes of mood. He had little confidence in his own ability and if required to make an effort he became sulky and abusive.

Remedial treatment resulted in little change of basic attitudes, though he improved in arithmetic.

19. MARTIN had never had a stable home and when his parents were divorced, he was received into care. Later, his mother remarried but refused to have anything to do with Martin, although making a home for his younger brother. At the age of 6 years, Martin came to the Caldecott and a foster home was found where he could spend his holidays.

At the beginning of treatment he showed a very defeatist attitude to learning, giving up at the slightest difficulty. Arithmetic he disliked the most.

Remedial treatment resulted in improved attainment in arithmetic but his attitude to work and to difficulties seemed unchanged. However, the school reported that Martin was working harder and showing a more positive, determined approach to difficult tasks.

20. PETER was the illegitimate child of a neurotic father, who died in a mental hospital, and a morally defective mother who gave up all claims to her son when he was 7 months old. Parental rights were assumed by a paternal uncle and aunt. However, they were not able to provide a stable home and Peter suffered many changes of home as well as from neglect. After attending a child guidance clinic, he was admitted to the Caldecott at the age of 9 years.

At the beginning of treatment he was reported to be a serious behaviour problem. He had few leisure time interests, showed homosexual tendencies and despite good intelligence, was doing badly in a secondary modern school, especially in arithmetic.

Remedial treatment resulted in a slight improvement of attitude and, in view of the serious nature and long standing of his difficulties, no more could perhaps have been expected. The school reported quite favourably on Peter's progress in arithmetic.

21. FRANK was the son of a grossly unstable Canadian soldier who left his family and returned to his own country. Having followed him and lived under very primitive conditions, the mother returned to England. Conditions remained very unsettled because Frank was enuretic and encropetic. He was rejected by his mother, a neurotic woman, and also by his grandmother. A period of residential treat-

ment in hospital did not alleviate these conditions. After some further changes of environment, he came to the Caldecott, aged 7½ years.

At the beginning of treatment Frank was described as a withdrawn, moody boy who had been very disappointed at his failure to win a place at the grammar school. Resentful of correction, he often seemed to be angry with himself and with life.

Remedial treatment could not be expected to resolve his fundamental difficulties and, in fact, psychiatric treatment was arranged for Frank subsequently. However, there was some improvement in arithmetic.

22. DAN came from a materially good, but emotionally unsatisfactory home. There was constant friction between his neurotic mother and ineffectual father, both of whom set very high social and intellectual standards for the boy. From time to time the family lived abroad. Because of his severe emotional disturbance, he entered the Caldecott aged 9 years.

At the start of treatment Dan was an extremely tense, anxious and solitary boy who was reluctant to try new tasks or experiences. He had found refuge in books and had a fund of general knowledge.

Remedial treatment resulted in a considerable improvement in Dan's attitude to challenge and difficulty. He became more self-confident and was able to remain relaxed in unfamiliar situations. There was also improvement in arithmetic, but he did not do himself justice on the occasion of the test.

23. BRIAN was of German parentage. After his father's death, his mother married an Englishman and came to this country when Brian was 3 years old. The stepfather, who suffered from violent temper outbursts, rejected Brian and when his mother had a nervous breakdown, he was sent to a foster home. At 8½ years, he came to the Caldecott.

At the start of treatment it was considered unlikely that he would succeed in the 11 + examination because of his low attainment in arithmetic. This proved to be the case. Though Brian had various hobbies and enjoyed outdoor activities, he showed many symptoms of anxiety neurosis, including compulsive masturbation.

Remedial treatment was successful, resulting in improved general adjustment and considerable progress in arithmetical understanding.

24. GWEN was illegitimate and, until the age of 3 years, lived with her mother, who was in residential employment. During the following six and a half years she was cared for in five different institutions

and foster homes and finally came to the Caldecott, aged $9\frac{1}{2}$ years. Meanwhile, her mother had married and Gwen was able to spend holidays at home.

At the beginning of treatment she lacked persistence although she had many interests. When unable to gain attention or recognition, she would be spiteful and disobedient. Moreover, she was rather unpredictable in mood and behaviour.

Remedial treatment resulted in greater persistence when tackling difficulties and her rate of progress in arithmetic became accelerated. Her basic difficulties of personality, however, remained unchanged.

25. ROGER was the illegitimate child of a highly intelligent, educated woman. The father, also an educated man, took no interest in or responsibility for his son. During his early years Roger suffered considerable physical neglect owing to his mother's instability which resulted in her having to go into a mental hospital when he was $2\frac{1}{2}$ years old. Eventually she was certified. Roger was placed in the Caldecott and during the holidays he went to a foster home.

At the start of treatment Roger was markedly lacking in confidence and his written arithmetic was particularly slow. Though he was not seriously behind in this subject he had stood still for some time and was refusing to learn new processes for fear of failure.

Remedial treatment proved of considerable help in changing his attitude to the subject. He became more confident in his approach, developed a reasonable speed of work, and just before being discharged, he expressed his own awareness of his new attitude by saying: 'I used to hate arithmetic and now I almost prefer it to reading.'

26. NIGEL was the illegitimate son of a mother who had herself been brought up in a children's home. First, he lived with his mother and a maternal aunt until the latter married. In order to keep Nigel with her, the mother then took a residential job. Soon afterwards the boy became a behaviour problem, being aggressive, generally uncontrolled and enuretic. He received psychiatric help for some time. The mother then unwittingly contracted a bigamous marriage and Nigel witnessed the scene when his mother discovered this fact from the first wife. The mother returned to live with the maternal aunt and Nigel was admitted to the Caldecott at 9 years of age.

Remedial treatment was not really justified on educational grounds. However, he was such a problem both in school and in the Community that it was decided to try this approach. He was a very tense, unhappy child, lacking in confidence and resentful of correction. His symptoms included lying, stealing, enuresis and greediness over food.

As was to be expected, there was only a slight change in attitude and attainment. Moreover, it proved to be temporary. Shortly after discharge, Nigel's behaviour began to deteriorate and he was again referred for psychiatric help.

27. PAUL had suffered in his early years from the obsessionally rigid as well as ambivalent attitude of his mother. There had also been continued tension between the parents and the situation was not improved by the family living with the maternal grandparents. Paul had become a serious behaviour problem and was placed in the Caldecott at the age of 6 years.

At the start of treatment he was an extremely disruptive influence in school because he interfered with other children, was physically and mentally restless and retarded educationally. Some progress was beginning to be made in reading, but he was at a standstill in arithmetic.

Remedial treatment resulted in some improvement in attainment and attitude. He was also responding more readily to school discipline and though still very immature emotionally, he was trying to control his impulses and to fit into group activities. While he was primarily treated as an arithmetic case, Paul was also given some help with reading for comprehension.

References

BIRCH, L. B. (1949) 'The remedial treatment of reading disability', *Educational Review*, 1, 107–18.

BURLINGHAM, D. and FREUD, A. (1954) *Infants without families; the case for and against residential nurseries*. London, Allen & Unwin.

EDUCATION, MINISTRY OF (1950) *Reading ability; some suggestions for helping the backward*. Pamphlet No. 18. London, H.M.S.O.

FERNALD, G. M. (1943) *Remedial techniques in basic school subjects*. New York, McGraw-Hill.

FRIEDMANN, S. (1958) 'A report on progress in an L.E.A. remedial reading class', *British Journal of Educational Psychology*, 28, 258–61.

GESELL, A. and AMATRUDA, C. S. (1947) *Developmental diagnosis; normal and abnormal child development; clinical methods and pediatric applications*. 2nd edn. New York, Hoeber.

LEWIS, H. (1954) *Deprived children; the Mersham experiment. A social and clinical study*. London, Oxford University Press.

MATHEMATICAL ASSOCIATION (1959) *Mathematics in secondary modern schools*. London, Bell.

MOORE, J. K. (1947) 'Speech content of selected groups of orphanage and non-orphanage pre-school children', *Journal of Experimental Education*, 16, 122–33.

PRINGLE, M. L. KELLMER (1957) 'The educational needs of deprived children', *Child Care*, 11, 4–9.

PRINGLE, M. L. KELLMER and BOSSIO, V. (1958) 'A study of deprived children. Part 1. Intellectual, emotional and social development', *Vita Humana*, 1, 65–92.

PRINGLE, M. L. KELLMER and BOSSIO, V. (1958) 'A study of deprived children. Part 2. Language development and reading attainment', *Vita Humana*, 1, 142–70.

PRINGLE, M. L. KELLMER and TANNER, M. (1958) 'The effects of early deprivation on speech development. *Language and Speech*, 1, 269–87.

SCHONELL, F. J. (1942) *Backwardness in the basic subjects*. Edinburgh, Oliver & Boyd.

7. The effects of early deprivation on speech development

*A comparative study of 4-year-olds in a nursery school and in residential nurseries**

with Margaret Tanner

Summary

Two groups of preschool children, matched for age, sex, intelligence and home background, were given a battery of verbal tests and their conversations were recorded during periods of free play. Data were obtained on vocabulary and sentence structure under controlled and spontaneous conditions, on the children's ability to understand and express themselves in simple sentences and on verbal expression in social intercourse. In all quantitative comparisons, the nursery school children were found to be in advance of the children in residential nurseries. Among qualitative differences noted, was the extent to which speech was used for establishing social contacts with contemporaries and for obtaining adult attention. Although there was considerable overlap in the achievements of the two groups, our evidence confirms that there is some retardation in the language skills of preschool children in care.

Introduction

The effect of early maternal deprivation on children's development has been the subject of many studies in recent years. There is a good deal of evidence to show that the various aspects of speech tend to be most seriously affected. A child's language development reflects the level of his intellectual, emotional and social growth. Though interrelated, these aspects can to some extent be studied separately. The gradual mastery of vocabulary, of sentence structure and of the logical expression of ideas is an indication of the extent to which the growth of intelligence has been influenced by experience. Using speech for making contact with adults and contemporaries reflects its social aspect. Verbally expressed feelings, whether in reality or

* First published in *Language and Speech*, 1958, 1, part 4, 269–87.

fantasy situations, give some insight into the child's emotional life. Thus 'the act of speech is a meeting ground for functions and activities of the organism (mental and physiological) at all levels. Speech production is achieved through the coordination of muscular, respiratory and neural activities on the one hand, and of cultural, intellectual and emotional factors on the other' (Goldman–Eisler, 1958).

This investigation aimed at a quantitative and qualitative analysis of the differences (if any) in speech development between preschool children in residential care and those living with their own families. Answers to four questions were sought: (*a*) Are preschool children in care retarded in their language development? (*b*) If so, are all aspects equally affected and in what specific ways? (*c*) Even if retarded, is their speech nevertheless developing along normal lines? (*d*) Are there any differences between the two groups in the use of speech for social intercourse?

Previous studies
All available results indicate that deprivation exerts the most adverse effect on speech development. Bowlby, reviewing recent literature, concludes that 'the least affected is neuromuscular development, including walking, other locomotive activities and manual dexterity. The most affected is speech, the ability to express being more retarded than the ability to understand' (Bowlby, 1951). How early the effects of environmental deprivation are manifested is shown in an investigation of newborn infants (Gatewood and Weiss, 1930). Given various stimuli such as light, sound, smells and temperature, neonates vocalised much more than in situations where they were 'allowed to lie naturally without any external stimulation'. Brodbeck and Irwin (1946) compared the frequency and variety of phonemes uttered by a group of orphanage children with those heard among a group living with their own families. Statistically significant differences were found in favour of the latter as early as the first two months. Freud and Burlingham (1954) reported retardation in language development during the second year of life.

Williams and McFarland (1937) applied a vocabulary test to sixty-four orphange children and compared them with a large group of children living in their own homes. The latter had a markedly superior vocabulary, much more so than could be accounted for on the basis of I.Q. or socio-economic level. Moore (1947), using the same vocabulary test, analysed two-minute samples of oral language of orphanage and non-orphanage children. Again, the former group was markedly retarded. Holding C.A. and M.A. constant, analysis of variance showed a statistically significant difference attributable to environmental influences. Goldfarb (1943 and 1945), in a comparative study of institutionalised and fostered children, investigated speech sounds, intelligibility of speech and level of language organisation at three age levels: in early infancy, at 6 to 8 years and in adolescence. At each age level the institution children showed marked language deficiency in all the areas measured.

That children in orphanages and institutions are seriously retarded in vocabulary and language development has been shown in a number of other investigations (Little and Williams, 1937; Skeels et al., 1938; Flemming, 1942). Although such children undoubtedly come from lower socio-economic levels, are somewhat below average ability and probably have restricted environmental experiences, their retardation appears to be so marked that it is necessary to look for additional causative factors. Even when matched with ordinary children for mental age, the deprived were much more retarded in vocabulary (Little and Williams, 1937). If association with adults facilitates language development, institutionalised children may show marked retardation because they associate most with other children, especially contemporaries; on the other hand they have far fewer individual contacts with, and attention from, adults (McCarthy 1930; Smith 1935).

Dawe (1942) planned a training scheme with a group of orphanage children aiming at increasing their understanding and use of language symbols. Matching eleven pairs of children for age, sex, school group, M.A., I.Q., and score on the Smith–Williams vocabulary test, one member of each pair received the training and the other served as a control. About fifty hours of individual and small-group teaching was given, providing the kind of enriching experiences children receive as a matter of course in good educated homes. The experimental group showed significant gains (at the one per cent level of confidence) in most language measures; moreover, these language gains were reflected in an increase in average I.Q. from 80·6 to 94·8 as a result of the fifty-hour training which was spread over a period of three months. During the same period the control group decreased slightly from a mean I.Q. of 81·5 to a mean of 79·5. The implications of these findings could be quite far reaching not only for deprived children, but for education generally, if they can be substantiated with larger groups.

Confirming the finding that infants brought up in institutional environments show severe developmental retardation, particularly in linguistic ability, Roudinesco and Appell (1950) introduced a change of regime; this was designed to provide the children with more individual attention from the nurses and other attendants. A retest after a period of eighteen months showed considerable gains in motor, social and adaptive behaviour, but the least improvement was brought about in language development. Gesell and Amatruda (1947), discussing the dynamics of environmental deprivation, stress that it operates by 'attrition' as well as by 'impoverishment', and that the results tend to be cumulative. The more monotonous and impersonal character of an institutional environment appears to reduce early vocalisation in contrast to the stimulation provided by the variety and warmth of normal family life.

The beneficial effect of regular contacts with adults outside the Children's Home was shown in a recent study of 8-, 11- and 14-year-olds (Pringle and Bossio, 1958). Backwardness in language development was least marked among those children who since their removal from home had maintained a continuing relationship with a member of their family or a family substitute. This supports the view (McCarthy, 1952) that language development depends to a considerable extent upon the child's identification with his mother. When there is a close contact with her or a mother substitute, the child continues to strive to communicate his thoughts and experiences; personal interest and continuity of contact seem to provide the motivational forces needed to stimulate this learning process.

The subjects

One nursery school and three residential nurseries were used to obtain the required number of children. It was decided to match the two groups for age, sex, intelligence and home background. To eliminate the complicating influence of mental dullness, only those whose level of tested intelligence was at least average, were chosen. Altogether fifty children were given a screening examination which made it possible to obtain eighteen matched pairs. The age, sex and I.Q. distributions are shown on tables 7.1 and 7.2. The difference between the mean I.Q.s is not statistically significant ($t = 1.4$).

Henceforth the nursery school group will be referred to as Group N and the children in the residential nurseries as Group R.

With regard to home background, only a broad similarity proved to be a practicable aim. It is known that the great majority of

Table 7.1. Age and sex distribution in the two groups of children

	Group N		Group R	
Age	Boys	Girls	Boys	Girls
Under 4 years	5	1	1	—
4 years to 4·5	5	6	2	4
4·5 years to 4·11	—	1	7	4
Total	10	8	10	8
Mean age	4 years 4 months		4 years 6 months	
S.D.	3·3 months		4·1 months	

children in care come from families where educational and cultural standards are low. Prior to separation most of them lived in homes where verbal stimulation is minimal. Overworked and under-privileged mothers, often burdened with too many pregnancies or forced by economic necessity to go out to work, have little time and

Table 7.2. Mental age and intelligence quotients on the Merrill Palmer Scale

M.A. range	Group N	Group R
3·6 to 3·11	0	1
4·0 to 4·5	1	3
4·6 to 4·11	3	3
5·0 to 5·5	8	6
5·6 to 5·11	3	1
6·0 to 6·5	3	4

	Group N			Group R		
I.Q. range	Boys	Girls	Both	Boys	Girls	Both
90–109	5	—	5	4	4	8
110–129	5	3	8	3	3	6
130–150	—	5	5	3	1	4
Total	10	8	18	10	8	18
Mean I.Q.	120			113		
S.D.	15·2			14·8		

Note. In calculating the mental ages and intelligence quotients, the verbal items of the scale were omitted although they had been administered. These items are considered separately (see page 144).

energy available to encourage the baby in his early experiments with sound and to elicit continued trial and effort by taking delight in his prespeech vocalisations. Similarly, once the child is beginning to speak there is likely to be less verbal stimulation in the form of nursery rhymes, stories, songs and general conversation. Thus it

Table 7.3. Age at which children in Group R came into care

Before 6 months	5
7–12 months	1
13–18 months	2
19–24 months	2
25–36 months	3
37–48 months	5

could be argued that most deprived children are already backward in language development before coming into care. A nursery school was therefore selected, which catered for children whose home background was likely to be similarly impoverished and unstimulating. The one chosen admitted only 'hardship cases', such as the children of unmarried or deserted mothers, or widows, or where there was severe overcrowding or serious illness in the home. Even so, the neighbourhood was such that the nursery school had a waiting list. Thus one would expect to find little difference between the language development of the two groups of children if the main adverse influence was an unfavourable home background. Moreover, half of the deprived group came into care before the age of 18 months (see table 7.3). It could be argued that their linguistic ability had been fostered predominantly by the life in residential nurseries.

The experimental procedure
Each child was given at least two individual interviews in a small room known to him, and in addition his normal free play in the nursery was observed. In a few cases it proved necessary, in order to obtain and maintain full cooperation, to give several shorter interviews or to administer the tests in a quiet corner of the playroom, because unusual surroundings seemed to have a disturbing effect on some of the more anxious children. Inevitably the amount of preliminary work necessary to gain a child's confidence varied considerably. With the most difficult children the formal testing had to be postponed until regular visits had been paid to the nurseries over a period of months.

It was aimed to explore the speech development of the two groups in as many directions as possible with such young subjects. First, two formal aspects of speech, vocabulary and sentence structure, were investigated both under spontaneous and controlled conditions. Vocabulary was assessed by the following means:

  a. the Picture Vocabulary Test from the Terman–Merrill Intelligence Scale, Form L, requiring object naming;

b. the Vocabulary sub-test from the Wechsler Intelligence Scale for Children, requiring definitions;

c. the vocabulary used in free play.

Secondly, the children's ability to understand and to express themselves in simple sentences, in response to both structured and unstructured test items, was assessed by the following tests:

d. the appropriate verbal items in the Merrill–Palmer Scale for Preschool Children, namely simple questions and action agent;

e. the Watts English Language Scale, involving the use of basic sentences and the ability to describe pictures.

Thirdly, spontaneous and undirected verbal expression was assessed by recording the children's conversation during periods of free play, supplemented by careful observation of the accompanying behaviour. Each child was observed for a minimum of half an hour, preferably playing with only one other child; if more children were taking part, the time allowed was proportionately greater. Since the play had to be entirely spontaneous and undirected, the total observation time was in many cases made up of a number of shorter periods since at this age social and group play is still fluid and frequent changes of partner and activity occur. The following general conditions were adhered to:

1. Speech was not recorded until the children were sufficiently accustomed to the experimenter to be able to play naturally and undisturbed by her presence.

2. If more than four children joined in, observation was discontinued since in a larger group more than one conversation was often carried on at once, thus making accurate recording difficult.

3. Sufficient play material was provided to give a choice of activity.

4. There was no adult participation. If a child spoke to the experimenter, the latter, though friendly, would give the minimum response and explain that she had some writing to do just now. Strict impartiality was observed when an appeal was made to her to arbitrate in a quarrel.

5. Every word spoken by the children was recorded for later analysis.

Discussion of the findings
General observations
Different attitudes and reactions to the tests and interviewing procedure were noted among the children in the nursery school and

those in the residential nurseries. In the former, the children responded readily when spoken to and in turn initiated many a conversation. When playing, all their energies and attention seemed to be absorbed so that it was easy for their activities to be observed and their speech to be recorded. On the other hand, invitations to accompany the investigator into a separate room (for the individual testing) met in some cases with a refusal at first; this was due not so much to shyness or lack of cooperation, as to a healthy preoccupation with their own activities, indicated by remarks such as 'I'm building a house' or 'we are going to have music now and it is my turn to be in the middle'. Eventually all but one very anxious boy came along willingly and then the nature of the test material held their interest. In the residential nurseries the problem was reversed. Invitations for the individual session were always met most readily; in fact, there was competition among the children to be singled out in this way, and to obtain the undivided attention of an adult their own play activities were willingly abandoned. On the other hand, the observation and recording of spontaneous and undirected speech proved rather more difficult. In the residential nurseries the presence of a visitor seemed to have a disruptive effect. The children stopped their activities when the investigator came into the room, watched her movements and then gathered around her. Thus it proved necessary to arrange a situation where spontaneous speech could be observed. Two or three children known to be friendly with each other, were taken into a room with a generous supply of play materials and the experimenter played with them for a short while. Then she explained that she had some writing to do and the observation period began. Even with these arrangements it rarely happened that the children became so absorbed in their play as entirely to ignore the investigator's presence.

In both groups there were a few shy children but they reacted differently: in the nursery school they showed some active resistance to leaving their group; in the residential nurseries they accompanied the investigator readily enough though remaining passive and refusing to talk during the early part of the interview. Perhaps it should be added here that the nursery school and one of the residential nurseries were excellently equipped; the other two residential nurseries seemed to have a rather inadequate supply, especially of materials suitable for imaginative and creative play.

K

Test and play observations

1. *Vocabulary*

a. The Picture Vocabulary Test of the Terman–Merrill Intelligence Scale, Form L, consists of eighteen pictures of common objects, such as a shoe, a cup and a house. 'The purpose of this test is to determine whether the sight of a familiar object in a picture provokes recognition and calls up the appropriate name' (Terman and Merrill, 1937). Table 7.4 shows the responses of the two groups.

Table 7.4. Terman–Merrill Picture Vocabulary. The mental age equivalents assigned by Terman and Merrill are given in parentheses

No. of words correctly named	Group N	Group R
9 words (2½-year level)	18	18
12 words (3-year level)	18	16
15 words (3½-year level)	16	9
16 words or more (4-year level)	12	7

From the 3-year level onwards, Group N received higher scores and the mean mental age level achieved by this group was 3 years 9 months as compared with a mean level of 3 years 4 months for Group R. Both groups tended to find the same words difficult. However, Group N obtained at least four more points than Group R on the following words: basket, glasses, umbrella and pocket-knife. This difference may be due to the fact that they represent personal possessions of a type less familiar to children in care.

Table 7.5. Wechsler Intelligence Scale for Children: Vocabulary Sub-test *

Standard score	Group N	Group R
4	18	15
6	18	14
8	18	11
10	17	9
12	13	7
14	10	6
16	4	2
18	2	1
20	2	0

* For norms, see *Report of the Committee of Professional Psychologists on the Wechsler Intelligence Scale for Children*, Appendix B.

b. The Vocabulary Sub-test from the Wechsler Intelligence Scale for Children consists of forty words of increasing difficulty for which the child is required to supply the meaning in his own words. The ability to define an object demands verbal skill considerably greater than that required for mere object naming. In table 7.5 are shown the standard scores received by the two groups. No child succeeded beyond the first sixteen words. Again, Group N made a better showing and obtained the mean score expected from an average 4·8- to 4·11-year-old child; the mean score of Group R was below that of an average 4-year-old.

Qualitative comparison. The following words tended to evoke different responses in the two groups: bicycle, knife, letter, donkey, fur, nuisance and brave.

i. BICYCLE. All but one of Group N gave an active definition in terms of 'ride it' or 'pedal'. Eight of Group R gave attributes such as 'wheels', 'goes ting-a-ling'.

ii. KNIFE. Twelve of Group N and thirteen of Group R defined it in terms of 'cut'; in addition four of Group N defined a knife in terms of 'to kill someone'.

iii. LETTER. All of Group R and half of Group N gave definitions of the 'posting' variety; the remaining half of Group N defined a letter as 'what you write'.

iv. DONKEY. All but one of Group N defined it in terms of 'ride'. Five of Group R gave similar definitions, but six gave descriptive definitions, e.g. 'goes cl-cl', 'he bites'.

v. FUR. Two of three definitions given by Group R were 'on a cat', also, three of six definitions by Group N. In addition three of Group N defined fur in terms of personal use, e.g. 'What you put on a cowboy suit'.

vi. NUISANCE. Group N: Four definitions involving 'naughty', two definitions involving 'smack'. Group R: Five definitions involving 'crying'; two definitions involving 'naughty'. Group N mentioned various types of aggressive naughtiness, e.g. 'getting mad', 'swearing'. Only Group R mentioned 'crying' and 'moaning'.

vii. BRAVE. Group N: Two definitions only 'kill every body' and 'go near things like tigers'. Group R: Two definitions only, both 'don't cry'.

Although many definitions given by the two groups were in similar terms, the differences described above seem to be significant. The definitions given by Group N for the first five words tended to be in terms of active participation, compared with a more passive mode of description on the part of Group R. Thus bicycles and donkeys are ridden, knives are linked with the expression of aggressive impulses and letters are written and not merely posted. In so far as definitions were attempted at all of the last two words, Group R had a more negative and passive conception of goodness. These differences suggest that Group N tended to give more definitions which were linked with and arose out of vital personal experiences.

c. Vocabulary used in free play. This was analysed into the main grammatical components of speech. As can be seen from table 7.6

Table 7.6. The number of different words used by the children

	Group N	Group R
Nouns	268	209
Verbs	209	107
Adjectives	84	57
Adverbs	24	19
Conjunctions	9	5
Pronouns	24	22
Prepositions	13	9
Miscellaneous	26	25

there was little difference between the two groups except that Group N used a greater proportion of verbs and adjectives. This may reflect their more developed descriptive power, a more active outlook on life and a rather more mature sentence form. There was a considerable overlap in all the categories, as can be seen from table 7.7. With the exception of nouns, Group R used comparatively few words not employed by Group N. The total number of words used by the

Table 7.7. The number and type of words common to the two groups and peculiar to each group

	Words used by Group N and Group R	Words used only by Group N	Words used only by Group R
Nouns	114	154	95
Verbs	84	125	23
Adjectives	35	49	22
Adverbs	15	9	4
Conjunctions	5	4	—
Pronouns	20	4	2
Prepositions	9	4	—
Miscellaneous	16	10	9

latter was 5,039 and by Group R 3,984. The ratio of the average number of different words to the average number of total words was practically the same for the two groups (0·39 for Group N, 0·41 for Group R). While these results give little indication of the total speaking vocabulary of the children, they give some information on their relative speech development.

i. *Nouns*. In table 7.8 are listed the words used exclusively by at least four children in one group. It is perhaps somewhat unexpected that the nouns 'dog', 'door' and 'window' were not mentioned by any child in Group R. The only nouns used exclusively by at least four children in group R were 'puzzles' and 'shop', words somewhat devoid of emotional content and descriptive of toys in their play room. Although one cannot base any conclusions on such slender

Table 7.8. Words used exclusively by one group

No. of children using word	Group N	Group R
8	dog	—
6	door, window	—
5	home	—
4	castle, policemen	puzzles, shop

evidence, it is tempting to speculate whether to Group R doors and windows are not exciting, policemen are neither feared nor admired, castles are not dreamed of, and dogs are never proudly owned.

An analysis of the nouns, common to both groups, but used to a markedly greater extent by one or the other, showed again a tendency for Group R to dwell on their actual playthings (table 7.9); in contrast the common use of the words 'car' and 'Mummy' by Group N suggests that their play activities are more related to experiences outside the nursery.

Table 7.9. Nouns common to both groups

	No. of children using each word	
	Group N	Group R
flowers	6	1
car	9	3
Mummy	13	1
ball	7	13
toys	2	8

(ii) *Verbs.* An analysis was made of the verbs most frequently used and a very similar range of verbs was found in the two groups. However, the verbs used exclusively by Group N tended to be more active and aggressive ones, whereas those of Group R suggested a rather docile, helpful attitude (for example, dance and push as against mend and worry).

(iii) *Adjectives.* Here, too, the range used by the two groups was very similar. Except that Group N used a greater number of adjectives, there were no suggestive differences in the adjectives used exclusively by either group.

2. *Ability to understand and to use simple sentences*

d. Verbal items in the Merrill–Palmer Scale for Preschool Children. In the 'Simple Questions' test, the ceiling of which is at the three-year level, both groups did equally well. In the more difficult 'Action Agent' test Group R attained a mean score of 9·2 as compared with 13·6 of Group N (total possible score 20). The number of children

Table 7.10. Response level on Action Agent Test

	No. of children giving correct responses	
Age level	Group N	Group R
2½ year	17	14
3 year	16	9
3½ year	14	6
4 year	14	6
4½ year	10	4
5 year	5	0

succeeding at the different age levels assigned to this test by Merrill–Palmer is shown in table 7.10. Qualitatively, the responses made by the two groups were very similar except for the question 'what swims?': all but one of the fifteen Group R children who answered correctly, replied 'fish' or 'ducks'; of the sixteen Group N children replying correctly, half gave the same answer but half mentioned 'men', 'people', 'boys', etc. Only one child in Group R mentioned a human being.

Table 7.11. Watts Language Scale

	No. of children	
Language ages	Group N	Group R
4·0 to 4·5	2	8
4·6 to 4·11	4	6
5·0 to 5·5	3	3
5·6 to 5·11	5	1
6·0 to 6·6	4	0

e. Watts English Language Scale. 'The pictures accompanying the scale were designed to measure, in as far as it is measurable, the progress of young children in mastering the basic varieties of the English sentence. By means of the scale . . . we should be able to decide with some approach to accuracy how one child compares with another of the same age in one important aspect of his linguistic development' (Watts, 1944). The scale consists of thirty-six pictures arranged in six groups of increasing complexity. The language ages scored by the children in each group are shown in table 7.11. Group N did considerably better than Group R, achieving a mean Language Age of

5 years 4 months, while the latter's was 4 years 7 months. The difference between the groups is most marked at the higher level where only one child in Group R obtained a score above the median score of Group N. The correlation between the Watts Language Age and the Merrill–Palmer M.A. was positive but low, 0·41 for Group N and 0·23 for Group R.

Every comment made by each child during this part of the interview was also recorded verbatim. A comparative qualitative analysis of these spontaneous remarks made while working on the Watts Scale showed that Group R made twice as many such comments. They seem to fall into six groups:

1. Questions concerning the content of the picture, e.g. 'Where are the children going?'
2. Interpretation of motive and elaboration of the story, e.g. 'The cat thinks the children will chase him, so he won't come down the tree.'
3. Comments to attract attention, e.g. 'Look at it'.
4. Comments anticipating the next picture or activity, e.g. 'I want to see the next one.'
5. Comments concerning the room, test material, etc. For example 'This is the school room.'
6. Self-references, e.g. 'I have a baby at home.'

The type of comments made by each group is shown in table 7.12. The differences found between the two groups are very suggestive. The children in the residential nursery made more attention seeking

Table 7.12. Spontaneous comments during work on the Watts Scale

Type of comment	Group N		Group R	
	N	%	N	%
Questions about content	7	10	38	25
Interpretations of motive	18	24	19	13
Comments to attract attention	6	8	42	28
Anticipatory comments	6	8	34	22
Comments on testing room and materials	9	12	14	10
Self-references	28	38	3	2
Total	74		150	

and anticipatory comments and asked more questions about the content of the pictures. Maybe they enjoyed receiving individual attention from an adult so much that they were anxious to prolong this opportunity. Group N did not apparently share this need to make the most of the situation. On the other hand, Group N's very markedly greater proportion of self-references suggests that these children are not only more accustomed to talking with adults about their own activities and possessions, but also assumed adult interest in their affairs. The other type of comment made to a greater extent by Group N was a reference to the motives of people or animals shown in the pictures. Probably this was due to a greater facility of the nursery school children to identify themselves with the events depicted in the test. This greater readiness to identify may also be related to the superior language development of Group N, since identification promotes imitation which itself is the basis of speech. There may also be a link here with the results obtained from the Wechsler vocabulary test where Group N more often gave definitions indicating active participation. Moreover, of Group R's nineteen interpretative comments, nine implied naughtiness on the part of the children, such as 'Someone's been bad, policeman want to send them to the police station and lock them up so they can't come out.' In view of the fact that there was nothing in the illustrations to evoke ideas of badness or punishment, this would seem to be of some significance; all interpretative comments of Group N arose naturally from the pictures.

3. *Spontaneous and undirected speech*
The verbatim records made during the free play sessions were analysed from three points of view: the incidence of (a) egocentric as against social use of language; (b) mature forms of conversations and (c) fantasy and humour.

a. The incidence of egocentric versus socialised speech. From being primarily an individual activity, speech becomes the major tool for social intercourse. Piaget (1959) attempted to measure the degree to which egocentric speech gives place to socialised speech. He found that at any given age, the proportion of egocentric to other spontaneous forms of language was approximately constant. The degree of egocentricity could be measured, he suggested, by the coefficient of egocentrism $= \dfrac{\text{egocentric language}}{\text{total spontaneous language}}$. The two main characteristics of egocentric language are that it is not addressed to anyone and usually does not evoke a response from others. The coefficients of egocentrism were calculated and though it was higher for Group R the difference was not statistically significant (0·387 for Group N and 0·510 for Group R).

Next the children's remarks were analysed into three categories: (i) those directed to the child(ren) with whom the speaker was playing; (ii) those directed to the investigator; and (iii) non-directed ones; for example, looking at some pictures a child would murmur 'look at this', while making no effort to attract anyone's attention nor looking whether anyone was heeding his remark. As can be seen from table 7.13 the total number of remarks made by Group N is somewhat larger. But the more marked difference between the two groups was in the proportion of remarks directed to other children. The considerably greater number of child-directed remarks made by

Table 7.13. Direction of children's comments

Type of remark	Group N		Group R	
	N	%	N	%
Child directed	596	56	358	37
Adult directed	247	23	315	32
Non-directed	226	21	301	31

Group N is in fact a reflection on the way in which these children played together. Many in Group R could hardly be said to be playing together at all, whereas in Group N a good deal of cooperative group play was observable. A small distorting factor was undoubtedly introduced by the presence of the investigator and this had a more distracting influence on Group R. At the same time Group N showed a degree of absorption in their play equalled by only a few children in Group R.

b. The incidence of maturer forms of conversation. Using a simplified version of Piaget's classification of socialised speech, an attempt was made to analyse the children's dialogue for examples of more mature forms of conversation. The following headings were chosen:

    i. collaboration in action or non-abstract thought;
    ii. collaboration in abstract thought;
    iii. clash of opinion;
    iv. arguments, differing from (iii) in that reasons were put forward for the differing points of view.

Though the first mentioned type of conversation occurred most frequently in both groups, once again Group N provided more examples. Collaboration in abstract thought did not occur at all in Group R but was beginning to show in a rudimentary and rather confused way among Group N. Clashes of opinion and arguments occurred with equal frequency among both groups but the nursery school children were more successful in reaching peaceful solutions or compromises.

c. The incidence of fantasy and humour. Although a detailed consideration of these two aspects is beyond the scope of this study, some mention of them must be made because of the marked difference between the two groups. Fantasy appeared in two forms: (i) objects or situations were interpreted imaginatively: for example, a boy playing in the sand pit said 'Have this ice cream, I made it for you'; (ii) pure make-believe: for example, a girl looking out of the window, called out 'there is a lion coming. Call a policeman.' Both these forms of fantasy occurred more frequently in the conversation of Group N (table 7.14). Some of the children in this group had

Table 7.14. Fantasy expressed in speech

	Group N	Group R
Imaginative interpretation	23	11
Pure make-believe	16	2
Total	39	13

already reached the stage where imaginative play no longer depended on, or arose from, the stimulation of the material world. The difference in the use of fantasy showed itself not merely in the number of occasions it entered into conversations but members of Group N showed greater persistence in developing an imaginative idea and would return to it after an interruption. Among Group R this was not observed.

At this age humour is, of course, very rudimentary and crude. Therefore, all occasions on which speech gave rise to laughter or where it was used for the sheer fun of it, were counted as instances of verbal humour; for example, a girl, pretending to be an old lady, said: 'I hurt my bones'; another girl: 'where are your bones?' (with both laughing); or a boy chanting amid the laughter of a small group: 'I fell on a banana and a butterfly picked me up.' Though some of these instances could hardly be described as intrinsically humorous, they proved to be amusing to the children. Moreover, they represented an attempt at experimenting with words. It was perhaps the beginning of an awareness that speech can be manipulated so as to arouse amusement in others and that words, like toys, can be used as vehicles for imagination. This awareness had hardly dawned on Group R. Whereas nine children in Group N took an active part in altogether eleven humurous exchanges, there was one example only in Group R.

Summary and conclusions

Wherever quantitative comparison was possible, Group N was found to be in advance of Group R. Differences ranged from fifteen months on the Merrill–Palmer verbal items, eleven months on the Wechsler Vocabulary and nine months on the Watts English Language Scale to five months on the Terman–Merrill Picture Vocabulary. In conversation, Group N used a wider vocabulary, showed rather better descriptive powers and a more mature type of sentence formation. On the other hand, there was little difference between the two groups in their use of the main grammatical components of speech; many definitions were given in similar terms and both groups tended to find the same words difficult to explain (in the Terman–Merrill and Wechsler vocabularies). Thus it seems that although Group R was retarded in the formal aspects of language, their speech was nevertheless developing along normal lines.

Some suggestive qualitative differences were noted. Group N tended to express in their definitions as well as in their free play a greater degree of active participation and aggressive self-assertion. The theme of naughtiness and crying seemed to preoccupy some children in the residential nurseries. But perhaps most marked were verbally expressed differences in attitudes both to adults and to contemporaries. A craving for adult attention is commonly observed by visitors to residential nurseries and our finding confirmed this. Group R were more anxious to be with and speak to the investigator, whether other children were present or not. Adult attention was actively sought instead of accepted in a matter-of-fact way. At the same time, Group R children spoke less of themselves or their belongings. In contrast, the nursery school children apparently took for granted adult interest in their doings and made frequent reference to their own activities and possessions. Among the factors which may account for this difference, the following are likely to be important: in residential nurseries play materials tend to be communally owned which must inhibit or at least delay the development of pride of possession engendered by having personally owned toys and belongings; therefore one would not expect the same desire to talk about and show off valued possessions. Secondly, it is very difficult to provide for children in care the range of experiences which occur as part of normal family life such as shopping, tradesmen calling, watching mother cook and father shave, visits to and from relatives, etc. This means that there are fewer non-routine and thus exciting happenings to absorb and to recount in conversations. Thirdly, nursery nurses who are in closest contact with the children are very young and their training is strongly biased in favour of physical health, hygiene and habit training. Usually matrons of residential nurseries are hospital trained nurses. It is the exception therefore to find emphasis placed on mental development in general and language growth in particular.

Just as there was more co-operative play activity among Group N, so speech was used spontaneously by them to a greater extent in social contacts with contemporaries. This was reflected in the rather lower coefficient of egocentrism and the higher proportion of remarks directed to other children. Again, Group N made greater use of verbally expressed fantasy and showed some persistence in following through an imaginative theme; even when fantasy did appear in the conversation of Group R, it was of a more fleeting nature. Lastly, Group N was beginning to appreciate the possibility of manipulating words and phrases for their own amusement and that of others, while only one child in Group R used language for this purpose.

If it be accepted that the medium of fantasy is one important way in which children learn to assimilate new experiences and come to terms with the difficulties and frustrations inseparable from growing up in a complex society, then children in care would seem to have a particularly great need in this respect. We cannot judge from our evidence whether Group R lacked to some extent the necessary verbal skills or whether their fantasies were too deeply repressed for overt expression to appear. Might the avoidance of the words 'mummy' and 'home' be an indication of the latter possibility? Similarly, deprived children tend to blame their own naughty behaviour or 'badness' as being the reason for having been sent away from home. One wonders whether the recurrence of themes of naughtiness and crying among Group R is linked to such fantasies.

Although there was considerable overlap in the achievements of the two groups studied, our evidence confirms that there is some retardation in the language skills of preschool children in care. In so far as Group R lacked the ability for verbalising fantasy and for using speech in making social relationships with contemporaries, to that extent their general emotional and social development may become adversely affected. Opinions may differ as to which should be regarded the cause and which the effect. But there is little doubt that such language difficulties as we found are likely to have long-term consequences unless remedied. For example, readiness to start school and ability to learn to read are the main educational tasks which will be adversely affected.

References

BOWLBY, J. (1951) 'Maternal care and mental health', *Monograph Series of the World Health Organisation*, **2**.

BRODBECK, A. J. and IRWIN, O. C. (1946) 'The speech behavior of infants without families', *Child Development*, **17**, 145–56.

BURLINGHAM, D. and FREUD, A. (1954) *Infants without families: the case for and against residential nurseries*. London, Allen and Unwin.

DAWE, H. C. (1942) 'A study of the effect of an educational programme upon language development and retarded mental functions in young children', *Journal of Experimental Education*, **11**, 200–09.

FLEMMING, V. V. (1942) 'A study of Stanford–Binet vocabulary attainment and growth in children in the city of Childhood, Mooseheart, Illinois, as compared with children living in their own homes', *Journal of Genetic Psychology*, **60**, 359–73.

GATEWOOD, M. C. and WEISS, A. P. (1930) 'Race and sex differences in newborn infants', *Journal of Genetic Psychology*, **38**, 31–49.

GESELL, A. and AMATRUDA, C. S. (1947) *Developmental diagnosis; normal and abnormal child development; clinical methods and pediatric application*. 2nd edn, New York, Hoeber.

GOLDFARB, W. (1943) 'Infant rearing and problem behavior', *American Journal of Orthopsychiatry*, **13**, 249–65.

GOLDFARB, W. (1943) 'The effects of early institutional care on adolescent personality (graphic Rorschach data)', *Child Development*, **14**, 213–23.

GOLDFARB, W. (1945) 'The effect of psychological deprivation in infancy and subsequent stimulation', *American Journal of Psychiatry*, **102**, 18–33.

GOLDMAN–EISLER, F. (1958) 'Speech analysis and mental processes', *Language and Speech*, 1, 59–78.

LITTLE, M. F. and WILLIAMS, H. M. (1937) 'An analytical scale of language achievement', *University of Iowa Studies in Child Welfare*, 13, 47–78, 88–94.

McCARTHY, D. A. (1930) *The language development of the pre-school child*. Minneapolis, Institute of Child Welfare Monograph 4.

McCARTHY, D. A. (1952) 'Language and personality development', *Reading Teacher*, 6, 28.

MOORE, J. K. (1947) 'Speech content of selected groups of orphanage and non-orphanage pre-school children', *Journal of Experimental Education*, 16, 122–33.

PIAGET, J. (1959) *The Language and Thought of the Child*. Routledge & Kegan Paul.

PRINGLE, M. L. KELLMER and BOSSIO, V. (1958) 'A study of deprived children. Part 2. Language development and reading attainment', *Vita Humana*, 1, 142–70.

ROUDINESCO, J. and APPELL, G. (1950) 'Les répercussions de la stabulation hospitalière sur le développement psychomoteur des jeunes enfants', *Semaine des Hôpitaux de Paris*, 26, 2271–3.

SKEELS, H. M., UPDEGRAFF, R., WELLMAN, B. L. and WILLIAMS, H. M. (1938) 'A study of environmental stimulation; an orphanage pre-school project', *University of Iowa Studies in Child Welfare*, 15.

SMITH, M. E. (1935) 'A study of some factors influencing the development of the sentence in pre-school children', *Journal of Genetic Psychology*, 46, 182–212.

TERMAN, L. M. and MERRILL, M. A. (1937) *Measuring intelligence; a guide to the administration of the new revised Stanford–Binet test of intelligence*. London, Harrap.

WATTS, A. F. (1944) *The language and mental development of children*. London, Harrap.

WILLIAMS, H. M. and McFARLAND, M. L. (1937) 'Development of language and vocabulary in young children', *University of Iowa Studies in Child Welfare*, 13.

8. Learning and emotion*

Introduction
The study of emotion is at present not very respectable academically. Lloyd Morgan's canon stipulated that the behaviour of animals should not be explained in terms of human attributes if it could be explained on a lower level (Morgan, 1900). Now, more than fifty years later, this has been subtly inverted: many psychologists are reluctant to attribute to humans any characteristics which cannot be demonstrated in lower animals. Similarly, the application of Lloyd Morgan's 'canon of parsimony' to human actions means that one must never explain them by 'higher motives' if they can also be explained by reference to 'lower motives'. Professor Mace has suggested that this reduces the interpretation of behaviour to the level of malicious gossip and that this may even be unfair to rats!

On the other hand, some psychologists, such as Ashley Montagu (1957), consider that learning theories have at present little to offer to students of personality and human development.

I shall take up a middle position: learning theories do have an important contribution to make but there is a great need for more systematic research in the field of human motivation, personality adjustment and mental health.

The meaning of emotion
Emotion is a label for a vast range of psychosomatic states which occur when something, either in the external environment or within the organism, thwarts or enhances the process of living. On the subjective side emotion involves feelings which may be quite clearly

* This chapter contains the substance of two lectures delivered during a course on the Psychology of Learning, organised by the University of Birmingham Institute of Education and held at the City of Worcester Training College in the summer of 1957.

defined (for instance when one experiences a surge of anger) or vague and difficult to describe (as when one feels anxious). Usually emotion involves perception or awareness or an event or circumstance, though strong feelings may occur without such awareness ('unconscious' motives). Emotion also involves an impulse to action, whether this be an actual physical act or a verbal reply. The objective features of emotional behaviour include a wide range of visceral activities, including glandular, digestive and muscular changes. Thus the term emotion covers both positive and negative conditions; at the one extreme it may be shown by highly explosive and disorganised behaviour, at the other by well organised and constructive behaviour. Though this point is simple it needs emphasising since 'often in psychological writing emotion is treated primarily as a form of disorder or distress. . . . But emotion is involved in the whole business of living' (Jersild, 1954).

Theories of Motivation

To understand emotional development a broadly conceived theory of motivation is needed. It must take into account the elementary physical needs as well as 'emotional (non-vital) basic needs' (Montagu, 1957). These Montagu defines as any biological urge which is not necessary for the physical survival of the organism 'but which must be satisfied if the organism is to develop and maintain adequate mental health'. As a definition of mental health he suggests 'the ability to love, i.e. to form relationships, and the ability to work'. Linton (1945) considers the following to be man's most important psychic needs: (a) the need for emotional response from other individuals, (b) the need for security and (c) the need for new experiences. Snygg and Combs (1949) maintain that the 'basic human need' is the 'preservation and enhancement of the phenomenal self', the self of which a person is aware. Maslow (1954) developed a system of 'basic needs' which he arranged in a hierarchy, from the most basic and biologic to the most advanced and socialised, according to the principle of relative potency. For example, the need for food is stronger than the need for safety, because the former dominates the organism when both needs are frustrated. Similarly the need for safety is stronger than the need for love and the latter is stronger than the need for prestige. According to Maslow, when the most potent need is satisfied, the next higher need emerges, so that man is a 'perpetually wanting animal'.

L

Lindgren (1956) has modified Maslow's original list to establish a more comprehensive system of basic needs. A fivefold classification is suggested: bodily processes (i.e. the need for food, water, oxygen, etc.) and safety (i.e. to avoid physical danger) are placed at the first and second level of importance; the need for love is given the third level of importance, second only to the need to maintain and protect the physical self. These three needs appear in infancy and hence are basic to the other needs. Unless they are met satisfactorily, the child cannot give the necessary attention and energy to meeting the other needs. For example, the child who is hungry or fears that his mother may have deserted the family by the time he returns home, is too preoccupied to do well in his school work. Needs at the fourth and fifth levels are concerned with the individual's relations with others. 'Status and acceptance by the group', which Lindgren places at the fourth level, involve self-respect and self-esteem, as reflected by the respect of others. Needs at the fifth level, which he terms 'general adequacy, creativity and self-expression', are concerned with the development and maintenance of a 'life role that is satisfying and worth while', based on a sense of personal adequacy and self-realisation. Needs at the lower levels involve behaviour which is relatively simple and direct; needs at the fourth and fifth levels are much more likely to involve behaviour that is symbolic or abstract, making greater demands on the intelligence and maturity of the individual. These basic needs are interrelated and interdependent; frustrating or blocking the needs at one level affects the ability to meet needs at other levels (for example inability to establish satisfactory relations with other people may affect the ability to sleep or to digest food properly).

Tilton (1951) holds that 'the best hypothesis upon which to proceed is that there is only one basic motivation and that it is not channelled along specific lines as are adult motivation patterns'. According to this viewpoint, there is originally only an excitement to activity as a result of physiological needs. Gradually under the influences of our culture and man's capacity for learning, this physiological basis is differentiated into motivational patterns. In spite of such commonness of pattern as comes from growing up in the same culture, there is to be expected a great deal of individual uniqueness, both because of the uniqueness of the individual's environment and because of his uniqueness as a physiological organism.

In the psychoanalytic field, most writers, from Freud and Horney to Fromm and Alexander, have for long stressed a view of human motivation where love and the development of close, secure relationships with the parents plays a central role. It seems significant that in recent years writers, holding different theoretical viewpoints have come to place the need for affection and belonging either equal to, or next in importance to, the basic physical needs. Some argue that this need is primary and essential for survival; others hold that it springs from the initial helplessness and dependence of the human infant; yet others believe that it is conditioned by the treatment of loving parents. Whatever the mechanism, it seems evident that babies need affection and, as they mature, also show a need to give love. Again, whether and to what extent the child's affectionate behaviour represents a primary drive or an acquired motive would be difficult to determine. The work of Dennis, for example, suggests that it arises spontaneously and with a minimum of social stimulation (Dennis, 1941).

The relationship between affection and learning

A basic and all-pervasive feature of parental love is that the child is valued for his own sake. In their relationship with him, the loving father and mother communicate affection through all their ways of dealing with him. The greatest impact of such love is on the development of the self, which has been defined as 'reflected appraisals' (Sullivan, 1948). Approval and acceptance by others are essential for the development of self-approval and self-acceptance. Whether a child develops a constructive or destructive attitude to himself and to other people depends in the first place on the parents' attitude to him. In the dependency relationship of the child to the mother, later to the father and then to other people, is to be seen the primary socialising pattern, the task of learning to become a human being. That the attributes of personality are a function of living in a human society and that the baby is born only with the potentiality to become a person but has to be taught to become human, is demonstrated clearly by two phenomena: first, by the development of children born without the necessary sense organs to perceive, communicate and interact with their environment, such as the deaf and dumb (Helen Keller being the most famous example); secondly, by the development of children who by some chance or mishap have been isolated from normal human conduct during early infancy (for example the case of Anna described by Kingsley Davis, 1940 and 1947).

The infant soon learns that in order to be loved he must satisfy the requirements of others and cooperate with them. Mothering to begin with ensures the sheer survival of the baby but the complete indulgence of all his wants is changed gradually into a series of regulatory pressures. 'By withholding adult cooperation, which is so essential to the infant, the parent has constantly at his command a device for increasing the infant's variable, exploratory behaviour, and for then selectively rewarding (by responding to) those new, more adultlike responses, which make their appearance' (Mowrer, 1944).

Experimentally, it is easier and more unequivocal to show the negative side, namely the results of development when babies are deprived of love and affection. In recent years there have been very similar findings in different countries regarding the unfavourable and often lasting effects on personality development of what has been termed maternal deprivation (Bakwin, Ribble, Bowlby, Spitz and Goldfarb, to mention a few). Frustration of the need to receive love from the mother or mother substitute, once such love has been experienced, produces in the very young infant anxiety, anger, despair and finally symptoms very akin to depression. Physically, too the child becomes much more vulnerable to infection, especially gastro-intestinal and respiratory disorders.

The development of anxiety

'The concept of anxiety is very important for understanding the emotional life of the child even though there is much diversity, at present, in the definition of anxiety, its origin and role' (Jersild, 1954). I propose to single out some of the theories which consider the development and role of anxiety in the parent–child relationship and later in classroom learning.

Once a child has learned through a loving mother's reaction to him that he is important and excellent, this satisfying experience is 'ever afterwards craved and so constitutes a powerful driving force of human nature' (Moore, 1948). Conversely, disapproval and possible loss of love arouses anxiety. Sensing the mother's displeasure or disturbed emotional tone, even very young infants become restless, irritable, show feeding problems, and so on. Thus anxiety is induced by the disapproval of people who are significant within the child's interpersonal world. There is research evidence to suggest that even prenatal conditions may predispose a child to anxiety (Sontag, 1941).

It was Freud who first worked out a theory of how human beings come to learn anxiety in the face of disapproval and loss of love. He held that children learn to become anxious about their mother's loss of love, because it is associated with pain. When she disapproves of her child, implying loss of love, she tends at the same time to punish in some way or other. Freud's solution was an associationist one and it can be reformulated in a stimulus-response terminology. It could be argued that maternal disapproval and withdrawal of love become conditioned stimuli eliciting anxiety and that the learning process obeys essentially the same laws as Pavlovian conditioning. To explain how children come to feel anxious not only about their mother's disapproval but other people's—Freud's 'moral anxiety'—one would apply the principle of generalisation: stimuli which are similar to the original conditioned stimulus, have the power of evoking the conditioned response by virtue of their similarity. Thus Lynn postulates that the acquisition of anxiety should be viewed as a task of discrimination learning (Lynn, 1957). Children can only be taught to associate disapproval and loss of love with anxiety if they are able to discriminate love from loss of love. The more distinctive the cues are, the more easily the learning is accomplished. Hence the apparent paradox that a child learns to be anxious more readily in the warm, accepting atmosphere of the happy family than in a rejectful or frigid situation, be it a broken home or an institution. The greater the child's general sense of love and security, the more distinctive are the cues of loss of love. This hypothesis supports the common clinical finding that it is over-protected children who are the most anxious. For rejected and deprived children the cues are blurred. A similar blurring may be caused by inconsistent handling. Burt, Healey, Bronner and others have drawn attention to the important role played by the inconsistent mother in the formation of the delinquent and psychopathic personality.

During the growth from infancy to childhood, anxiety continues to play an important part. It appears whenever others criticise, snub or disapprove of the child. Anxiety is such a painful and disturbing emotion that most children will go to considerable lengths to avoid behaviour that might arouse it. In everyday life anxiety has positive as well as negative value. Because he wishes to avoid this feeling, the child learns to be considerate in his relations with others and to conform to laws, customs and taboos.

The role of anxiety

'The function and role of anxiety in learning is so far only partly understood' (Lindgren, 1956). It seems, however, that much of the motivation for learning stems from what one might term 'normal anxiety'. This is particularly true of the learning that occurs within the context of social situations. Children learn to modify their behaviour in order not to disappoint or offend their parents, teachers or playmates. Even those skills classed as 'intellectual' may be mastered, at least in part, as a means of reducing or avoiding anxiety. For example, children may learn to read because their parents and teachers expect them to do so and because their contemporaries are acquiring this skill; failure would lead to feeling different from the group and would evoke the disapproval of the powerful adults; by learning to read these anxieties are avoided.

The practical implications of research carried out so far on the effects of anxiety on learning are not easy to see. Only a beginning has been made in exploring this problem systematically and some of the findings may seem conflicting. Snygg and Combs (1949) found that over-anxiety has the effect of 'narrowing the perceptual field', thus interfering with successful problem-solving. This conclusion is confirmed by Beier (1951) who states that 'individuals who are faced with threat and who are in a state of anxiety show a loss of the "abstract" qualities, or more specifically, face a loss in flexibility of intellectual function'. Lynn (1956) suggests that anxious children do better at reading than at arithmetic and postulates that some pupils do not learn to read because they are not anxious enough. Clinical experience, including my own, suggests, however, that among reading failures one can distinguish at least three groups: some children fail because neither they nor their parents set great store by this achievement; for a second group of children serious anxieties about other matters, such as parental disharmony, make learning to read an area of comparatively minor anxiety; lastly many fail to learn to read for the opposite reason, namely too much anxiety.

Montague (1950) found that a high level of anxiety helped in the learning of simple material but interfered with the learning of complex material. This suggests that the over-anxious person, when reassured by the realisation that the task to be learned is easy and within his capacity, can then proceed to learn it more effectively, since his anxiety has been reduced; on the other hand, complex material reinforces his already considerable anxiety, thus interfering with effective learning. These findings are supported by another study which showed that people with a high degree of anxiety were less able to improvise and hence less successful in learning complex and novel tasks (Ausubel, Schiff and Goldman, 1952).

Janis and Feshbach (1953) showed that deliberate attempts to arouse strong anxiety produced less favourable results in the behaviour of learners than more moderate methods. Mandler and Sarason (1953) compared the abilities of people with high and with low levels of anxiety to learn a manipulative task. At first a high level of anxiety interfered with the performance of the task. However, as the experiment proceeded, the anxiety drive appeared to help the 'high-anxiety' group to improve their scores. Informing the two groups of their success or failure resulted in improvement in the scores of the 'low-anxiety' group but depressed the scores of the 'high-anxiety' group. There was greater variability in the scores made by the 'high-anxiety' individuals, indicating that anxiety is not a stable factor in learning but has a different effect on different persons.

Thus it may well be that some anxiety is conducive to learning and that for each individual there is an optimum level of anxiety which eads to maximal learning; perhaps it is this level which should be called 'normal' anxiety. On the other hand, a level of anxiety which is too high or too low seems to lead to ineffective or insufficient learning. With regard to children's educational failure, there is a great deal of evidence to suggest that 'most teaching problems stem from a super-abundance of anxiety rather than a lack of it' (Lindgren, 1956).

The role of competition

One factor that increases anxiety is competition. It is now fairly generally accepted that it is an acquired and not an innate drive and that cultural values determine the development, the extent and the direction of competitive traits. The results from animal experiments show that different competitive experiences in early life have an observable effect upon 'adult' behaviour. For example Fredericson's work with mice supports the hypothesis that a limited period of competition for food during infancy will result in competitive behaviour at a later stage despite absence of hunger (Fredericson, 1950). Of course competition has its satisfying effects, and is rewarding in terms both of socially approved achievement and of the increased security of those who compete successfully. But encouraging competition in the classroom gives rise to two difficulties: first, if all children were of equal ability, competition (characterised by weekly or monthly class lists) would only be a measure of effort made; in practice, even when there is streaming, pupils are of mixed abilities so that the less able group remains comparatively unsuccessful. If a goal is felt to be unattainable there is a tendency for effort to diminish partly because a long record of failure and a sense of rejection are liable to lead to excessive anxiety. An over-emphasis on competition leads to an emotional climate where winning or being first is the important goal; learning is no longer important for its own sake or for the basic needs it can meet. Under an intense system of competition, most children are doomed to failure since only a select few can succeed. For example the most serious objection to the eleven-plus examination is that in many areas less than a quarter of those entering have any hope of succeeding.

The second difficulty lies in the fact that encouraging competition interferes with the development of cooperative attitudes. This has now been shown experimentally (Grossack, 1954) though clinicians have for some time expressed concern about the disruptive effect of competition. Adler (1932), for example, stated that 'under our present system we generally find that when children first come to school they are more prepared for competition than for co-operation. This is a disaster for the child; and it is hardly less of a disaster if he goes ahead and strains to beat the other children than if he falls behind and gives up the struggle.' That this is not only an individual disaster would be held by those who believe that cooperative behaviour has great survival value and that evolution in man has been increasingly directed toward the fuller development of cooperative behaviour. If this be accepted, then the skills of cooperation are far more basic to successful living than the skills of competition. Yet many children experience a severely competitive climate at home and siblings or other children may be held up as examples even when emulation is beyond the child's capacity. Similarly, parental pressures and expectations bear a measure of responsibility for the competitive atmosphere which prevails in many schools.

Practical implications
How to use anxiety and competition constructively in a predominantly competitive society is a complex problem. 'One of the characteristics of successful learning is to produce tension and anxieties. . . .

When learning really takes place, it means that there has been some change in the learner. We seldom welcome change. All that is childish and immature within us struggles against the necessity for change. . . . In effect, we realise that we are unable to meet our basic needs successfully, and we become anxious for fear that we might never be able to meet them' (Lindgren, 1956). Frustration and anxiety are not only inevitable in the process of growth and development but may be conducive to it, provided they are appropriate to the individual's level of tolerance. 'In order that effective integration may take place in the child's mental development, conflicting drives, impulses, external demands and ideas must be balanced, not eliminated' (Tyler, 1948). How easy is it to achieve such a balance? There are many conditions in presentday life which intensify anxiety and uncertainty. To mention just a few: the emphasis on economic competition; rapid and major scientific and technological developments such as atomic science and automation; a change in social and moral standards developing in the aftermath of a world war and a social revolution; the increasing instability of family life. If parents and teachers suffer from feelings of anxiety, personal conflict and doubt, these feelings are likely to be communicated to the children in their care. The most stable and 'emotionally tough' children may be able to resist the effects of an atmosphere laden with anxiety; the rest—possibly the majority—may, to a greater or lesser extent, become predisposed or conditioned to excessive and thus harmful anxiety. Early parental handling will influence children's later attitudes to learning. For example, Hattwick and Stowell found that children who were either 'pushed' or 'babied' had more social and academic difficulties at school than those not subjected to such parental treatment (Hattwick and Stowell, 1936). And it has been argued 'that all of a child's worries, fears, anxieties, self-consciousness, feelings of inadequacy, his relations to his parents, siblings and to himself, tend to gain reflection in the school situation' (Klein, 1945).

On the other hand, many of the circumstances that affect a child's self-esteem and respect, arise in connection with his life at school where he is 'exposed to failure or the threat of failure on a colossal scale' (Jersild, 1954). By the nature of the academic and social setting children become involved in many competitive situations of their own making in addition to those provided by the teacher. Children try themselves out in countless ways, realising their strength and discovering their limitations.

The teacher who sees his role in a wider framework than the inculcating of skills and information can counteract or at least mitigate the unfavourable consequences of over-anxiety and competition. He will endeavour to gauge the emotional climate of his classroom as well as the degree and extent of anxiety shown by individual children, particularly those who are failing; he will plan to reduce anxiety where it interferes with successful learning and to increase it where it seems lacking; he will limit the use of competition in situations where only a minority have any chance of success and instead provide all pupils with opportunities for positive achievement. Thus 'normal' or 'tolerable' anxiety is utilised as a motivating force in the learning of tasks which are within the child's capacity though he may have to make a considerable effort in order to succeed. Competition will be used as a group incentive only for those of similar standing; where there are considerable individual differences in learning capacity, competition will be used positively by encouraging a child to surpass his own past achievement, i.e. competing with his own efforts.

The effects of emotion on learning need to be given greater practical recognition, especially in the classroom, by relating material to be learned to the self-concept, ego-ideal or level of aspiration of the learner. Research has shown that the successful pupil tends to set his aspirations at a realistic level, whereas the failing child is liable to set them too high or low. The level of aspiration a learner sets himself is related in part to past experience and in part to his self-concept or ego-ideal. Moreover, the child who is made to feel guilty or anxious because of his failure often becomes more concerned about avoiding anxiety than about analysing and profiting from the reasons for his failure. Whatever their level of ability, children need to experience in their learning the stimulus of success as well as the discipline of failure, without a feeling of guilt or despair. Divorcing or isolating the intellectual from the emotional side of life, is unlikely to lead to the successful teaching of any but a minority.

Case studies

To illustrate the relationship between anxiety, competition and successful learning at home and in school, the cases of two children will be described in some detail.

1. *A six-year-old boy*

Gordon, aged 6 years, was referred for refusing to speak though he had been at school for over two terms. In her report the headmistress added that he was very apathetic, would not talk to the other children, not even in a whisper, and that he was tolerated rather than disliked by his contemporaries. The diagnostic psychological examination, consisting of two interviews lasting an hour each with the mother, and a morning spent with the child, brought to light the following factors which seemed to have some bearing on Gordon's present difficulties.

Family circumstances. The father, a semi-skilled worker, had been with the same firm ever since starting work; before marriage the mother worked in an office. There were three children: an older sister, a younger brother and Gordon, whom mother described as a slow, sulky and shy child. There seemed to be a marked difference in temperament between him and his siblings who, from the mother's description, seemed intelligent, quick and responsive children. For some time the mother had been concerned about Gordon's slowness, refusal to talk to strangers and reluctance to speak except to members of the family—'People might think he is really stupid the way he acts when we meet anyone.' He had no friends and never talked about school. Father took the line that he himself had also been shy and that Gordon would grow out of it.

Maternal attitude. There were a number of circumstances during

Gordon's early life which had made the mother more anxious than she had been with his siblings. Because of her pregnancy she had to leave her flat (only one child was permitted) and housing difficulties continued for some time. Though she had hoped for a boy, his comparative slowness (i.e. in sucking and toilet training) disappointed her. She then discovered that her husband was illiterate, which greatly increased her anxiety since she feared Gordon might be like him. Apparently the parents had been close neighbours for many years before marriage and there had never been any need for correspondence. Mother had made various suggestions to help him to learn to read and write, but the father was adamant in refusing to do anything about it. Lastly, the youngest child was born only 14 months after Gordon and he proved to be a quick, responsive baby. Toilet training had been severe, partly because Gordon was slow and stubborn and partly because mother in any case believed in very early habit training.

The child. Despite mother's evident irritation and embarrassment Gordon would not say a word in her presence. When he was left alone with the examiner and realised that he was 'not being made' to talk, he became quite friendly and soon whispered though he never used a normal voice. He was found to be of average intelligence and there were a number of indications that this was likely to be an underestimate. Though slow in everything, he took great care, showing considerable persistence and a determination to finish what he had started. This painstaking, almost obsessional attitude was also noted in his drawings.

Working hypothesis. Gordon had been both over-protected and dominated by his mother who had tended to identify him with her husband (whom she regarded as a failure). This led her to make unfavourable comparisons between the boy and his brighter siblings, to hurry him over his early learning (partly because of her own quickness) and at the same time to do too much for him because of his very slowness (partly passive resistance on his part?). There was a real loss of love after the birth of his younger brother, who needed his mother's attention and soon proved more satisfying to her, and a further felt loss of love was caused by her increasing impatience and disappointment with him. As a result of her rejection and ambivalent handling, Gordon had become shy, asocial, infantile and submissive; but combined with his insecurity and uncertainty, there developed a strong streak of hostility and stubbornness, shown by his refusal to be hurried or to talk outside the family circle despite, or perhaps because of, his mother's strenuous attempts to make him do both. Thus Gordon showed many features characteristic of the dominated, over-protected child who is distrustful of the world and follows a pattern of non-cooperation in situations requiring give and take (Levy, 1943; Symonds, 1949).

At school the home situation seemed to be re-enacted. Anxiety was provoked by the competitive setting of a large class and by an elderly teacher who, although quite kindly, treated Gordon's silence as defiance which had to be broken down and his slow passivity as laziness which would respond to 'jollying along' and to comparisons with other children. This attitude resulted in Gordon feeling 'un-loved' once again and retreating from the competitive challenge into stubbornness and silence.

Aims of treatment. At the first case conference it was decided that emotional re-education should be along the following lines:

a. With the home: to enable the mother to appreciate the positive qualities in Gordon's personality, such as his persistence, neatness and thoroughness; to accept the fact that he is not mentally dull but needs to be allowed to learn at his own pace; to encourage him to talk not by pressure in public but by helping him to stake his claims *vis-a-vis* his more forceful siblings (according to father Gordon 'never gets a word in edgeways'); to encourage mother to see father's positive qualities and accept the fact that despite his illiteracy he is not a stupid man (though refusing promotion and thus a higher wage at work, he is a most gifted handyman in his own home); to encourage father to play a more active part in his children's upbringing, especially Gordon's.

b. With Gordon: to give him the experience (which he may have missed in early childhood) of being accepted unconditionally and valued for his own sake; to allow him, once he has formed a secure relationship, to express his hostility and ambivalence towards the adult world; to let him set the pace in a permissive, unstructured environ-ment rich with opportunities for creative, imaginative activities.

Thus our work aimed at integrating the boy into his family setting as a loved, accepted member, restoring his self-confidence and self-respect and enabling him to face competition and possible failure without retreating into his shell.

Results of treatment. Though considerable changes have taken place it is too early to say whether they will be lasting since Gordon has only been attending for a period of five months (once weekly). At our Centre he not only talks freely but shouts and laughs loudly; at home he is becoming increasingly able to hold his own and though still slow, is less sullen and stubborn. His mother has been delighted to see him so active and lively when at the Centre and recently reported with unexpected pride: 'He even cheeked me the other day.' He is asking boys in to play and is learning to prevent his siblings from interfering with his activities. At school he is not yet talking normally but is now replying in whispers and beginning to take a more active interest in what goes on.

2. *A nine-year-old girl*

Shirley, aged 9 years, was referred because of retardation in all English subjects. The headmaster stated in his report that she seemed an intelligent girl and in a recent non-verbal group test had scored an I.Q. of 118; she lacked confidence and was a poor mixer.

Family circumstances. Born illegitimately to two doctors, one of whom was married already, Shirley was adopted when 2 weeks old. Since her real parents played no further part I shall refer to the adoptive parents as 'mother' and 'father'. The latter, a foreman in a car factory, was not educationally ambitious for the child, but expected her to do well educationally because of her 'superior background'.

The mother had very much wanted a daughter and when she realised she could not have any children, decided to adopt one. She was then just over 40 years old. Awareness that the child came 'from a much higher social class' led her to feel a mixture of pride, ambition and a sense of heightened responsibility 'to make up for what she has lost'. The mother had left school at 14 and worked in a shop until marriage. Now they were quite comfortably off but it was not a cultured home and neither parent was interested in books.

Maternal attitude. Being an over-anxious and fussy woman, the mother set great store on cleanliness, tidiness and politeness. Shirley had conformed to these high standards of behaviour by being 'a good, easy baby' and a 'gentle, obedient toddler'. The fact that she was fussy over food and apparently needed little sleep was attributed by her mother to her 'refined nature and superior heritage'. Until she started school Shirley had been discouraged to play with other children since they were 'not the right type'. When she started school, her attendance was rather irregular, partly because she tended to suffer from bronchitis and partly because mother kept her at home at the slightest provocation. However, Shirley was fairly happy while at the infant school. It seems that her difficulties began when she went up to the juniors and that they were linked with three circumstances: her teacher was a rather strict women, who frightened Shirley by frequent shouting and punishment; she found that compared with her contemporaries she was rather backward in reading, perhaps because of her frequent absences as well as fear of the teacher; thirdly, she was told by another child that she was adopted. The parents had kept this fact from her all along. Now they dismissed it as 'stupid gossip', told her to ignore it and reassured her that it was untrue. At the same time the mother was very upset and decided to move to a different neighbourhood, ignoring the fact that all her relatives knew that Shirley was adopted and that the child was likely to have overheard discussions long before going to school. Though she did not refer to her adoption again, Shirley developed nightmares, screaming and walking in her sleep. She was no happier at her new school, becoming increasingly timid and solitary. At home she loved helping but was rarely allowed to do so, partly because her mother wanted her 'to enjoy childhood' and partly for fear of accidents.

The child. Throughout the interview, Shirley was over-anxious to please. Her manner was gentle and diffident, she spoke in a soft, pleasant voice and in appearance, dress and bearing conveyed the impression of a rather old-fashioned 'young lady'. The precociousness of her conversation further enhanced this impression. She was found to be an able child (I.Q. 128) but seriously retarded in all English subjects (4 years in mechanical reading, 3 years in comprehension reading, 5 years in spelling and composition). In the personality test Shirley readily expressed her fears and worries as well as her knowledge of being adopted.

Working hypothesis. Shirley's emotional and educational difficulties seemed to be caused mainly by three circumstances: maternal over-anxiety, over-protection and high social aspirations, leading to the child's over-dependency, lack of confidence, fear of failure and inability to mix; anxiety over her adoption which had never been brought out into the open though she clearly knew about it; absences from school and a fear of teachers.

Aims of treatment. It was decided that emotional re-education should be along the following lines:

a. With the home: to help the mother to accept the necessity of telling Shirley that she is adopted and to give her some guidance on the kind of questions she must expect from the child; to suggest various ways of giving the girl an increasing measure of independence, allowing her to have some responsibilities in the home and to encourage her to make friends with her contemporaries; to modify the maternal stereotype of a 'well-bred, high-born young lady'.

b. With the child: to support her through any stress that might arise when the mother tackled the adoption problem; since she seemed ready to express her anxieties through projection material, to give her opportunities for doing so in miming, puppetry and drama which might also lead to increased social contacts; to begin remedial work in English straight away but well below her present level of attainment to help her to regain confidence.

Results of treatment. As we came to know the mother better, it became clear that she was a much more anxious and obsessional woman than was apparent at first. Her days and weeks were arranged according to a strict and unalterable routine, she was always worrying about something and she proved resistant to suggestions. Despite agreeing with us that it would be wise to talk to Shirley about her adoption, she kept postponing it 'until the right opportunity comes'. On the other hand, she began to allow the child greater independence, encouraged her to bring one or two girls home and arranged for her to have dancing lessons; this the child had longed for and we thought it might help her to gain confidence. When Shirley's educational attainments began to improve, the mother's anxiety became directed towards the 11 + examination; previously she had condemned parents who pressed their children educationally but now she felt that she 'would never forgive herself if Shirley missed the opportunity of going to the Grammar school, seeing how intelligent her real parents were'. She also worried lest 'failure' would make the child again lose confidence.

Shirley made considerable improvement all-round during her period of attendance (six university terms, forty-six individual sessions). Thus her reading age increased by $5\frac{1}{2}$ years, her spelling age by 3 years and her written composition, though still slow and much inferior to her oral work, was average for her age. The nightmares and sleep-walking ceased, her dislike of school changed to cheerful acceptance (though not a positive liking) and she made one or two friends. Remarks made to her mother and to us showed not only that she knew about her adoption but that she had come to terms with it. For example, when out shopping with her mother one day, she met another girl who attended her school and said: 'I wish you or some other mother would adopt her; she never has any nice clothes, or ribbons or nice things to eat during the morning break.' Her mother replied: 'But she has a mother of her own', which Shirley countered by saying: 'But her mother is not good to her like you are to me. It doesn't matter having an adopted mother if she loves you and looks after you.' Even such remarks did not persuade the mother to broach the topic but it reassured both her and us that Shirley was no longer bewildered and unhappy about the adoption.

We prepared mother for the fact that Shirley was unlikely to succeed in gaining a special place, partly because she was still educationally retarded, and partly because she never did her best under examination conditions. In the particular area, children were given a second chance of entry into the Grammar school at 13 + and it was suggested that she might stand a better chance then. Since Shirley seemed much improved in emotional adjustment and was making steady educational progress, it was felt that she could be discharged. Moreover, it would enable her to make a completely fresh start at the secondary modern school without being singled out in any way. A follow-up examination two years later showed continued but rather slower progress both educationally and emotionally: she was in an A stream but only in the bottom section; she had only a few friends; at home she had many more responsibilities which she enjoyed and she was beginning to 'mother' her mother (for example at the Centre she turned to her mother before following the examiner and said soothingly: 'Now don't worry, dear, everything will be all right.') There had been no recurrence of symptoms denoting emotional disturbance but for a girl of her age she had unusually high standards of orderliness and politeness.

Thus it seems that only partial success was achieved with mother and daughter. Being an elderly, over-anxious and aspiring woman the mother continued to set too high standards for the child and to create an emotionally tense atmosphere in the home. The process of emotional re-education brought about some reduction of the child's anxieties, through creative activities, social stimulation and educational improvement, all of which enhanced her self-confidence. Though no direct interpretations were given, she was also helped to come to terms with the problem of her adoption. Yet she remained

M

to some extent socially timid, educationally retarded and emotionally vulnerable.

Conclusion

The complexity of the relationship between learning and emotion stems from several sources. Perhaps chief among them are the complexity of the 'material' itself and our comparative ignorance of the intricate workings of human beings; it also derives from our approach which, perhaps inevitably, is piecemeal. This leads to the danger of creating false questions. We are forced to investigate the various aspects of human personality separately but then may go on to discuss how these arbitrarily distinguished aspects are related to each other. Yet cognitive and orectic aspects are indivisible and I have outlined how they develop together from early childhood. The mother–child relationship provides both the incentive and the condition for learning. The way to maladjustment and the way to educational failure are often along the same path. That is so just because of the very close and constant interrelationship between learning and emotion. Conversely, satisfactory relationships and successful learning together with the ability to tolerate 'normal anxiety' are shown by children who have been reared in homes where unconditional parental love has been balanced by appropriate demands for increasing social and emotional independence. I have concentrated upon early learning processes because the greater part of children's most basic learning experiences take place in the home, particularly during the preschool years. Attitudes towards oneself and others, standards of right and wrong, the ability to love and work, in short the development of all human potentialities depends to a considerable extent upon the stimulation and handling received during infancy and childhood. Of course learning—defined behaviouristically as the alteration in behaviour resulting from experience—continues throughout life. It is the extent of this ability which appears to be determined early in life.

References

ADLER, A. (1932) *What life should mean to you.* London, Allen & Unwin.

AUSUBEL, D. P., SCHIFF, H. M. and GOLDMAN, M. (1953) 'Qualitative characteristics in the learning process associated with anxiety', *Journal of Abnormal and Social Psychology*, **48**, 537–47.

BEIER, E. G. (1951) 'The effect of induced anxiety on flexibility of intellectual functioning', *Psychological Monographs*, **65**, no. 326.

DAVIS, K. (1940, 1947) 'Extreme social isolation of a child', *American Journal of Sociology*, **45**, pp. 554–65; **52**, 432–7.

DENNIS, W. (1941) 'Infant development under conditions of restricted practice and of minimum social stimulation', *Genetic Psychology Monographs*, **23**, 143–89.

FREDERICSON, E. (1950) 'The effects of food deprivation upon competitive and spontaneous combat in C57 black mice', *Journal of Psychology*, **29**, 89–100.

GROSSACK, M. M. (1954) 'Some effects of co-operation and competition upon small group behavior', *Journal of Abnormal and Social Psychology*, **49**, 341–8.

HATTWICK, B. M. and STOWELL, M. (1936) 'Relation of parental over-attentiveness to children's work habits and social adjustments in kindergarten and the first six grades of school', *Journal of Educational Research*, **30**, 169–76.

JANIS, I. L. and FESHBACH, S. (1953) 'Effects of fear-arousing communications', *Journal of Abnormal and Social Psychology*, **48**, 78–92.

JERSILD, A. T. (1954) 'Emotional development', *in:* Carmichael, L. (*ed.*) *Manual of child psychology.* London, Chapman & Hall, ch. 14, 833–917.

174

KLEIN, E. (1945) 'The reluctance to go to school', *Psycho-analitic Study of the Child*, **1**, 263–79.

LEVY, D. M. (1943) *Maternal overprotection*. New York, Columbia University Press.

LINDGREN, H. C. (1956) *Educational psychology in the classroom*. London, Chapman & Hall.

LINTON, R. (1945) *The cultural background of personality*. New York, Appleton-Century-Crofts.

LYNN, R. (1957) 'Conditioning and the psychopathic personality.' Paper given to the British Psychological Society.

LYNN, R. (1957) 'Temperamental characteristics related to disparity of attainment in reading and arithmetic', *British Journal of Educational Psychology*, **27**, 62–7.

MANDLER, G. and SARASON, S. B. (1952) 'A study of anxiety and learning', *Journal of Abnormal and Social Psychology*, **47**, 166–73.

MASLOW, A. H. (1954) *Motivation and personality*. New York, Harper.

MONTAGU, M. F. ASHLEY (1957) *The direction of human development; biological and social bases*. London, Watts.

MONTAGUE, E. K. (1951) 'The role of anxiety in serial rote learning.' Ph.D. Thesis, University of Iowa.

MOORE, T. V. (1948) *The driving forces of human nature and their adjustment; an introduction to the psychology and psychopathology of emotional behavior and volitional control*. New York, Grune and Stratton.

MORGAN, C. LLOYD (1900) *Animal behaviour*. London, Arnold.

MOWRER, O. H. and KLUCKHOHN, C. (1944) 'Dynamic theory of personality', *in:* Hunt, J. McV. (*ed.*) *Personality and the behavior disorders*. New York, Ronald Press. Vol. 1, ch. 3, 69–135.

SNYGG, D. and COMBS, A. W. (1949) *Individual behavior; a new frame of reference for psychology*. New York, Harper.

SONTAG, L. W. (1941) 'The significance of foetal environmental differences', *American Journal of Obstetrics and Gynaecology*, **42**, 996–1003.

SULLIVAN, H. S. (1948) *The meaning of anxiety in psychiatry and life*. New York, The William Allanson White Institute of Psychiatry.

SYMONDS, P. M. (1949) *The dynamics of parent-child relationships*. New York, Bureau of Publications, Teachers College, Columbia University.

TILTON, J. W. (1951) *An educational psychology of learning*. New York, Macmillan.

TYLER, R. W. (1948) 'Co-operation and conflict in the mental development of the child', *Mental Hygiene*, **32**, 253–60.

9. The educational needs of deprived children*

The problem
Listening to the comments of their teachers would lead one to think that deprived children have greater educational difficulties than those living in their own homes. Similarly, the remarks made by superintendents and house staff of children's homes suggest that they accept a disproportionate number of unfavourable school reports as a usual occurrence. This raises two questions: first, whether the incidence of educational difficulties is in fact higher among deprived than ordinary children; and second, whether this is inevitable.

Incidence of backwardness and retardation
A recent study carried out by one of my research students clearly shows that the problem of school failure is at least twice as serious for children in care. We took attainment in reading as a measure of educational achievement because this subject is the most basic educational skill. Particularly in the Primary School, backwardness in reading has an adverse effect on a child's progress in most other work. Moreover, it is only for this subject that the extent of backwardness in the ordinary school population is known, so that a standard for comparison is available.

Before the second question can be answered, namely whether this greater backwardness found among deprived children is inevitable, the nature of educational difficulties needs to be considered. The term 'backward' tends to be used for a number of different conditions. First, dull children who suffer from limitations due to inborn factors and show all-round limited capacity to learn, are described as backward (I.Q. range approximately 70–85). Second, children who experience learning difficulties in school are usually called

* Reprinted from *Child Care*, January 1957.

backward. But when educational achievement is taken as the criterion, two subgroups can be distinguished: first, the backward; and second, the retarded. The attainments of backward pupils are below the standard reached by the majority of their contemporaries by 15 per cent or more. Mentally dull or backward children are inevitably backward educationally. Even when working up to capacity, dull children, by the very nature of their handicap, are unable to do as well as the majority of average intelligence.

Retarded or underfunctioning pupils fail to reach a level of educational attainment commensurate with their mental ability, i.e. their achievement falls seriously below the level of their capacity. Thus while in backwardness a child's attainments are compared with those of his contemporaries, in retardation a pupil's achievements are considered in relation to his own mental capacity.

Exact information regarding the proportions of dull children in the school population is not available, but estimates vary between 10 per cent and 15 per cent. Even less information is available for deprived children, but the results of our work suggest that the incidence of mental dullness is at least twice as high among them. This higher proportion is not unexpected since children in care come predominantly from that section of the community which deals less adequately with the complex problems of modern life. Among the important causes for their inadequacy is limited intelligence. Therefore one would expect to find a greater number of dull children among the deprived than in a random section of the population. Because of this, a higher incidence of educational backwardness is inevitable.

In the ordinary population about 15 per cent are dull, 70 per cent are of average, and 15 per cent of very good intelligence. On the other hand, among deprived children we found only five of very good intelligence, 60 per cent in the average group, and 35 per cent who were dull. Nevertheless, the majority are of average intelligence just as in the ordinary population. This is of relevance when one considers the extent of educational retardation. Again quoting from my own research, twice to three times as many deprived children are retarded at the age of 11 years than is the case among ordinary children (the respective proportions being 35 per cent against 12 per cent). While mental dullness, and educational backwardness caused by it, is irremediable, most cases of educational retardation respond to remedial treatment. Clearly the need for such help is even more urgent for deprived children than for those living in their own homes.

A third aspect that has a bearing on educational needs is speech or language development. Other work has suggested that deprived children tend to be rather limited in this respect and we also found that, compared with normal children, they are severely limited in their capacity to understand and use their mother tongue. For example many 8-year-olds did not know the name for a safety-pin, razor blades, the plumber, the postman, nostrils and eye lashes.

Causes of language and educational retardation

Why should deprived children be more retarded educationally and in language development than ordinary children? As in most psychological work, there is unlikely to be just one cause but rather a multiplicity of interacting and interdependent factors. In recent years the close link between emotional factors and learning in childhood has come to be recognised. To look only at the failing school child or only at his intellectual capacity does not get to the root of the trouble. Intellectual development—particularly in its early stages—depends on the existence of a satisfactory relationship with a loved adult whose approval and appreciation is needed for every small achievement. Thus a loving, educated and cultured home provides a sound foundation for success at school. Needless to say, few children in care come from such homes. Many have grown up in a family broken in spirit or in reality, or afflicted by mental illness; they have been moved around among relatives, institutions, and foster homes and have lacked a continuous, loving relationship with a mother or a mother substitute. The child whose early learning efforts met with little interest will now bring his apathetic, discouraged attitude into the classroom. Being emotionally insecure and having only a limited speaking vocabulary, educational difficulties are likely to follow. Moreover, a vicious circle is often set up on starting school. Because he is insecure and discouraged he fails to do as well as other children. The teacher, very understandably, is disappointed at a lack of response and progress, and this disapproval makes the deprived child feel yet more hopeless and apathetic.

The meaning of remedial treatment

It must be stressed that this term is not synonymous with coaching. For the child who is otherwise well-adjusted in school and has a positive attitude to learning, intensive help with one particular subject may be sufficient. For seriously retarded children coaching is ineffective. In remedial teaching the problem is tackled on a wide front. Before teaching in the narrower sense of the word can be undertaken, it is essential to widen his horizon, broaden his interests, develop his power of self-expression, and stimulate his desire to talk and communicate. Moreover, severe educational failure is almost invariably accompanied by emotional difficulties, ranging from lack of concentration, day-dreaming, and apathy to aggressiveness, truancy and delinquency. Therefore, creative and therapeutic activities such as puppetry, miming, modelling, painting, sand and water play, are an essential part of remedial treatment. When successful, it results not only in considerable acceleration in the rate of educational progress, but more important, perhaps, children's attitudes to learning, to difficulties, and to challenge improve. This may also lead to a remission of symptoms such as aggressiveness or timidity.

Educationally retarded children require remedial treatment until they have caught up on the basic subjects and are able to succeed without special attention. Thus remedial help need be given for a limited period of time only, until the child is working approximately up to his mental level. It is of greatest benefit to children of average and above average ability, though underfunctioning dull children can also be helped. However, the latter tend to make slow progress unless daily help can be given. Dull children are best catered for in special classes (where the whole teaching programme can be adapted to their slower rate of learning) unless the ordinary classes are small enough for the teacher to devote individual attention to them.

Organisation of remedial work

It would be best if a variety of schemes were tried: first, because there are different needs in different areas as well as differing facilities and resources; second, because different methods might be appropriate for short-term and long-term cases; and third, because there is need for experiment in a new field, such as this, to find suitable methods. Specially trained remedial teachers are, of course, best qualified to undertake this work, but if none are available it should be entrusted to experienced teachers who have special interest in this field. The most essential personal qualities needed are patience, an understanding of emotional difficulties and flexibility.

According to the size of a children's Home, one or two teachers might be employed full-time. Some children will arrive with detailed psychological and educational reports which will show whether remedial teaching is required before they attend ordinary schools. Others will need to be given a diagnostic examination before this decision can be made. According to the severity and nature of their difficulties they may either be given all their teaching in the home or, alternatively, receive special help for two or three periods during the week, otherwise attending school in the usual way. Children who are fostered out or who live in small family homes could also benefit by attending for remedial help either full- or part-time.

For short-term cases coming into care it might be argued that having to adjust to life in a children's Home and to a new school during a brief period of time is making things doubly difficult for a child who has already been an educational problem in his previous school. The time away from home might be made profitable for those who are seriously retarded by providing intensive remedial help instead of the children attending local schools.

If full-time teachers cannot be employed, either because of the cost or because of lack of premises or because the size of the problem does not warrant a full-time person, part-time teachers may be used to give children extra help after school hours, in the evenings or during the weekend. Such teachers could be peripatetic, calling at different residential Homes as well as visiting foster homes. An alternative, which would save the teacher's time, would be to have central premises to which the children could go.

Present facilities

If it is accepted that, for a variety of interacting conditions, the incidence of emotional difficulties and educational backwardness is higher among children in residential care than among the population at large, then more provision would seem to be necessary for the former. However, at present the opposite is the case. It is well known that there is a severe shortage of psychotherapeutic and remedial provision in the country as a whole, the more serious the further away northwards an area is from the Home Counties. Deprived children are doubly handicapped by being at a disadvantage regarding the availability of appropriate treatment: psychotherapy is usually provided less readily for them than for the child who lives with his own family on the grounds that the child guidance team must work with the parents in order fully to help the child; and that in any case, his emotional disturbance is to some considerable degree due to his deprivation. With regard to receiving remedial treatment for his educational backwardness, here too he has to compete for limited facilities. Again he is at a disadvantage because of his often low scores on verbal intelligence tests and because of his frequently apathetic attitude to school work; both these are considered contra-indications to successful remedial results and so he is less likely to be selected for it.

Since remedial treatment has a stabilising influence and enables children to fit in more happily at school, it seems even more urgent that it should be provided for deprived than for ordinary children. This leads to the thorny question of who should pay for it. To make adequate educational provision is of course the duty of Local Education Authorities and not of Children's Committees. However, only few authorities provide remedial facilities, due mainly to the shortage of teachers, buildings and finance. One may hopefully look forward to the day when all areas will have remedial treatment available for everyone who needs it, or, even more Utopian, to a time when classes will be so small that teachers can afford to give individual attention to all failing children. Meanwhile, it might be of interest to mention the facilities at present available specifically for deprived children.

When, two years ago,* I first reported the results of our research regarding the educational needs of deprived children, the only remedial provision specifically available for them was an experiment begun by the Church of England Children's Society (and described by Dr A. Bowley in *Child Care*). Since then, partly as a result of our findings, three further schemes have been started, each organised and financed in a different way.

The Children's Officer of Birmingham, Mr E. J. Holmes, was successful in securing his Committee's consent to employing part-time remedial teachers. By this action a welcome precedent has been set. In the first place the scheme will run for a limited period, four trained remedial teachers carrying out the work in two larger Homes after school hours. Results achieved so far are encouraging, despite the fact that out-of-school work is not ideal, since both children and teachers are not at their best at the end of the day.

The second scheme owes its inspiration to the Superintendent of

* i.e. in 1955.

one of the larger L.C.C. children's Homes. Having grown increasingly concerned about the children's educational difficulties and concomitant behaviour problems, he succeeded in gaining his Committee's support for a remedial unit to be established on the premises. This is staffed by a full-time teacher who is employed and paid by the Local Education Authority. Again, results achieved so far are reported to be satisfactory.

The third scheme owes its existence to the pioneering spirit and foresight of Miss Leila Rendel of the Caldecott Community, who decided to devote some research funds made available to her by the Nuffield Foundation to an experiment in this field. She hoped that if results proved satisfactory, they would stimulate the setting up of similar units and the development of remedial work for deprived children. The unit, consisting of two self-contained, fully equipped rooms (a classroom and a play room) is in charge of a fulltime, trained remedial teacher and children attend for varying periods according to their needs (from daily sessions to twice a week), while spending the rest of the day in their ordinary schools. Organised as a pilot research project, the methods of work used are closely similar to those developed at Birmingham University's Remedial Education Centre. Regular case conferences are held, attended by the teachers and house staff concerned, to discuss children's progress and to select new cases to be admitted to the unit. Very detailed records and test results are being kept so that a full evaluation can be made at the end of two years.

It might be of interest to mention briefly the progress made by a boy who has attended this unit for only four months. Billy was referred by the Children's Officer for serious difficulties at school; both his work and behaviour were stated to be 'appallingly poor'. Billy's story is not untypical of children in care: an illegitimate child of a rather feckless young woman, he had been placed in a children's Home at the age of 18 months. His mother kept up a spasmodic contact, making extravagant promises of taking him home, when in fact she has never had one, being either in residentwork or living 'with a friend'. By the age of 8 he had been to four different homes and three different schools. He was then befriended, through the 'Uncle and Aunt Scheme', by a couple who had two children of their own and who eventually offered to accept him as a foster child. As was to be expected, there were a number of crises, when it looked as if the arrangement would break down, but now a year and a half later Billy was settled happily with them, except that his foster mother was very concerned about his lack of educational attainments, because his reports stated with monotonous regularity that 'he does not concentrate and shows no interest in his work. A slow child who could, however, do much better than this.' His foster parents had tried to help him. This was not a success as he seemed to resent it, and became surly and stubborn. At first this attitude also characterised his manner when he began to attend the remedial unit. Though aged $9\frac{1}{2}$, he had hardly made a start with reading and his achievement in arithmetic was only slightly better. Contrary to his school reports he was found to be of average intelligence (I.Q. 90) and not mentally dull. At first his behaviour was similar to that shown at school: he bullied other children, lacked concentration, was sullen in his attitude to the remedial teacher and resented any direct suggestions. No teaching was attempted during the first few sessions (he attended once a week for two hours together with three other boys), but his play activities clearly showed his need to explore all available media. Gradually his attitude to the remedial teacher changed and not only did he greatly look forward to his visits, but he began to talk freely and spontaneously and to accept suggestions from her. Having explored his interest, prereading activities were introduced in the form of games which eventually led to the making of his own illustrated reading book and to keeping a simple diary in cooperation with the other boys. Though at the end of his first term's attendance no measurable or testable improvement in attainments had taken place, his attitude to learning and to being taught had become considerably modified. He is likely to respond next term to a more formal and systematic approach to reading in the first place, and later to the other basic subjects. Meanwhile, some improvement in behaviour has been reported by his school.

Present needs

Great strides have been made since the passing of the Children Act in almost every aspect except the educational field. There is an urgent need for remedial treatment among children in care and little hope, at least for the near future, that Local Education Authorities will be able to make the necessary provision. It is therefore suggested that as a temporary emergency measure Children's Committees accept responsibility for making such help available and, if necessary, pay for it. At the same time they should, as ordinary parents can and do, continue to bring the seriousness of the problem to the notice of the Local Authority and press for remedial facilities to be made available at the earliest opportunity.

Some help can also be given by housemothers and foster parents. As much time as possible should be devoted to talking to the children, reading and telling them stories, getting them to make up and act simple plays about everyday occurrences, encouraging them to relate small happenings that take place during the day to express their feelings, ideas and thoughts. This kind of help needs to be given to most deprived children much longer than is usual, because so often they have missed these experiences at the right time. Quick returns can therefore not be expected, but if there is a slow growth in their capacity to enjoy and use language, there is likely to follow also an improvement in adjustment both in the Home and at school. With children under school age such activities can be regarded as preventive. The system of family units, which is being increasingly introduced into children's Homes, may also help to foster language development among all ages; the younger ones will learn from and imitate the older, while the older children can be encouraged to read and talk to the little ones, ostensibly to help houseparents and the family unity, but in fact also improving their own power and wish for self-expression.

10. Speech development in residential nurseries*

'Just baby talk?'

In recent years many studies have been devoted to the effects of early deprivation on children's development. There is considerable evidence that the various aspects of speech tend to be most seriously affected. Does it matter? Even if toddlers in residential nurseries are backward in this respect, does baby talk really matter? It matters enormously. Speech helps children to learn to reason, to think and to understand the world around them; it helps them to make relationships, both with adults and with their contemporaries; and eventually the child's response to school and the progress he is able to make will depend in no small measure on his ability to express himself, and on his mastery and enjoyment of the spoken word.

Recent findings

Perhaps I might here briefly summarise the findings of a recent investigation (see Chapter 7). It aimed to study the difference (if any) in speech development between preschool children in residential care and those living with their own families. Answers to four questions were sought: (1) Are preschool children in care retarded in their language development? (2) If so, are all aspects equally affected and in what ways? (3) Even if retarded, is their speech nevertheless developing along normal lines? (4) Are there any differences between the two groups in the use of speech for social intercourse?

For this study children between the age of 4 to 5 years were chosen and matched for age, sex, intelligence and home background. To eliminate the complicating influence of mental dullness, only children of average ability were selected. Half the children came from residential nurseries, the other half attended a nursery school and lived

* Reprinted from *Child Care*, July 1959.

at home. It is sometimes argued that deprived children are already backward in language development before coming into care. Therefore, a nursery school was chosen which caters for children whose background is also unstimulating and impoverished. In fact, 'hardship' cases only were admitted, such as children of unmarried mothers or widows, or from homes where there was severe overcrowding or serious illness. Thus there should be little difference between the language development of the two groups of children if the main adverse influence was an unfavourable home background. Moreover, half of the deprived group came into care before the age of 18 months. It could be argued that their linguistic ability had been fostered mainly by life in residential nurseries.

Quantitative differences

Wherever quantitative comparison was possible, the children in the nursery school were found to be in advance of those in care. Thus, on items testing the ability to name common objects, such as a shoe or a leaf, or to define simple words such as a knife or an umbrella, the children in the residential nurseries were 6 to 9 months retarded. Similarly, the vocabulary they used in free play was found to contain fewer verbs and adjectives and a narrower range of words. Regarding the ability to understand and to use simple sentences, the children in care were again retarded by about 9 months.

Lastly, the spontaneous and undirected speech of the two groups was studied. Verbatim records made during free play sessions were analysed from three points of view: the incidence of (*a*) egocentric as against social use of language; (*b*) mature forms of conversation and (*c*) fantasy and humour.

a. The two main characteristics of egocentric language are that it is not addressed to anyone and usually does not evoke a response from others. The most marked difference between the two groups was in the proportion of remarks directed to other children. The considerably greater number of child-directed remarks made by nursery school children was in fact a reflection of the way in which these children played together. In the residential nurseries real co-operative group play was rare and sporadic only.

b. Dialogue which indicated some collaborative action or thought was accepted as the beginnings of a more mature form of conversation. The following examples may serve as illustrations:

JOHN: 'We don't know how they go in.'

GRAHAM: 'I do. This is how you do it. This goes there.'

JOHN: 'No, it doesn't—it goes there.'

Or the following:

GEORGINA: 'Now I build a big castle.'

SANDRA: 'It might go bang.'

GEORGINA: 'Any minute it will fall.'

SANDRA: 'Yes. Build it up to light.'

GEORGINA: 'It will fall on lady's head, not my head.'

SANDRA: 'No. It will fall on Shirley.'

GEORGINA: 'It will fall on her. I'm not going to build it any more because it falls down every time.'

This kind of conversation occurred more frequently among the nursery group children. Similarly, verbal clashes of opinion and arguments occurred among both groups, but in the residential nurseries the children were less able to reach peaceful solutions or compromises.

c. Fantasy appeared in two forms; objects and situations were interpreted imaginatively; for example, Phillip bangs on the door and Eric shouts: 'Stop banging. That's thunder!' Eric retorts: 'No, it's a car, I am going to the sea-side.' Secondly there were expressions of pure make-believe; for example, Annette, looking through the window, called out, 'There is a lion coming; quick, get a policeman.' Or:

BRIAN: 'What shall we do?'

BEVERLEY: 'Play as little girl.'

BRIAN: 'That the mum. You the mum, I the father and you the little girl.'

BEVERLEY: 'No. You the dad and our little boy has died and I the little girl.'

Again, both these forms of fantasy occurred more frequently in the conversations of the nursery school group. Some of the children had already reached the stage where imaginative play no longer depended on, or arose from, the stimulation of the material world. Moreover, the nursery school children showed greater persistence in developing an imaginative idea and would return to it after an interruption. These features were not shown by the children in care.

Lastly, to consider the incidence of humour. At this age, humour is, of course, rather rudimentary and crude. Therefore, all occasions on which speech gave rise to laughter or where it was used for the sheer fun of it, were counted as instances of verbal humour: for example:

PHILLIP: 'Ullo, big head.'
ALLAN: 'Ha, ha, same to you, big head.'
PHILLIP: 'Ha, ha, same to you.'
etc., etc.

Or:

ERIC: 'You're a fish. You're a big octopus.'
ROBERT: 'A big busy bee—hee, hee.'
ERIC: 'Stop it, stop it.'
ROBERT: 'Bee, bee, hee, hee.'
ERIC: 'Hee, hee, bumble bee.'
ROBERT: 'That silly old bee, hee, hee.'

Or a boy chanting amid the laughter of a small group:

'I fell on a banana and a butterfly picked me up.'

These examples, even if hardly humorous from an adult point of view, proved to be amusing to the children. In any case, they presented an attempt at experimenting with words for the joy of juggling with them. Thus there was growing awareness that speech can be manipulated so as to arouse amusement in others and that words, like toys, can be used as vehicles for the imagination. This awareness had hardly dawned on the children in the residential nurseries.

Qualitative differences

Some suggestive qualitative differences were noted. The nursery-school children tended to express in their definitions as well as in their free conversations a greater degree of active participation and aggressive self-assertion. On the other hand, some children in the residential nurseries seemed to be preoccupied with themes of naughtiness and crying. But perhaps most marked were verbally expressed differences in attitudes both to adults and to their contemporaries. A craving for adult attention is commonly observed by visitors to residential nurseries. We, too, found that these children were more anxious to be with and to speak to the investigator whether other children were present or not. Adult attention was actively

N

sought instead of accepted in a matter-of-fact way. At the same time the children spoke less of themselves or of their belongings. In contrast, the nursery-school children apparently took for granted adult interest in their doings, and made frequent reference to their own activities and possessions.

Conclusions

What then are the answers to the questions posed at the beginning of this enquiry? From the results quoted they appear to be as follows:

There is some retardation in the language skills of preschool children in care; all aspects are affected but to varying degrees. At the same time, there is considerable overlap in the achievements of the two groups studied and the speech of the deprived children seems to be developing along normal lines. However, they make less frequent and less full use of language in social intercourse, be it in cooperative or in fantasy play.

The medium of fantasy is one important way in which children learn to assimilate new experiences and to come to terms with the difficulties and frustrations inseparable from growing up in a complex society. Children in care would seem to have a particularly great need in this respect. We cannot judge from our evidence why the children in the residential nurseries made little use of verbal fantasy. They may have lacked to some extent the necessary verbal skills. Alternatively, their fantasies may have become too deeply repressed for over expression to appear. The fact that the words 'mummy' and 'home' were not mentioned once by any of the children in care supports the latter possibility. Similarly, deprived children tend to think that their own naughty behaviour or 'badness' is the reason for having been sent away from home. The recurrence of themes of naughtiness and crying among our deprived group may be linked to such fantasies.

This lack of ability to verbalise fantasy and to use speech for making social relationships with contemporaries is likely to have an adverse effect on the general emotional and social development of young children in care. Opinions may differ as to which should be regarded as the cause and which the effect. But there is little doubt that such language difficulties as we found will have long-term consequences unless remedied. For example, readiness to commence school and ability to learn to read are the main educational tasks which one would expect to be affected. There is evidence available to show that the incidence of educational backwardness is in fact higher among children in care than among the ordinary population. In many cases the basis for these learning difficulties may well have been laid in the preschool years.

Among the factors which may account for the differences between the children in the residential nurseries and in the nursery school, the following are likely to be important: coming into care is the end product of a chain of adverse circumstances; but however adverse, the child had previously lived in a familiar environment and had been looked after, however, inadequately, by people he knew and loved. To be removed to a residential nursery (excellent though it may well be) means the collapse of the world the toddler has implicitly accepted and trusted—after all he knew no other. Bewilderment and shock are almost inevitable and are likely to result in at least a temporary setback in development. When, and how fully, recovery takes place, is a problem that needs investigation.

Secondly, it is difficult to provide for the preschool child in care the whole range of experiences which occur naturally as part of normal family life; events such as tradesmen calling, shopping, watching mother cook and father shave, visits from and to relatives and friends, all foster the growth of vocabulary. Thus there are fewer non-routine and, for the child, exciting happenings to absorb and recount in conversation.

Thirdly, in residential nurseries, play materials tend to be communally owned, which is likely to inhibit or at least delay the development of a pride of possession engendered by having personally owned toys and belongings; therefore one would not expect the same desire to talk about and show off valued possessions.

Fourthly, nursery nurses, who are in closest contact with the children, are themselves very young and inexperienced; does their early theoretical training give them an understanding of the fact that the toddler's seemingly inexhaustible supply of questions is his way of learning about the world? Though his incessant 'why' may become tiresome, though it may be exhausting to live with a kind of walking question-mark, this process of question and answer is vitally important for helping the child to reach mental maturity. May it be that too many of his questions go unanswered so that eventually he learns not to ask them?

Lastly, I would suggest that the general training of nursery nurses tends to be unduly biased in favour of physical health, hygiene and habit training. Similarly, matrons of residential nurseries are usually hospital-trained nurses. It is the exception, therefore, to find emphasis placed on mental development in general and language growth in particular.

Practical implications and suggestions

Although many residential nurseries have been closed it may be impractical to advocate their abolition in the near future. Yet there are certain considerable difficulties in the way of improving the staffing position in residential nurseries. The cost of running them is already high and, even if enough well-trained staff were available, the increased cost may prove too high. Of course, on the face of it, staffing is quite satisfactory—usually about two trained child-care officers for every five children. But allowing for time off, holidays and changes in personnel, each member of staff while on duty looks after at least six to seven children. There is evidence to show that associating mainly with contemporaries during the preschool years is less stimulating to language development than adult contacts. Might the early integration of toddlers (say after 18 months of age) into cottage Homes or, better still, into family-group homes, be preferable alternatives? Then the younger ones could learn from and imitate the older children, while the staff would have to deal with only one or two toddlers at the 'eternal questioning' stage. Now that a number of Children's Committees have closed all their residential nurseries there is an opportunity to make a comparative study of the language development of children cared for in foster homes and attending nursery schools.

Secondly, in the training of nursery nurses, it might help if there were a stronger and earlier emphasis on the importance of language development. In the absence of a loving and cultured home it is fostered most readily through the kind of activities practised in the best nursery schools. Fairy tales, stories, songs, nursery rhymes and poems should not be regarded as merely incidental activities to amuse the children when nothing more urgent requires attention; such experiences are vital to emotional, social and intellectual growth. Regular daily periods need to be provided for these activities. In addition every opportunity should be used during the course of the day for conversation and verbal stimulation.

Thirdly, while large toys and equipment must remain communally owned, all children should also be given personal toys if none are supplied by parents or relatives. Only if such ownership is fully granted will a toddler gradually learn to develop a sense of responsibility for his own belongings and a pride in them. Moreover, possessions are a talking point, as much for children as for adults.

Just baby talk? On the contrary, only if we talk to babies, will they outgrow the need for baby talk. The more children are spoken to and read to, the more readily will they learn to enjoy the give and take of conversation with contemporaries and adults. This enjoyment and skill will in turn form the basis for mastering the three R's in school and, more important still, for participating to an increasing extent in our predominantly verbal culture.

11. Emotional adjustment among children in care:
*I. A firm friend outside**

It is now generally accepted that it is in early childhood that the foundations are laid not only for physical but also for mental health. At present we can define only in very general terms the conditions and experiences which seem to promote good mental health. For example, harmonious, happy and loving families which provide a dependable framework of security and acceptance and which set definite moral standards, appear to produce children who are emotionally stable. Clinical work with maladjusted children suggests that it is the quality of the emotional relationships between the child and his family, which is of central importance.

By studying an even more special group, such as children separated from their own families and living in residential care, we might be able to narrow the problem down still further. All who work with such children agree that among them there is a high incidence of emotional disturbance. Yet among them also are some who are quite stable and well adjusted. Why should this be so? What characterises such children? Is it possible to tease out from the life pattern of these well-adjusted children any specific conditions or circumstances which have contributed to their stability? The study which I am reporting here was designed to investigate these questions.

Outline of the study
In a previous investigation (Pringle and Bossio, 1958) we carried out a comprehensive enquiry into the development and achievement of 188 children who were 'in care' and living in a large children's Home. As expected, we found a considerable proportion of children who showed signs of maladjustment. However, some 30 per cent were

* First published in *Child Care*, January 1961.

considered to be quite stable and adjusted. To gain further insight into the relationship and dynamics of separation and institutionalisation on the one hand, and emotional adjustment on the other, it was decided to make an intensive, clinical study of two groups of children selected from the main sample: the one group was to consist of the most severely maladjusted, the other of the most stable children. Both groups were to be long-term cases and should have spent the major part of their lives away from their own parents. In both groups the first separation from the mother was to have occurred at an early age. Perhaps the most difficult problem was to decide on criteria for adjustment and maladjustment respectively. It is notoriously difficult for different people to arrive at an agreed definition or description. This is due to our comparative ignorance at the present time. Therefore it was decided to use four independent assessments or measures, and select only those children considered either 'severely maladjusted' or 'notably stable' on all four assessments. Lastly, we confined our choice to children of average intelligence. In this way we selected the most severely deprived children and excluded the possibly complicating factor of low or high intelligence. The following then were the criteria by which we selected the two contrasting groups of children from our main sample:

1. The first removal from home had occurred before the age of 5 years.
2. The child continued to live apart from his parents for more than half of his life.
3. He should be of average intelligence (i.e. I.Q. range on the full WISC between 85 and 114).
4. He had been rated either 'notably stable' or 'severely maladjusted' on all the following assessments:
   a. The Bristol Social Adjustment Guides completed by the staff of the children's Home.
   b. The same Guides completed by the class teachers.
   c. The results from a Personality Test (the Raven's Controlled Projection Test).
   d. The clinical observations made by the psychologists throughout the individual testing and interviewing of each child.

Applying these criteria, we found eleven 'severely maladjusted' and five 'notably stable' children; they were some from each of the age groups of the main sample, namely, 8-, 11- and 14-year-olds. A detailed case study was made of each of these sixteen children, eleven boys and five girls.

Summary of the case studies

First, the main sample and the two intensively studied groups were compared with regard to their results on all the individual tests and assessments. On all these the performance of the stable group was consistently superior to the other two groups. For example, the main sample and the maladjusted group were markedly backward in language development and reading attainment. The stable group did as well as the average child of the same age. This finding supports the view that emotion and learning are inseparably linked. We tend to create artificial questions by discussing emotional maladjustment and learning difficulties separately and by giving labels to children such as 'problem children' and 'learning failures'. Then we speculate about the nature of the link or relationship between these conditions. In fact they are closely and almost inextricably linked. In most cases, the same conditions which lead to emotional problems also produce difficulties in the field of learning, be it at school or college.

Now to turn to the children's personality traits. Perhaps the most outstanding feature was the inability of the maladjusted group to make relationships with adults or children or both. Descriptions such as 'craves affection and attention', 'has no real friends', 'moody, restless and spiteful', were characteristic. They were usually over-anxious for adult approval and over-attentive to newcomers. This attachment was, however, only temporary and soon gave way to indifference, uncertainty or even hostility. The contrast with the stable group was again marked here. They were described as 'helpful, friendly and well-liked' and were on good terms both with adults and with their contemporaries.

Next to turn to the family background of our cases. The records relating to the children's parentage were found to be rather scanty. This may well have been because both groups had been in care for a long time and there had been several placements. Thus there is insufficient information for a comparison between the two groups except on one fact. The rate of illegitimacy was much higher among the maladjusted children.

The life histories of the children show that the first separation from their mother occurred at a rather earlier age for the maladjusted group. All but two children had this experience by or before one year of age. For the stable group it occurred between the age of two to four years. In this group the first separation seems to have been caused by ill health or other unfortunate circumstances. In the maladjusted group, more than half the children had been deserted or abandoned by their mothers. Both groups had experienced a number of different placements, either in different children's Homes or foster homes. The maladjusted group had had more changes of environment, partly because their difficult behaviour led to repeated breakdowns in fostering arrangements.

However, the most marked difference between the two groups is in the amount of contact maintained with parents or parent substitutes. We classified contact maintained into three categories, namely regular, occasional and none at all. 'Regular' meant that contact had consistently been maintained over many years by the same people, in the form of letters, parcels, visits, outings and holidays for the children; 'occasional' meant that for some years there had been little continuous or regular contact; moreover, in many cases even this limited amount had only been forthcoming at the repeated requests of the Children's Officer; 'none at all' meant that the child had never known a continuing relationship with any adult outside the children's Home, be it with a relative or a friend. We found that all the stable children had experienced a dependable, lasting relationship with a parent or parent-substitute. Only one child in the maladjusted group had known such a contact.

Discussion and conclusions

On the basis of our findings, three hypotheses might be put forward to account for the difference in emotional adjustment between the two groups of children. One hypothesis would be that the maladjusted group was constitutionally inferior and thus more susceptible to emotional instability. What is the evidence in support of this view? It is rather meagre since little information was available on the child's parents. However, the very high incidence of illegitimacy among the maladjusted group could be one pointer; the subsequent parental indifference or rejection shown by failure to maintain regular contact with the child, could be another. If one accepts these as indications of parental instability, then one would conclude that the maladjusted group were likely to be constitutionally inferior. However, on the same premises one could argue that the loss of contact and rejection in the maladjusted group may have been due largely to the social stigma of illegitimacy. This may also have been the reason why these children came into care at such an early age. In our society the unmarried mother encounters many practical difficulties which militate against her providing a home for her baby. One cannot assume that a woman who has had one illegitimate child is necessarily unstable; the fact that some of these women were known to have married subsequently and to be providing a home for their legitimate offspring, supports this view. Thus we must conclude that we have insufficient evidence regarding the influence of hereditary or constitutional factors. In any case our knowledge of the inheritance of human traits is too limited as yet to warrant such an over-pessimistic and defeatist point of view.

The second hypothesis is based on the claim that very early separation does irreparable harm to the basic personality structure. For most of the maladjusted group, the first mother/child separation occurred before the first year of life. Subsequently, the children were reared in an institution where care is given in a more or less impersonal way by a variety of adult figures. Thus it could be argued that our maladjusted group were in early infancy deprived of the experience of establishing a stable and secure relationship with a mother figure; and that they failed to do so subsequently for this very reason. It has certainly been shown that later stages of development depend on the occurrence and consolidation of preceding ones. The hypothesis that a child will become an 'affectionless character' unable to form lasting human relationships if he has lacked the early experience of a warm, intimate and continuous relationship with his mother (or permanent mother substitute) had fairly wide support for a time; however, it has been criticised recently as being too sweeping, narrow and deterministic a view of emotional development (e.g. O'Connor, 1956; Clarke, A. D. B., and Clarke, A. M. 1959; Wootton, 1959). It would be unwarranted, therefore, to argue that early separation from the mother was the sole or even the most important circumstance differentiating the stable from the maladjusted group. To view it as a contributory factor is reasonable.

The third hypothesis rests on the observation that all children in the stable group have had the opportunity to maintain a continuous and regular contact with an adult outside the children's Home. Even if their own family was indifferent and rejecting, someone had cared sufficiently to maintain a stable, enduring relationship with them.

It is worth noting that two children had never lived permanently in the homes of their mother substitutes but were visited regularly and spent holidays with them. In neither case were the people relatives of the child. Thus both groups were deprived of normal family life. The stable group was, nevertheless, loved and supported by adults important and loyal to them; but the maladjusted group was psychologically or emotionally deprived. None had found an adult willing consistently to devote the care and time required to build and maintain a lasting relationship. Thus we could postulate that children—at least in our type of society—need to feel that they matter and are valued as individuals; that they are valued in this way for their own sake, not only by someone paid for the job of looking after them. Our maladjusted group had failed to establish or perhaps had never had the opportunity for forming such a relationship.

It may well be that if a child never experiences lasting love and unconditional loyalty from an adult, he eventually becomes unable to develop these qualities in his human relationships. Probably, too, the later the opportunity is given to establish such a relationship, the more difficult and the longer it will be before the child learns to trust adults and eventually to reciprocate affection.

Thus a vicious circle is likely to develop: not having known a secure relationship, the child fails to learn in early infancy the responses appropriate and expected in such a relationship. When in later life he is offered affection, he does not know how to reciprocate. His reactions will be immature, like those of a very young infant who takes our love for granted and demands unceasing devotion. In a normal family, the child learns that he is expected to reciprocate: by delaying his demands for immediate or exclusive attention; by controlling his anger and selfishness; by considering the feelings of others; by conforming to social expectations. Not having learned all this at the usual time, the emotionally deprived child will later alienate and often lose any affection and goodwill offered because he seems selfish, greedy and ungrateful. This deprives him of the opportunity to learn the very skills needed in making close human relationships; instead he learns to mistrust affection when offered. Because of this mistrust, coupled with his emotional immaturity, he is likely to grow increasingly unable to respond when offered further opportunities for building up close, emotional ties. The more his ability to respond becomes stunted, the more his chances to build a warm relationship recede.

Eventually the vicious circle is closed: unloved and friendless, he is in turn unloving and hostile towards others.

Some of the children in our maladjusted group were beginning to show some characteristics of the so-called 'affectionless character'; many more seemed still to be searching for and attempting to form affective ties. It is perhaps not surprising to find that children who are rejected very early in life and appear to remain unwanted and unacceptable, become increasingly insecure, maladjusted and educationally backward. After all, a sense of personal worthiness, of belonging and of being important to someone, remains a basic human need even in adulthood.

Thus our evidence supports the hypothesis that susceptibility to maladjustment and resilience to the inevitable shock of separation appear to be determined by the quality of human relationships available to the child.

By themselves, neither physical separation from his family or parent substitutes, nor prolonged institutionalisation lead necessarily to emotional difficulties or character defects. Further research is needed to verify this hypothesis and to investigate whether and when an inability to form lasting relationships becomes irreversible.

Two case studies

A detailed account of two fairly typical cases illustrates in concrete terms the differences we found between the stable and the maladjusted group. First, the life history of Kathleen, aged 10½ years; one of the severely maladjusted children.

The illegitimate child of a 17-year-old girl, Kathleen spent the first months of her life with her mother. A casual labourer was said to be the father but he had left the district and was never traced. The mother had been a domestic servant since the age of 14 years when she had left her own home because of continued friction and her father's drunkenness. Since the baby's birth she had encountered all the difficulties usually met by the unmarried mother—finding work to enable her to keep her child, finding accommodation and, perhaps most important, finding some moral support. After five months she gave up the struggle and deserted Kathleen who was taken into care. During the following ten years, the mother paid one visit and for a short period had the child to live with her. For nineteen months Kathleen stayed in a residential nursery but then had to be moved because in this particular area babies under the age of

2 were cared for in a separate establishment. She was described as very restless, difficult to feed, and prone to gastric and throat infections. In the second residential nursery which catered for 2- to 5-year-olds, her late speech development and persistent tantrums were commented upon.

A visitor to the nursery became interested in Kathleen when she was about 4 years old. The lady concerned, a Mrs Allen, had lost her own daughter some two years before in a motor accident and had remained in a very nervous condition ever since. To occupy her mind, she had undertaken some voluntary work which brought her into contact with the nursery. Kathleen reminded her of her own daughter and she began to take an interest in the child. After visiting her regularly, Mrs Allen had Kathleen to stay every other weekend. The husband did not approve, partly because he was not particularly fond of children, but mainly because he considered the situation unhealthy. His wife insisted on calling Kathleen by the name of her dead daughter, dressed her in the dead child's clothes and seemed determined to mould her into the pattern of the one she had lost. At first Kathleen was easy to handle, biddable and apparently affectionate; then, however, her restlessness, temper outbursts and fluctuations in behaviour, from over-affectionate to hostile, began to alienate Mrs Allen's feelings. Her visits and invitations to her home grew less frequent and regular.

When Kathleen was old enough to start school, she had to be transferred to another children's Home. It was situated some considerable distance from the Allens' house, though visiting would still have been possible. This transfer probably gave Mrs Allen the excuse she had been trying to find for breaking off her contact with Kathleen. Unfortunately detailed enough reports were not available to show Kathleen's reaction to this break. Superficially there seemed little change since both the nursery she had just left and the children's Home she now found herself in, described her in terms very similar to those used by her first residential nursery: an immature, restless child who craved for attention but made only facile attachments to children and adults.

At first she seemed to like school; but soon she was regarded as a nuisance in the classroom, because she was always seeking the limelight, while her backwardness in speech proved a barrier to progress with reading. These emotional and educational difficulties were, as is inevitably the case, accompanied by the teacher's disapproval and punishment. Denied the approval and success she craved, Kathleen's behaviour deteriorated and a stammer also developed. She grew to dislike school and there were often scenes in the morning because she refused to get ready. For some eighteen months she attended for speech therapy and though the stammer did not improve much, her behaviour became a little more acceptable. Then the speech therapist left to get married and could not be replaced for some time.

One day, Kathleen's mother turned up. Delighted by the child's apparently immediate affection, she promised that she would soon be able to come and live with her 'own mummy and daddy'. Meanwhile she would write and send her presents. None of these promises was kept and Kathleen became most difficult in the Home and at school. After some months she did in fact leave the children's Home, although the accommodation to which her mother took her was only just adequate. The mother was cohabiting with a married man, named Porter, whose wife had deserted him. Three of his own children and two children which Kathleen's mother had had by him made up the household. In the new school which Kathleen was now attending she was placed in a small class for backward children in charge of a very sympathetic and knowledgeable teacher. Kathleen began to like going to school and to make some progress. She was devoted to her teacher and demanded to take home every tick and star given for correct work. After school she was always wanting 'to do jobs' and never seemed in a hurry to get home. Gradually a change came over Kathleen. Instead of being her restless, excitable, but by now quite hardworking self, she became listless, pale and tired-looking. A note to the mother asking her to come to school produced no results. Then the teacher noted that very often Kathleen was sitting outside the classroom when she came to unlock the door; she looked as if she had slept in her clothes. Eventually it came out that that was exactly what she had been doing more and more frequently. Mr Porter had taken a dislike to her from the beginning, partly because he had been unaware of her existence until very recently. He had always beaten and illtreated Kathleen's mother and now meted out similar treatment to her child. Being the oldest of the five other children at home he had made her into the household drudge. When she fell short of her duties, he beat her and kept her short of food. Kathleen's mother was too much under his domination to stand up for the child; her motives for wanting Kathleen home remained obscure. The child was too terrified of him to tell anyone, but took to sleeping out in bombed buildings and open spaces. When winter came, she hit upon the idea of hiding in the school till the caretaker had locked up. Thefts of biscuits and other food had been noted but were only traced to her when she was discovered in school one night. Whenever Kathleen had spent a night away from home Mr Porter had beaten her. On this occasion he gave her such a terrible beating that when she returned to school it was decided to notify the N.S.P.C.C. Kathleen was again placed in a children's Home and Mr Porter was taken to Court charged with cruelty and neglect. Since then she has lost all contact with her mother.

Unfortunately she had to change school again, losing the benefit of a special class and a gifted, understanding teacher. In the Home her behaviour was very difficult; she was sullen, moody, and developed a number of fears and also began to bite her nails quite badly. At school she soon acquired the reputation of being a problem child, from the point of view of both behaviour and educational attainment. Though rising 9, she was still virtually a non-reader.

About this time a Mrs Wells befriended Kathleen. Having offered her services as an 'official aunt', Mrs Wells had stated to the Children's Officer that she would like to find a girl who might be a companion to her own daughter, Sheila, aged 9 years. Mrs Wells also had a 14-year-old son, Michael, who attended a Grammar school. For many years Sheila and a girl cousin, who lived next door, had been inseparable friends. Since the cousin's family emigrated to Australia, her daughter had been rather lonely, especially at the weekends. There followed for Kathleen a succession of weekend outings since this was during the school holidays; picnics, trips on the river, visits to a museum and other treats, all exciting adventures for both girls. These were deliberately planned by Mrs Wells in the belief that it would enable the girls to get to know each other on 'neutral ground' and without Kathleen becoming too quickly aware of the difference between her own and Sheila's home life. The plan seemed to work and there was comparatively little friction, despite Kathleen's immaturity when compared with Sheila, who was only a few months her senior. Eventually Kathleen came to spend weekends at the Wells' home. The older boy took an intense dislike to her which was only heightened by his parents' disapproval of what they called his childish jealousy. Sheila on the other hand, rather mothered Kathleen, and generously shared her toys and sided with her against Michael. At the children's Home Kathleen's behaviour deteriorated, but the Wellses had no fault to find with her. Eventually they offered to accept her into their home as foster child. The Children's Officer was pleased but considered it her duty to sound some warning about likely behaviour difficulties. However, Mrs Wells felt that it was just because Kathleen needed a normal family life that she showed this difficult behaviour and cited as proof the fact that she was such a responsive child when in their home. So Kathleen was fostered with them. Except for frequent bickering between her and Michael, she seemed to settle down quite satisfactorily. Glowing reports reached the Children's Department. Inevitably this blissful period came to an end, apparently suddenly and dramatically but in fact a number of pointers had been appearing, such as quarrels with Sheila, which were probably due to jealousy on both sides. It had been much easier for Sheila to be generous and protective to the occasional visitor than to a daily rival for attention and affection. Kathleen, moreover, had become increasingly demanding towards the foster parents, who also had to face more difficult behaviour from their own children. The crisis came when Kathleen destroyed a bad school report, telling them she had not been given one because she was a new girl (having had to change school on coming to live with the Wells family), had a violent temper outburst against Sheila when, in addition to an uncontrolled physical attack, Kathleen poured out threats and curses; and finally, when attempts to calm her were of no avail and she was locked into her bedroom, she climbed out of the window and ran away. An anxious time was spent until she was picked up two days later by the police. She refused to give her name and address and was temporarily placed in a reception home. Then she made wild accusations against all the members of the Wells family, reminiscent of what in fact had been done to her in the Porters' home. After all the ensuing unpleasantness, the Wells' patience and understanding had worn too thin to risk having Kathleen return to their home. Moreover, the whole affair had created a local scandal, so Mr Wells decided it would be best for them to leave the district.

Thus, once again, an attempt at forming a relationship had ended in total failure and a complete break with the people concerned. What about Kathleen's relationships with house parents? She had by now been in five different children's Homes and had been looked after by over a dozen different nurses and house mothers. In no case had the bond been deep or lasting enough to make a real impact upon her, but she still retained a craving for attention and affection.

Her stammer, bitten nails and temper tantrums were much in evidence now and her educational failure was severe.

Secondly, the life history of Peter, aged 10 years, one of the stable children. Until the age of 2 he lived with his parents. His mother had always been a very delicate girl and after the boy's birth, remained weak and ailing. In addition the home was chronically short of money, as the father, an unskilled labourer, deserted his family periodically to live with another woman by whom he had two illegitimate children. When Peter was 2 years old, his mother was found to suffer from T.B. and had to enter a sanatorium. At first he was placed in a residential nursery, but soon afterwards was transferred to hospital because of chronic catarrh and laboured, almost asthmatic, breathing. He remained in hospital for four months and during that time was befriended by a nurse who felt sorry for the small boy who never had a visitor. His mother wrote quite regularly but his father took no further interest in him. When Peter returned to the residential nursery, Miss Hall, the nurse, kept in touch with him, visiting and sending small gifts. As it became evident that his mother's illness was going to be very protracted, Miss Hall began to spend a good deal of her time off with him. At Christmas and in the summer she took him on holiday with her, he spent occasional weekends at her flat or in her parents' home and she never forgot his birthday and other special occasions.

At the age of 5 years, Peter was transferred to a large children's Home. There, as in the nursery, he showed himself to be a lively, likeable and responsive child who was on good terms with both adults and children. Starting school proved to be an enjoyable experience for him and he loved his school uniform, which Miss Hall had bought for him. Just before his seventh birthday, his mother was discharged from hospital but had no home to go to since her husband had sold their belongings and disappeared, Miss Hall's parents came to the rescue by offering temporary accommodation. The mother was anxious to have Peter with her and so he left the children's Home and shared his mother's room. Before she had managed to find somewhere else to live, she had a relapse and had to return to the sanatorium.

As there was no vacancy for Peter at the children's Home from which he had come, he was placed in another some considerable distance away. Since this made visiting much more difficult for Miss Hall, she decided to change her job and she obtained a nursing post

o

in a nearby hospital. It was only to be expected that this period, and especially the deterioration in his mother's health, had a very unsettling effect upon Peter. Though he hardly knew his mother, he idolised her and had been overjoyed at the prospect of living with her in a home of their own. Very wisely, Miss Hall encouraged the boy's affection for his mother, and in turn her unpossessive devotion had its own reward in seeing Peter regain his former even emotional keel. Once again he became well-liked in the Home and popular with other boys, settled down successfully in his new school and kept up a regular correspondence with his mother. Miss Hall saw as much of him as her own work permitted.

Thus it seems that although Peter's own family life was broken quite early and his first separation from his mother occurred when he was very small, he had found security and stability through the love and friendship given to him by Miss Hall. That she could not provide a permanent home for him, that his father had rejected him and that he hardly knew his mother at all—none of these appear to have been inimical to his emotional adjustment.

References

CLARKE, A. D. B. and CLARKE, A. M. (1959) 'Recovery from the effects of deprivation', *Acta Psychol.*, **16**, 137–44.

O'CONNOR, N. (1956) 'The evidence for the permanently disturbing effects of mother/child separation', *Acta Psychol.*, **12**, 174–91.

PRINGLE, M. L. KELLMER and BOSSIO, V. (1958) 'A study of deprived children', *Vita Humana*, **1**, 65–91, 142–69.

WOOTTON, B. (1959) *Social Science and Social Pathology.* London, Allen & Unwin.

12. Emotional adjustment among children in care:

*II. Practical implications**

Introduction

In the previous chapter an investigation was described in which a group of very stable and very maladjusted children, living in residential care, were studied. The most marked difference between them was in the amount of contact maintained with parents or parent substitutes; all the stable children had experienced a dependable, lasting relationship, whereas only one child in the maladjusted group had known such a contact. The hypothesis was put forward that susceptibility to maladjustment and resilience to the inevitable shock of separation appear to be determined by the quality of the human relationships available to the child.

There are four groups of people for whom these findings have practical implications: a child's own family; the interested public willing to help in the emotional rehabilitation of children in care; professional child care workers; Government Agencies, Children's Committees and administrators.

Preparation for family life and preservation of family ties

Many schools are now willing to include sex education in the curriculum for adolescent children. As important—probably even more so—would be the giving of some insight into human relationships, how they are learned, built up and maintained; how and why the relationship between the married couple changes with the arrival of the first baby; why parental love not only gives a sense of security but enables the child to grow emotionally and intellectually; and the likely effects of being completely deprived of enduring human relationships. If adolescents were given such understanding they might, on becoming parents themselves, be more reluctant to break

* First published in *Child Care*, April 1961.

up their marriage when there are children. Even if this does happen, they might at least avoid severing all ties with their offspring.

Secondly, though parents whose children come into care for long periods are often unstable, ineffectual or otherwise inadequate people, most of them are fond of their children. They break off contact with the child partly because of difficulties such as the time and money involved in regular visiting and partly because of feeling ashamed and guilty at giving up parental responsibilities. Blaming 'them' (i.e. authority) and avoiding contact with the child reduces to a minimum the occasions when the parents are reminded of their failure; it also avoids the need to answer the child's questions about why he had to leave home and when he can return. But the child feels abandoned and worthless if he knows that his parents are alive but do not even want to visit him.

There is evidence to show that a young child tends to interpret separation as the withdrawal of his parents' affection. Losing all contact with them subsequently would appear to the child conclusive evidence that his assumption was correct. It has been argued that the degree of psychological disturbance which the child suffers is greatly influenced by the quality of his relationship to his parents both before and after separation; and that belief in their affection for him will make it easier for the child to make new relationships with other people (Trasler, 1960). Should it not, therefore, be considered worth while, even from an economic point of view, for case workers to take all possible steps to prevail upon parents or parent substitutes to keep in touch with their children and to give them every help in doing so? Maintaining family ties seems to foster emotional adjustment and the capacity for making other human relationships.

'Uncle and aunt' schemes and fostering

How can interested people help to foster and maintain emotional stability in deprived children?

First, I would suggest, by appreciating the need for a continued relationship on which the child can come to depend. In many areas 'uncle and aunt' schemes make it possible to befriend a child in residential care. Before embarking on this venture the nature of this commitment ought to be fully realised. One should be prepared to see it as a long-term relationship which, if humanly possible, will continue despite a change in circumstances, such as moving house or a new baby in one's own family. At times the contact may have to be more infrequent than at others. As long as the child appreciates the reasons for this and as long as the contact is maintained by letter during periods when personal visits are not possible, no harm will be done. Even if the child can never live with his 'uncle and aunt' this relationship will give him a sense of security. If he can stay in an ordinary home, though it may only be for limited periods, he will learn a great deal that it is difficult, if not impossible, to teach in even the best institution.

The second point of practical importance is this: if gratitude is expected for what is offered, it would be wiser not to attempt this particular kind of social service. It needs a patient, intelligent understanding of the circumstances which usually precede a child's coming into care; and of the likely effects of these experiences on his social and emotional development. It also needs persistence and faith in human nature to continue being a dependable and loyal friend to a child who appears to lack appreciation and responsiveness. This task is made the harder by the fact that deprived children seem initially to respond quickly and affectionately. Soon the superficial nature of their reaction becomes apparent. Only patience, understanding and loyalty on the adult's part can, slowly and painfully at times, teach a child the nature of true and unconditional human relations. The older the child, the more stormy and disturbing this process is likely to be. Only adults who are themselves mature, warmhearted and secure are able to give such undemanding and longterm friendship. The reward for success is great: a human being willing and able to accept his place as a member of the community, and who in turn may become a parent capable of warm feelings and a sense of responsibility towards his own children. Thus the vicious circle may be broken of maladjusted children growing up to become the problem parents of the next generation.

The above considerations apply with even greater force to people willing to become foster parents. At present the breakdown of all longterm foster placements is quite considerable. For various reasons no adequate statistics are available but it is estimated that one-third to two-fifths of them are unsuccessful. Out of a total of over 30,000 such placements, this constitutes in human terms a great deal of misery coupled with a sense of failure for both the children and foster parents concerned. Recent research in this aspect of child care sheds considerable light on possible ways of reducing this rate of breakdown (Trasler, 1960).

Professional child care workers

Though the roles of the Child Care Workers and house parents are closely interrelated and to some extent overlap (for example in their dealings with the child's own parents), they will be discussed separately.

Child care workers

The keynote of their work should be the prevention of the break-up of a family. Though increasing attention has been paid to this aspect during the past ten or more years, we are still doing too little and too late.* Because of what is already known about the time and way in which human relationships are learned in early childhood, efforts in preventive work should be concentrated upon the preschool child.

Dealing adequately with the inevitable shock of being for the first time separated from home and parents might also be discussed under this heading of prevention. Of course it is an everyday occurrence for child care officers, but such over-familiarity with the problem must not be allowed to blunt one's sympathetic awareness of what it must feel like for the child; for the young infant it is a break in the first, and probably only, relationship he has as yet made. When removing a child from a squalid and neglectful home it is easy to feel that the change must be for the better: the toddler will sleep in a clean cot, get fed properly and regularly, and have plenty of toys to play with. But the child has learned to live in that slovenly home, has known no other and, in the vast majority of cases, has derived a measure of security and affection from it; thus he may fear and even dislike the new, orderly routine. How to deal with and to minimise the shock of first separation will vary according to the child's age. It helps to explain as much as he can understand, in language simple enough for his age, to tell him what has happened and why, and what is going to happen to him. It is best never to tell even white lies but at the same time we shall only alienate his feelings and prevent his accepting the new environment if we criticise or condemn his parents. The fact must also be accepted that for a time the child will not be his real self. This is important in relation to the next point, namely correct placement.

Except where a child comes into care temporarily, the best

* In a recent issue of *Child Care* (Vol. 1, no 4, Oct. 1960) Dr Somerville Hastings argued that possibly one-third or more of the total cases coming into the care of the L.C.C. need never have done so.

methods devised so far are observation or reception centres. Initial placement in them gives time for collecting together all the relevant reports—and these can be very numerous in view of the many agencies that may have been concerned already with a problem family. However, no reports can take the place of firsthand observation. They also provide the opportunity for carrying out any tests and assessments which would help placement. All this information can then be brought together and discussed in a case conference because child care is essentially a team job. The wider the choice of placement, the more likely the chance of success.

Once a placement is decided upon, the case worker has the delicate task of guiding and supporting both the child and the adult who will become responsible for his care, through the process of getting to know and to trust each other. Parents whose own child has become maladjusted often speak of their great sense of relief when they can confide their anxieties to a skilled and sympathetic social worker. This need for support and guidance is all the greater when, as a foster parent or house parent, one is dealing with a difficult child who is all the more unpredictable for being a stranger. In any case, previous failure or severance of emotional ties makes the building up of new ones a lengthier and more difficult task.

The reintegration of the family unit is another task not as yet sufficiently recognised, at any rate in practice. It is of course generally accepted that one function of the child care officer is to work for the child's return to his own home. But is enough thought and time given to guiding the family through the period of adjusting to live together again? Neither the child nor his family are the same on his return, they have been changed by the experience itself; for example, there may be a lack of trust on the part of the child and feelings of guilt on the parents' side. Moreover, while separated, both the child and his family tend to idealise each other; this may lead to disappointment when they come to live again with the real people. If the family is successfully reintegrated, a repetition of the breakdown is perhaps less likely.

Lastly, some professional case workers may need to change their attitudes to problem parents. It may have to be accepted that some such parents can never be rehabilitated permanently so as to lead a normal family life. But they should nevertheless be given every encouragement and help to maintain some contact with their children who are in care. It is sometimes argued that visits 'upset' a child, especially if there are tears at parting. When contact is regular and dependable, this does not usually lead to upset. Even if it does, such upset is temporary and children in care must learn to accept separation from their parents and the disappointment of partings. For the same reason it used to be held that children should not be visited while in hospital. Now it is recognised that the 'settled' child, who quietly accepts being ill in unfamiliar surroundings and being cared for by unfamiliar people may be emotionally much more adversely affected than the child who sheds some tears at the end of his parents' daily visit. It is for this reason that most children's hospitals now allow such visiting. After all, tears and sorrow are signs of positive feelings, and all children have to learn to suffer unhappiness at some time or other. What are deeply upsetting and unsettling to children in care are lavish but unkept promises, or sporadic, unpredictable contacts, or complete rejection by their own family. In such cases children may need to be protected by the professional worker.

But may it not be possible to modify even the behaviour of such problem parents, unstable and unreliable though they are? Is enough being done to bring home to them the misery which they are causing their children by making unrealistic promises? And that they could instead give a sense of belonging to the child, simply by visiting him regularly? Is it not their sense of inadequacy which drives them into making these promises and then they stay away, ashamed of having once again failed the child? Should case workers be prepared to give support to such parents for the sake of the child? It implies accepting that some homes will remain permanently broken, and that despite this, one or both parents can still contribute to their child's mental health, given professional guidance. Problem parents may become more ready to act on advice if they feel accepted rather than despised and rejected by the child care workers. One of the hardest things for the child to learn is to accept such parents as they are.

House parents

In our study, not one of the stable children had formed a dependable, lasting relationship with an adult within the residential Home. It could be argued that this was due to chance, or to the smallness of our sample, or perhaps both. But is it possible in practice to provide even in the best residential Home the kind of relationship we have discussed? When the national rate of turnover for house staff is 30 per cent, or 40 per cent, is it realistic to expect children to form close and permanent ties with them? Off-duty periods and the competing demands of the other children are added obstacles. As W. Clifford (1960) put it: 'If our Homes are characterised by too frequent changes, then we have exchanged one unsuitable environment for another. Committal may become a medicine as deadly as the disease.' The reasons why staff do not stay long in residential work is beyond the scope of this chapter. Suffice it to say that until the status, level of training and conditions of pay are considerably raised, it is unlikely that the necessary number of suitable staff can be attracted for this highly skilled, exacting and responsible work.

The growing emphasis in child care on prevention, short-term placement and boarding-out, has gradually brought about a change in the work of house parents. On the one hand, there is a shifting child population in the Homes and on the other hand, many of the long-term cases are children who are handicapped physically, emotionally or mentally. As I see it, this may require a change in the attitude of house mothers to their work. Instead of aiming to become mother substitutes, might a more detached, professional attitude be more appropriate? Such an attitude might be defined as one of unpossessive involvement. Like the teacher or social worker, one is responsible for the child's welfare and happiness for a period of time, which is often a critical and difficult phase of his life; but this emotional involvement goes hand in hand with an awareness that the child's affection has to be shared with other people. Such a professional attitude may help towards a greater understanding of why more affection and loyalty is given to feckless parents than to devoted house parents and why even unworthy parents are idealised during separation.

The change of attitude suggested here would take place more readily if house parents were treated as professional workers by all concerned: regular case conferences of all the people dealing with the child to review his present behaviour and to consider any change in his circumstances, would lessen the sense of isolation felt by house parents; to be fully informed of the child's past and any plans likely to be made for his future; to hear from time to time what has happened to the children who have returned home or been boarded out; all these measures would make house staff feel that they are members of a team and that their responsibilities and skills are recognized and valued.

Government agencies, children's committees and administrators

It will be evident that some of the suggestions made in this discussion could only be adopted with the support of the various agencies financially responsible for child care. Indeed, in many instances, the initiative must come from them. Training schemes for house parents can develop on a sufficient scale only with Treasury support; suitable placement cannot be made unless a wide range of alternatives is available, such as large and small children's Homes, foster homes, 'scattered' family homes, hostels and schools for maladjusted children, etc. To prevent the break-up of family life, long-term and intensive social work is essential; this can only be done by social workers whose case load is small. This may appear too costly a procedure. Yet when the L.C.C. appointed some special case workers to undertake such work it was found that if each of them succeeded in preventing the break-up of only two families a week, the social worker's own salary was in fact saved. Similarly, a small case load is essential if house parents and foster parents are to be given regular support and guidance to enable good relationships to be developed between the children and those who care for them. These are merely a few examples of some of the conditions which must be provided by executive and administrative bodies if more than lip service is to be paid to the paramount importance of building and maintaining close personal relationships between children in care and the adults interested in them.

Conclusions

To sum up, our findings support the hypothesis that the child who is rejected very early in life and subsequently fails to find dependable relationships, is likely to become emotionally maladjusted. Never having experienced lasting love and loyalty from any adult, the child becomes unable to develop these qualities in his human relationships. The main practical implication of our evidence lies in the need to ensure that every child in institutional care has the opportunity to make a stable, emotional tie with an adult in the outside world. Those willing to befriend a child must be helped to realise why it is essential to maintain their contact with the child regularly and reliably over a period of years. Some reorientation in attitude and emphasis may also be required on the part of professional child care workers. And lastly, the support of Government agencies, children's committees and administrators is essential.

References

CLIFFORD, W. (1960) 'Professionalism and vocation in residential work', *Child Care*, **14**, 1, 9–10.

GRAY, P. G. and PARR, E. A. (1957) *Children in care and the recruitment of foster parents; an enquiry made for the Home Office.* London, Social Survey.

TRASLER, G. (1960) *In place of parents; a study of foster care.* London, Routledge & Kegan Paul.

13. The nurse and the educational needs of children*

During the last decade a revolution has begun in many parts of Europe in the psychological concepts underlying child care. The work of pioneers such as Bowlby, Spence, Spitz, Goldfarb and Roudinesco, to mention just a few, has led to the recognition of the possible ill effects of prolonged mother–child separation and of deprivation of a normal home life. Of course, practical application of this knowledge is by no means general yet; partly because established practice can only gradually be modified and partly because of shortage of personnel and accommodation. What has hitherto been less widely recognised is the close link between emotional and educational development. Usually it has been thought that intelligent children do well and dull children do badly in their school work. Now we are beginning to realise that a happy, harmonious and supporting home plays a vital part in scholastic progress. Even further than that, views on the nature of intelligence are changing: its innate basis is admitted; but intelligence is also being considered as something that grows and develops in the course of a child's active experience of his environment. Increasing emphasis is being placed on the realisation and direction of intelligence by experience. And the earliest, most basic experiences to stimulate this growth take place during infancy in the home. It is then that the basis is laid for later scholastic success.

The educational needs of children must be considered in a much wider sense than simply school learning. Emotional and social learning are prerequisites for intellectual learning. In the first place it is

* Presented at the European Seminar on 'Nursing Education for Child Care', organised by the World Health Organisation's Regional Office for Europe and held in Vienna in 1960.

through the close bond of affection between mother and baby that the link is forged between emotion and learning. The all-pervasive feature of parental love is that the child is valued for his own sake. In their relationship with him the loving father and mother communicate affection through all their ways of dealing with him.

Thus through being loved by his mother the baby learns to feel love for her and this makes him wish to please her. Later this wish is extended to other people who become significant in the child's world so that eventually he wants—most of the time—to please his parents, friends, teachers and nurses. Given this basic experience of love, the child will have learned to make a relationship with another person; this implies not only receiving but giving affection; not only making demands but being willing to satisfy the demands of others; no longer demanding immediate satisfaction but being able to wait and to accept frustration; no longer being completely selfish and self-centred but subordinating one's wishes to those of others. Thus children become willing to be dry and clean, to walk, to talk and eventually to succeed with school learning. But if this early, basic experience of love has been lacking, if the child has been rejected and deprived, he will be apathetic and unresponsive or will fight and protest (according to his temperament) against every new demand which is made upon him. His learning will remain slow, difficult and inadequate.

The mother–child relationship provides both the incentive and the conditions for learning. The way to maladjustment and the way to educational failure are often along the same path. That is so just because of the very close and constant interrelationship between learning and emotion (Pringle, 1958). Conversely, satisfactory relationships and successful learning together with the ability to tolerate frustration are shown by children who have been reared in homes where unconditional parental love has been balanced by appropriate demands for increasing social and emotional independence. This balance can only be achieved if a child's basic psychological needs are satisfied. These needs have been variously described but the following seem to be the most essential (Tansley and Gulliford, 1960):

a. the need for security;
b. the need for giving and receiving affection;
c. the need for new experiences;
d. the need for recognition and self-esteem;

e. the need for acceptance by other children;

f. the need for independence and responsibility.

These needs are closely interrelated and the growth of mental stability and intellectual development depends upon their satisfaction at each stage from infancy to adolescence. The order in which they are listed shows their relative importance during childhood. Security and affection are the essential needs of infancy; if they have not been fully met, as in the case of many deprived and handicapped children, there is a poor foundation for later personality development. The needs for recognition, for acceptance by the group and for independence become increasingly important as the child gets older. New experiences are the mental food required for intellectual growth.

These needs are also important in relation to the child's motivation for school learning. This depends as much, if not more, on the pupil's willingness to learn as on his intelligence, the teacher's skill and the methods and materials which are employed. While there are many ways in which one can try to influence positively children's school learning, the basis of stable and enduring motivation lies initially in the satisfaction of these six psychological needs. At a later stage— possibly not until adolescence—higher forms of motivation will be developed leading eventually to learning for its own sake, and for the intellectual satisfaction of having mastered a problem or skill. This is unlikely to happen in the child who remains at odds with adults and thus with society.

Children whose basic psychological needs have been inadequately met, are usually difficult to motivate. If they are preoccupied with their relationships to parents or parent substitutes, learning to read or do arithmetic is a problem of minor importance. If continually under stress through feelings of hostility, jealousy or anxiety, children cannot organise their emotional energies for school learning. Research into the causes of educational failure has shown that anything which interferes with the satisfaction of the basic needs may result in an impaired capacity for school learning, be it in bright or dull pupils (Lewis, 1954; Wall, 1955; Pringle, 1958 and 1960).

In what follows I shall briefly discuss each of the six basic, psychological needs in relation to children in hospital and in various residential institutions and make suggestions regarding the part the nurse can play in contributing to the satisfaction of these needs.

a. *The need for security*

Children need the security of a stable family background; the security of a familiar place in which to live, play and work; the security of familiar people whose attitudes and behaviour are consistent and predictable; and the security of a known routine. The younger the child, the more important is this sense of security since his dependence is on a few adults as yet and his intimate experience of a place and a routine is limited to one setting, namely his own home. However, to the infant and toddler one cannot readily give verbal explanations and reassurances so that a change of routine or environment is made more traumatic by its unexpectedness and inexplicability.

What then are the implications for sick children? What a child feels about his own illness will depend a good deal on the nature and severity of the illness; on whether it is his first experience of being ill and on whether illness is a rare or frequent event in his life. His feelings will be much affected by the feelings and behaviour of his parents, particularly of his mother. Not only what happens while he is ill but all that they have felt and expressed to him earlier in his life, will influence his reaction.

If he can remain in his own home, there will be little threat to his sense of security. However, the visiting nurse can help in two ways: first, by being able and willing to establish a friendly relationship both with the mother and the child, the latter will be more ready to submit to unpleasant or painful treatment. Secondly, if she can give a brief but truthful explanation of what she has to do with some warning if it is likely to be painful, the child will be more trustful, particularly on subsequent occasions. If the same nurse can attend throughout the child's illness, it helps greatly.

If the child has to go to hospital as an out-patient, he will be more insecure from the start. It tends to be (especially to a young child) a large and bustling place, full of strange sights, sounds and smells. An audience of students during his examination and treatment may add to his distress. In addition to keeping the waiting period to a minimum and keeping the examination (and possible distress) of other patients out of sight and hearing, a calm, unhurried and gentle attitude on the part of the nurse, reassures both mother and child.

The sense of security of a child who has to become an in-patient, is inevitably more severely undermined. (Space prevents me from considering the case of children receiving in-patient treatment in a special unit with their mothers present.) Everything is strange, unfamiliar and frightening, and the sense of loneliness and desertion by his mother are only increased by witnessing the distress of other children. Until he gets to know one nurse and learns the new routine, he will be utterly bewildered and insecure. Time spent on settling him in, on letting his mother be with him, on showing him that nurse and mother are on friendly terms, will be time well spent since he will be easier both to manage and to treat when reassured. Being able to have some familiar objects with him acts both as a link with home and as a talking point with the nurse.

Children respond with great sensitivity to the moods, gestures and movements of adults, partly because we do not give them clearly expressed information. They draw their own conclusions, which whether right or wrong, are often very frightening. I need not elaborate how much greater this danger is of guessing the unsaid for lack of saying in hospital. Of course I am not pleading for a full, medical exposition even to an older child, but a simple explanation is usually possible. Even if he does not understand all we say, the tone of voice can convey to him sympathy and reassurance.

Now to turn to children admitted to residential nurseries, children's Homes and residential schools. Even if removed from a 'bad' home, this is bound to have given the child a sense of security through its familiarity and routine, however haphazard. Thus there is inevitably shock and fear to begin with. Unfortunately there is a very great turnover of staff, in England at least, in residential homes for children, especially in residential nurseries where young nurses train. Thus it is virtually impossible to give a sense of security through continuity of daily handling by the same person.

b. *The need for giving and receiving affection*

Both experience and research have shown how vitally important it is for the children to have someone who loves them and who watches and encourages each new step they take in growing up (Bowlby, 1951; Bowley, 1954; Stott, 1956; Pringle, 1960). This need is particularly closely linked to learning, be it skills such as walking or talking or educational attainments such as reading and arithmetic. The loving mother naturally shows joy and pride in every new achievement and in one sense the child learns 'for her'.

The satisfaction of this need only marginally concerns the nurse working in infant welfare centres, home nursing and short-term

P

hospital treatment. It is worth stressing, however, that children sense whether the people handling them are genuinely interested and fond of them or are merely 'doing a job'. Long-term hospitalisation still too often produces in children a sense of being unwanted, uncertain and isolated. Maintaining contact with his family must be regarded as the first principle. Secondly, if nurses can be assigned to particular children to care for them in *all ways*, each child may come to build up a real relationship of mutual knowledge and affection. But she must also be given more time than is allowed normally for ordinary nursing duties. Spence (1947) advocates that long-stay hospitals should be reformed so that children 'lived in small groups under a housemother, and from there went to their lessons in a school, to their treatment in a sick-bay and to their entertainment in a central hall. There would be no disadvantage in the housemother having had a nursing training, but that in itself is not the qualification for the work she will do. Her duty is to live with her group of children and attempt to provide the things of which they have been deprived.'

In fact, these principles apply with equal force to convalescent homes, residential homes and schools. Only through building up a relationship can this need for giving and receiving affection be adequately satisfied.

c. *The need for new experiences*
For the young child, everything is a new experience, from exploring his own body to meeting an increasing range of his environment; learning to walk and talk and read all can be new and rewarding experiences, giving a sense of pride and achievement. All normal children have a strong urge to explore and find out, welcoming the challenge of new situations and new learning.

This need concerns the nurse mainly with regard to the long-stay patient and the child in residential care. If she is to help here, a knowledge of normal child development and what is appropriately introduced and learned by children at the various age levels is essential. Only then is it possible to judge which experiences a child is missing and to what extent it is possible to give them to him or to compensate in some measure for their loss. For example, the child aged 12–14 months will need to be talked to a great deal in order to develop his own speech and the 2- to 3-year-old will need to have his eternal questions answered to enlarge his understanding of the world around him and to feel that his curiosity is not sheer naughtiness;

otherwise he may sink into a quiet, listless passivity which will inhibit his interest and curiosity not merely at this age but at later stages of learning, including at school. Here it is worth remembering that trauma, shock and unhappiness often produce regression; it is the most recently acquired behaviour which is the most easily lost. Emotional strain makes it impossible for him to maintain new and still precarious acquisitions. Once he has come to terms with his new situation, he needs every encouragement not only to relearn his achievements but to go on to new ones.

In addition to what the nurse herself can do in this direction, others such as hospital teachers, occupational therapists and ordinary school teachers will provide the child with new experiences. There the nurse can help in two ways: first, by understanding the importance of these activities for the child's mental health and thus not regarding them as an irritating interference with the smooth running of hospital routine; secondly, by taking an interest in what the child may be achieving, whether the learning of a new nursery rhyme, making a drawing, or learning another page in his reading book. In this way she can share his interests and make him feel that learning new skills is a worthwhile activity. For him such activities and experiences are psychologically therapeutic giving him confidence and taking him out of his preoccupations with illness or the loss of his family, even if this respite is only temporary. The retarding influence of residential Homes on children's intellectual, emotional and social development, as well as on their language and reading attainments has been shown in recent studies (Pringle and Bossio, 1958; Pringle and Tanner, 1958). Conversely, the beneficial effects of new experiences, carefully graded according to learning capacity, have in recent years been demonstrated by work with low grade mentally defective patients both children and adults (Mundy, 1957; Clarke and Clarke, 1958; Kirk, 1958; Oliver, 1958). These findings are most promising since they suggest that re-education may be a form of therapy and rehabilitation.

d. *The need for recognition and self-esteem*
A child needs to feel successful and to get recognition for what he can do. Though mastering new skills is exciting, at the same time it brings with it frustration and failure. If despite them the child is to continue wanting to try and eventually to succeed, he needs recognition, not only for what he has actually achieved but also for his

attempts at new tasks. Otherwise he may give up the struggle, preferring to remain babyish and dependent; alternatively he may seek recognition in socially unacceptable ways, such as delinquency.

Here the nurse can help in all her contacts with children. In outpatient departments, welfare clinics and home nursing she can, to begin with, praise some obvious achievement, such as that he has learned to walk or talk or read so well—whatever she can glean that he has mastered. Similarly, she can praise his attempts at cooperating with her, even if these are not altogether successful. Realising that even many a stable child finds injections frightening, let alone such experiences as the examination of nose and throat or lumbar punctures, she can praise the child for showing courage, even if he has been very distressed. Children vary very much in their sensitivity to physical pain and to mental stress and thus it is impossible to assess how trying a particular experience has been to an individual child. But by praising his pluck and endurance, we give recognition to the fact that he may well have made an effort; in any case we help to restore his shattered self-esteem when he is aware that he has lost control.

Very similar considerations apply to long-term patients. Of necessity they will have to undergo unpleasant, if not painful treatment; in many cases, they will have to endure much boredom and to forgo boisterous play activities normally enjoyed by children. Moreover, being confined in hospital necessarily reduces their opportunity of earning the recognition of their parents. It is thus all the more desirable that the nurse should be aware of her power to satisfy or stultify this need.

In residential nurseries and Homes even the casual visitor quickly becomes aware that this need often remains unsatisfied. Children often crowd round him, vying for his attention and his recognition of their achievements. In many residential schools the matron in the surgery or sickroom is a favourite refuge. The seriousness of small cuts and feelings of sickness are exaggerated since they may earn him a respite from being one of a group and instead give him the individual attention and recognition of a mother substitute.

e. *The need for acceptance by other children*
Companionship of other children and acceptance by his contemporaries becomes of increasing importance to the child as he grows from childhood into adolescence. Even temporary rejection by play-

mates can cause real distress, while more lasting social isolation leads to loneliness and misery. The socially isolated child may either increasingly withdraw into himself or, alternatively, try to gain acceptance from the group by boasting, showing off and other attention-getting devices.

How can the nurse help in the satisfaction of this need? Primarily, of course, it is a matter of administration and physical conditions whether children are placed in appropriately sized groups to make social contact possible. Mixed age groups and both sexes are the ideal; the younger the children the smaller the group needs to be to facilitate real interchange of experiences and group activities. This applies equally to hospitals and to children's Homes and residential schools. Conversely, for this reason as well as others, it is inadvisable to place children in adult wards.

f. *The need for independence and responsibility*

The urge to become increasingly independent, self-reliant and responsible is a marked feature of normal development. With chronically or incurably ill children this is easy to overlook since they are usually much more dependent on nursing care. Moreover, like the physically handicapped they have more limited capacities for taking responsibilities which in any case is not readily encouraged within the framework of hospital routine. Yet the satisfaction and pride in themselves when they do accomplish a step forward is most marked in all children. Thus the nurse can help the child's development if she gives him as many opportunities as possible for learning to become more independent and responsible. The same applies to residential schools and Homes. Of course, it is often quicker and more convenient to do things oneself; but it not only deprives the child of opportunities for personal satisfaction through the achievement of independence and a measure of responsibility but also adversely influences his chances of standing on his own feet one day in the outside world.

Now I want to discuss children's educational needs in the narrower sense of the term, namely specific learning during the school years as well as the preschool experiences that lead to readiness for formal schooling. To begin with preschool experience: mastery of his native language, at least for everyday use; familiarity with a multitude of objects, animals, plants and other aspects of his environment; and an exploration of the feel, smell and touch of a wide variety of materials, all provide the necessary foundation on which later school learning will be built. Thus the endless questioning of the 2- to 4-year-old is not merely an attention-getting device, but an attempt to learn to understand his world. Similarly, playing with sand and water, clay, paints and other materials is not merely messy play to be discouraged as much and as soon as possible; on the contrary, it is from these activities that children learn the uses and limitations of these particular materials, learn to express themselves imaginatively in various media and also develop hand–eye coordination and control which will later be needed for learning to write, to sew and for other manipulative skills. In the same way, riding a tricycle, scooter or truck, climbing on a frame and simply running or skipping, not only provide outlets for children's physical energies but help them to achieve the greater muscular coordination needed in more difficult tasks such as learning to swim, play football or roller skate.

What does all this imply for the nursing care of preschool children in hospital? First, that room is needed if there are to be full opportunities for these experiences. Secondly, that the better the nursery school teacher, the more she will be trying, in consultation with the nurse, to find ways to give even the handicapped and bed-ridden patient as wide a range as possible of these experiences by adapting and inventing new equipment and apparatus. Thirdly, that the better the teacher, the less neat and tidy the ward will look during 'school time'. Lastly, that the quiet passive child who is content to watch instead of playing himself, though easier to manage, is in fact mentally not as healthy as the active, boisterous and inquisitive one. And that later this limited range of experience and undeveloped sense of curiosity may well show itself in educational backwardness.

Very similar considerations apply to children in residential nurseries. Neat and orderly playrooms can only be achieved at the cost of restricting the children's range of activities and experiences. Emphasis on hygiene and physical care may be achieved at the cost of neglecting to talk with the children, telling them stories and nursery rhymes and encouraging their ability at self-expression. A great deal of research evidence is available to show that the one aspect of child development affected most adversely by institutional care is the growth of language skills. This in turn has an adverse effect on intellectual development and scholastic achievement.

Next to consider the primary school child (5 to 11): learning to read, write and do arithmetic together with widening his cultural horizons and social contacts are the main tasks to be accomplished during this stage. But there is no abrupt change from one stage to the other so that many activities valuable during the preceding years will now be pursued at a more skilled level; for example, painting, clay work, building and climbing. The more gifted and imaginative the teacher, the more she will devise means to stimulate the children's imagination and to compensate for the limitations inevitably imposed on learning in a hospital setting. The better the teacher the greater is the need for understanding on the part of the nurse. Both must acquire great flexibility and an understanding of each other's role. The more conservative and pedestrian the teacher, the less will she 'upset' hospital life and routine.

This problem does not arise quite so acutely in residential Homes and schools since children usually go out to separate school buildings.

At the next educational stage, namely the secondary level, specialist subjects of various kinds begin to play an increasing part. These may be of an academic, practical or prevocational kind. If the child is mobile, or at least can use his arms and hands freely, there will be a good deal of equipment and apparatus that his teacher will want him to use. Moreover, by now the child will no longer work mainly when the teacher is able to give guidance and supervision, but he will want to do some work in his spare time too. This is a sign of good motivation and personal involvement which one hopes all adolescents will achieve before reaching the school-leaving age. If the nurse recognises that self-imposed work makes a positive contribution to the patient's mental health, she will be more ready to be flexible in the management of the ward and give due warning when the child's work must be interrupted.

In residential schools for handicapped children whether they be blind, cerebral palsied, slow learning or maladjusted, each of the learning stages I have just outlined will last longer because the child needs more practice to achieve mastery. Moreover, many handicapped children are aware of their difference from the normal and have a sense of inadequacy and inferiority (partly due to parental attitudes). Thus it is all the more important that they should be given the chance for achieving a measure of educational success. By her sympathy and encouraging attitude the nurse can play a vital role in that task.

Both experience and research have shown how vitally important it is for the child to have someone who loves him and who encourages each new step he takes in growing up (Bowlby, 1951 and 1954; Stott, 1956; Pringle and Bossio, 1960). Giving and receiving affection is closely linked to learning and educational success. At the same time some recent investigations strongly suggest that education or re-education may, itself, be a form of therapy and rehabilitation, both intellectually and emotionally (Mundy, 1957; Clarke and Clarke, 1958; Kirk, 1958; Oliver, 1958; Pringle, 1958; Pringle and Sutcliffe, 1960). Because hospitals are more prepared now to take responsibility for providing a substitute home for the sick child, the nurse can also now take an active share not only in satisfying the basic psychological needs but also in furthering the children's educational achievements.

References

BOWLBY, J. (1951) 'Maternal care and mental health', *Monograph Series of the World Health Organisation*, **2**.

BOWLBY, J. (1954) *Child care and the growth of love*. Harmondsworth, Penguin.

CLARKE, A. M. and CLARKE, A. D. B., ed. (1958) *Mental deficiency; the changing outlook*. London, Methuen.

KIRK, S. A. (1958) *Early education of the mentally retarded*. Illinois, University of Illinois Press.

LEWIS, H. (1954) *Deprived children; the Mersham experiment. A social and clinical study*. London, Oxford University Press.

MOORE, T. V. (1948) *The driving forces of human nature and their adjustment; an introduction to the psychology and psychopathology of emotional behavior and volitional control*. New York, Grune & Stratton.

MUNDY, L. (1957) 'Therapy with physically and mentally handicapped children in a mental deficiency hospital', *Journal of Clinical Psychology*, **13**, 3–9.

OLIVER, J. N. (1958) 'The effect of physical conditioning exercises and activities on the mental characteristics of E.S.N. boys', *British Journal of Educational Psychology*, **28**, 155–65.

PRINGLE, M. L. KELLMER (1958) 'Learning and emotion', *Educational Review*, **10**, 146–68.

PRINGLE, M. L. KELLMER and BOSSIO, V. (1958) 'A study of deprived children. Part 1. Intellectual, emotional and social development', *Vita Humana*, **1**, 65–92.

PRINGLE, M. L. KELLMER and BOSSIO, V. (1958) 'A study of deprived children. Part 2. Language development and reading attainment', *Vita Humana*, **1**, 142–70.

PRINGLE, M. L. KELLMER and BOSSIO, V. (1960) 'Early prolonged separation and emotional maladjustment', *Journal of Child Psychology and Psychiatry*, 1, 37–48.

PRINGLE, M. L. KELLMER and SUTCLIFFE, B. (1960) *Remedial education; an experiment. An account of two years' work by a remedial unit for maladjusted and deprived children at the Caldecott Community.* University of Birmingham and Caldecott Community.

PRINGLE, M. L. KELLMER and TANNER, M. (1958) 'The effects of early deprivation on speech development', *Language and Speech*, 1, 269–87.

SPENCE, J. C. (1947) 'The care of children in hospital', *British Medical Journal*, no. 4490, 125–30.

STOTT, D. H. (1956) *Unsettled children and their families.* London, University of London Press.

TANSLEY, A. E. and GULLIFORD, R. (1960) *The education of slow-learning children.* London, Routledge & Kegan Paul.

WALL, W. D. (1955) *Education and mental health.* Paris, Unesco.

14. The emotional and educational needs of handicapped children

It has been said that our educational system has been devised by the clever for the clever. Be this as it may, there is no doubt that the educational principles and methods used with the handicapped have been devised (but for a few exceptions) by those who have had no first-hand experience of serious and lasting handicaps. This may have led to an assumption which, though only rarely made explicit, seems to exert a very powerful and all-pervasive influence on the treatment of handicapped children: the yardstick commonly applied in judging their success is the extent to which their achievements equal those of the more fortunate majority; this means that unrealistic goals are set up which almost inevitably lead to a sense of failure. A second assumption is implicit in all educational thought, namely that emotion and learning are separate and distinct from each other. This belief derives from our approach to developmental problems which, perhaps inevitably, is piecemeal and which results in posing false questions. Being forced to investigate the various aspects of human personality separately because of their complexity and our ignorance, we then go on to discuss how these arbitrarily distinguished aspects are related to each other. Yet cognitive and orectic aspects, intellect and emotion, are indivisible. I propose to outline briefly how they develop together from early childhood, both in the normal and the handicapped child. The basic emotional and educational needs are shared by all children but the presence of a disability poses some special problems. These will be specially considered and illustrated by two case studies. They have been chosen because the children and their parents have received educational and psychological guidance from our department for many years (six and twelve years respectively); both children have multiple handicaps; and their backgrounds contain many contrasting features.

Different schools of psychology offer a different list of basic human needs, varying from as many as sixty to as few as two. The following fourfold classification seems to be sufficiently all-embracing for most practical purposes:

1. The need for love and security.
2. The need for new experiences.
3. The need for recognition and achievement.
4. The need for responsibility.

The need for love and security

This need is perhaps the most important one during the long and difficult business of growing up. It is unconditional acceptance which gives the child this sense of security, the sense of being cherished whatever he may be like and whatever he may do. The basic and all-pervasive feature of parental love is that the child is valued for his own sake. In their relationship with him, the loving father and mother communicate affection through all their ways of dealing with him, long before there is conscious understanding or speech. The greatest impact of such love is on the development of the self, which has been defined as 'reflected appraisals' (Sullivan, 1958). Approval and acceptance by others are essential for the development of self-approval and self-acceptance. Whether a child develops a construc-tive or destructive attitude to himself and to other people depends in the first place on the parents' attitude to him. In the dependency relationship of the child to the mother, later to the father and then to other people, is to be seen the primary socialising pattern, the task of learning to become a human being. That the baby is born only with the potentiality of becoming a human being but needs the oppor-tunity to learn how to do this, is shown by two phenomena: firstly, by the behaviour patterns of children born without the necessary sense organs to perceive, communicate and interact with their environ-ment, such as the deaf-blind (for which there is an educational unit at Condover Hall School); secondly, by the extremely deviant de-velopment of children who by some chance or mishap have been isolated from a normal human environment during early infancy (for example the child described by Kingsley Davis in 1940 and 1947, or the very recent case of a boy who until the age of 4 years was made to live in a chicken coop).

Once the child has learned, through a loving mother's reaction to him, that he is important and excellent, this satisfying experience is 'ever afterwards craved and so constitutes a powerful driving force of human nature' (Moore, 1948). Conversely, disapproval arouses anxiety. Sensing the mother's disturbed emotional tone or displeasure, even very young infants become restless, irritable, show feeding problems, and so on. Thus anxiety is induced by the disapproval of people who are significant within the child's interpersonal world, first by the mother, then by other members of the family and later by teachers. Anxiety is such a painful and disturbing emotion that most children will go to considerable lengths to avoid behaviour that might arouse it. Conversely, there is evidence to show that the tack of a close, continuous relationship with the mother or a mother substitute, especially in early childhood, is associated with emotional maladjustment including an impaired capacity to make relationships (Bowlby, 1951; Clarke and Clarke, 1960; Pringle and Bossio, 1960). Unconditional acceptance within an affectionate family circle satisfies the need for love and security. Similarly, at school the child will feel secure and wanted if he is able to establish a satisfactory relationship with his teacher and feels able to win her approval.

Does the handicapped child face any special problems in relation to this need? To give a sense of security, one needs to feel secure oneself. But this is just what many parents of handicapped children do not feel: some are overwhelmed by their lack of knowledge and afraid of being unable to meet the special needs of their handicapped child; others feel guilty or ashamed; others may be completely at a loss, especially parents of slow-learning children who themselves are of limited ability and thus too bewildered by all the other demands of modern life to give adequate emotional support to their handicapped child. In the vast majority of cases not enough is done to help them to face and come to terms with their own unconscious attitudes. (Tizard and Grad, 1961).

At school, too, special difficulties are likely to arise unless the child is among the lucky few for whom an early and correct diagnosis is made; a place is available in a suitable school (whether ordinary or special); and long-term educational guidance (in the fullest sense of the term) is provided throughout his school life. If, on the other hand, he has to try and hold his own with normal children, he will almost inevitably come to feel inferior and a failure, the more so the less obvious or easily understood the nature of his handicap. To the blind and to certain kinds of physical handicap, sympathy is readily extended; mental handicaps of any kind are more often met with ridicule or contempt. If his teacher lacks knowledge of and experience with handicapped children, she may be worried by this special problem and feel unable to cope adequately; if in addition she is faced with a large class (as over two-thirds of all junior school teachers are) it is in no way surprising that the handicapped pupil may seem to her, and thus feels himself to be, a severe burden.

That parents feel concerned, and often extremely anxious, about their handicapped child is entirely natural. Indeed, this concern should be harnessed to provide the motivation for giving throughout the handicapped child's life that extra care, time and thought to him which can make such an important contribution to helping him to overcome, as far as possible, the adverse effects of his disability. Instead, this natural concern often turns into over-anxiety or resentment: left without any clear idea of the nature of the handicap and its short—as well as long-term—implications, parental uncertainty may show itself in insecure and inconsistent handling of the child. The more severe, complex or multiple the handicap, the more urgent is the need for comprehensive diagnosis and continuous guidance.

To be of value, all efforts to help handicapped children should be regarded as being team work in which parents, teachers and specialists are active partners. No one specialist, however eminent, is capable of making a complete diagnosis singlehanded. Assessing the type and extent of defect, be it mental, physical or both, is of limited value if it is not related to other factors such as the child's emotional maturity and adjustment, educational needs, home background and available facilities for treatment and teaching. Essentially the approach must be multidisciplinary; the more complex the condition, the greater the number of specialists who need to be consulted. This entails one danger: unless there is close cooperation between the various members of the team, preferably culminating in a case conference, several, at times conflicting, recommendations may be made. Not only is this confusing to parents and teachers who cannot be expected to disentangle overlapping or contradictory advice, but the resulting insecurity is also likely to communicate itself to the child.

While the need for a medical examination is generally accepted, this is not yet so with regard to a psychological examination. The view that the psychologist's role is confined to mental testing has persisted for far too long; with the handicapped such a role is even more sterile and harmful. Test results are only one aspect in the total assessment of the child's emotional and educational needs. Moreover, at present many of our measuring devices are, in part at least, unsuitable for the handicapped. Since trained educational psychologists have also had teaching experience, their main contribution should lie in framing practicable educational recommendations based on all the available information and in providing long-term and continuous guidance to parents and teachers in applying them. Diagnosis and treatment should be viewed as continuous and interlinked processes; rather than claiming finality, diagnosis should aim at an increasing awareness of the needs of each individual; treatment either verifies the original diagnostic hypotheses or else leads to the framing of modified or new ones. (Pringle, 1960 and 1964).

There is evidence to suggest that, due to improved methods of medical and pre- and ante-natal care and to rapidly increasing surgical skills, more children with multiple handicaps survive now. Perhaps the time has come to consider the most appropriate agency to carry out the initial psychological diagnosis and to give continuous guidance to parents and teachers on the fostering of the children's emotional and educational development. Are child guidance or school psychological services the most suitable units? Are hospital clinics more appropriate? Or should there be new diagnostic-therapeutic centres for handicapped children? If deprived children in care (for whom traditional child guidance clinics have so far failed to provide psychological guidance) are added to the handicapped, some 140,000 children would come under the care of these new centres at some time or another. Since the number of handicapped children in any one area (except large conurbations) is likely to be small, should there be regional centres which could call upon a wide range of specialists? Should these units be linked in some way to Universities so as to be in touch with current developments and to stimulate research?

A more widespread provision of facilities for a comprehensive initial diagnosis and for periodic reassessments would greatly contribute to meeting the need for security among handicapped children. When parents and teachers understand and accept his particular condition they inevitably convey this to him by their confident, affectionate and continuous encouragement and support. A happy, harmonious community—be it a family or a school staff—radiates warmth, confidence and hope which are just as easily felt by the child as anxiety, uncertainty and despair.

The need for new experiences

The second, basic emotional need is for new experiences. For the small baby everything that goes on around him becomes a new experience as soon as he is able to perceive it; so is every one of his earliest achievements, be it the ability to move his limbs and body at will or to examine the texture, taste and general appearance of materials and objects; similarly, learning to crawl, walk, run and climb are new experiences in themselves, quite apart from the increasingly wider world they open up for his firsthand exploration; while learning to understand speech and to talk himself, makes possible a vast range of new experiences. At a later stage still, play and creative activities of all kinds, visits to places outside the immediate neighbourhood, mastering the basic subjects, all these and many more provide new fields to be conquered, making life for the normal, active child a series of challenging and rewarding adventures. Indeed, new experiences can be regarded as a prerequisite for growth. At each developmental stage from birth to maturity, tasks appropriate to the particular stage of growth are presented to the child and their mastery provides in turn the stepping-stone towards more difficult achievements. If denied the opportunity of new experiences, no learning can take place; for example, in a non-speaking environment, the child will not learn to speak even though his hearing and speech apparatus is perfectly normal. Modern psychology has taught us that educability—a child's capacity to respond to all the growth tasks to which education, in the widest sense of the word, exposes him—depends not only on inborn capacity or intelligence, but on environmental opportunity and stimulation. Thus the emotional and cultural climate of the home, parental concern and ambition, realistic standards of expected achievement at home and at school, all these can foster or limit and even impair intellectual growth. Potentialities for learning may be developed to the full or may remain stunted according to the nature of the environment in which the child develops.

The handicapped child is inevitably placed in a less advantageous position regarding the satisfaction of this second need. By its very nature a handicap distorts or delays or even makes impossible the acquisition of new experiences. As yet little is known about how each of the various handicaps distorts learning; for example, the physically handicapped may fail to acquire adequate experience of space and movement which may distort concepts of distance, dimension and later of number; the deaf, having to remain unstimulated by speech until much later than normal children, may fail to acquire an adequate basis for abstract thought; and slow-learning children are unable to benefit from new experiences at the time that normal children do; thus they may miss the opportunity for learning altogether if these experiences are not deliberately provided at a later stage than is usual; and the blind are permanently debarred from getting to know the physical attributes of the world around them in the way the sighted majority do. Not only is this distortion of learning inevitable but it inevitably becomes cumulative and progressive. The way in which this affects the quality of learning is so far little explored. What is clear is that the ingenuity of parents and teachers will be taxed to the full in trying to provide and adapt new experiences to the child's limitations without curtailing the range of these experiences more than is absolutely necessary.

The danger is that new experiences may become a source of anxiety and defeat instead of an exciting challenge. Modifications may be needed in the order and manner in which new experiences are presented; more careful grading and control may have to be used and the aid of specially devised tools, gadgets and apparatus may have to be invoked to minimise difficulties and failure. Of course one cannot, and indeed should not, avoid all sense of failure and frustration either with normal or handicapped children; all learning involves the capacity to tolerate and accept obstacles and difficulties. But the handicapped have inevitably to tolerate strain, frustration and failure on a much larger scale than their more fortunate contemporaries; if the load becomes unbearable, the child may refuse to cope with new experiences and withdraw into passivity, looking on but refusing to participate. Though an effective way of avoiding failure, it is harmful since it blocks further growth through continued learning.

One effective way of learning open to all handicapped children, except the deaf, is through speech. For some, such as the blind and physically severely disabled, it may well become a compensatory way of broadening their experience and understanding. Research with deprived children living in residential care has shown severe language retardation. Though no similar investigations have been carried out

Q

with children attending residential schools, it may well be that conditions in them have a similarly limiting effect on language development, particularly where untrained 'house' staff are responsible for the 'home' side of school life. Hygienic living conditions and neat class- and playrooms are far less important than the promotion of language development through conversation, story telling, puppetry and other activities. In the same way, emphasis on the spoken word must take precedence over the written; indeed, if a child has little to say, he will have even less to write about. The more varied and richer his range of firsthand experiences, the more incentive he has for talking; the less he is able to have first-hand experiences, the more parents and teachers need to strive to bring alive what he can obtain only at secondhand, for example, by watching television. Talking with him is likely to be the most effective way of doing this, provided the level of verbal communication is geared to his level of comprehension.

The need for recognition and achievement

This need is closely linked to the one discussed previously. Just because learning, even for the normal child, is a slow, arduous process, eset by difficulties and setbacks, a strong incentive is needed. This is found in the pleasure shown at success and in the praise given to achievement by the adults whom the child loves and wants to please. Encouragement and a reasonable level of expectation act as a spur to perseverance. Too little expectation leads the child to accept too low a standard of effort and achievement; too high a level of expectation makes him feel that he cannot live up to what we require of him which leads to discouragement and again diminished effort; an optimum level of expectation is one which is geared to each individual's capability at a given point in time and stage of growth, a level where success is possible but not without real effort. He needs also to feel that learning is unhurried and that mistakes and failure are an integral part of learning for which he is neither scolded nor disapproved of. (This does not mean a child should never be scolded or punished; refusal to do something he can do, disobedience or destructiveness are quite different from mistakes due to imperfect mastery of a task.)

Here we are faced with a difficult problem regarding the handicapped child. Though most of us do not realise it, we habitually praise for achievement. What we ought to give praise and recognition to is not only achievement but the amount of effort which is being made. For example, a dull or physically handicapped child may have made much more effort to write a few lines of composition whereas a bright child, who produced a whole page could have done twice as much while still making less effort than the former did for his comparatively limited achievement. Linked with this difficulty is another touched upon at the beginning, namely the general tendency to judge the success of the handicapped by the extent to which their achievements equal that of the normal majority. Sooner or later the handicapped child is bound to become aware of this and thus is forced to realise the extent to which he has failed. The fact that the highest praise and admiration is accorded to the handicapped adult who successfully competes with the normal, means that the more severe the handicap the less likely is the child to be rewarded genuinely and unreservedly by recognition and success. Indeed this attitude towards the handicapped may well make for strain and often maladjustment among handicapped children, particularly in adolescence. There is a tendency for thinking to be limited to: 'John is deaf or physically handicapped or mentally retarded. Therefore he has severe problems of adjustment.' Rather the true explanation is along these lines: 'John, who is deaf, physically handicapped or mentally retarded, lives in a society whose members pity and/or despise the handicapped. They are thought of as helpless, dependent and inferior. They cannot compete for many of the desirable things of life. Though this may not be consciously formulated, John nevertheless becomes aware of this pity, prejudice and low social esteem. Thus he himself comes to feel that he is less worthy, less able, less privileged than those who can hear or who can move about easily or are not mentally retarded. In short, John has learnt to feel inferior and therefore he has severe problems of social and emotional adjustment.'

If the psychological need for recognition and achievement is to be met, the handicapped child must be permitted fulfilment of another need aptly described by Mallinson (1956) as 'the need to be different and the need to be the same'. The latter is met by recognising that basically handicapped children have the same needs as all children; but that at the same time we can only do them justice if we make all necessary allowances for the differences imposed upon them by the nature of their handicap. This implies permitting each child to compete only with himself, since if every individual is unique, the handicapped child is even more so. Hence even the slightest improvement over his previously reached standard is worthy of praise and recognition: the cerebrally palsied chairbound boy who manages to stand up unaided for a few minutes; the deaf girl who repeats imperfectly a word previously beyond her; and the slow learner who manages to read a simple book normally mastered by pupils who are his juniors by many years. The amount of effort, practice and frustration involved in mastering these simple skills is colossal compared with what is expected and given by the normal child for much greater returns in terms of success and achievement. To persevere in the face of the heavy odds against him, the handicapped needs every encouragement and praise for each small step he learns to make. If this is denied him, he may be driven to seek recognition and power by neurotic means: by refusing to learn, by remaining dependent, by carrying a chip on his shoulder and by insisting that the world owes him a living.

The need for responsibility

The need for responsibility is met by allowing the child to gain personal independence, first through learning to look after himself in such simple ways as feeding, dressing and washing himself; later in permitting him increasing freedom of movement without supervision about the home, street and neighbourhood as well as increasing responsibility for his own possessions, such as toys, money, clothes and pets; and finally, by encouraging him to become entirely self-supporting until eventually he may assume responsibility for others at work or within his own family. The nature of a child's handicap may inevitably set a limit to the ultimate degree of responsibility he will become capable of exercising. But it is necessary to guard against the tendency to withhold responsibility either from a sense of pity or over-protection, or else through underestimating what he might become able to do or because of a lack of ingenuity in devising means by which, despite his handicap, he can shoulder a measure of responsibility. At home one must strive to prevent the whole household revolving around the needs of the handicapped child, sometimes at the price of neglecting the legitimate demands of the other members of the family; similarly, at school the child must be given opportunities for shouldering some responsibilities, however limited. The more a school is run as a community, the easier it is to make each child feel that he has a contribution to make. By making every effort to satisfy the need for responsibility, self-respect and self-acceptance are fostered. The handicapped child is thus encouraged to develop an attitude of the mind which aims at helping himself as far as lies in his power and at achieving an optimal level of independence. There is evidence to suggest that how a child feels about himself and his handicap is a much more potent factor in determining his personal and social adjustment than the nature or even degree of the handicap itself.

Lastly, I should like to quote some of the conclusions to which I came as a result of surveying the literature on the emotional and social adjustment of physically handicapped children (Pringle, 1964).

While most comparative studies show the handicapped child to be less mature and more disturbed than those without any disabilities, the consensus of opinion and weight of evidence, at present at any rate, seem fairly heavily balanced against the view that the handicapped are inevitably maladjusted. That behaviour and personality are bound to be affected where the disabled physique has seriously limiting, depriving effects, whether physically, socially or both, is unlikely to be disputed. However, even then it would be argued by most that 'physique was only one factor in an extensive context of environmental and personal conditions acting together' (Barker et al., 1953). Furthermore, available data have failed to show any evidence of a definite association between a particular disability and a particular behaviour characteristic. So much then for negative conclusions.

On the positive side, there seems to be wide agreement that parental attitudes towards the child and his handicap are of paramount importance. To quote some early American workers (Allen and Pearson, 1928): 'The child seems to adopt the same attitude to the disability that his parents do. If they worry about it, so does he. If they are ashamed of it, he will be sensitive too. If they regard it in an objective manner, he will accept it as a fact and will not allow it to interfere with his adjustment.' This view has been summed up most succinctly by one who himself succeeded in triumphing over severe physical disability: 'Success or failure does not depend on what we lack but rather upon the use we make of what we have' (Carlson, 1941). There is one final point on which all investigators are agreed: more and better research is needed.

Case studies

To illustrate the relationship between learning and emotion as well as the fateful consequences on a handicapped child's development if one or more of the basic needs remain unsatisfied, the cases of two children will be described. They have been chosen because the children and their parents had received long-term educational and psychological guidance (6 and 12 years respectively) although neither child was given regular weekly treatment; both children have multiple handicaps; and their backgrounds contain many contrasting features, including the fact that the physically more handicapped boy has never attended a special school.

The case of Terence

TERRY, aged 8½ years, was referred by his headmistress. She stated that the boy had been accepted as a very slow learner until a young, newly qualified teacher recently began to take an interest in him. To begin with, she had felt sorry for him since he seemed timid and anxious, had a bad speech defect, few friends and an obvious fear of teachers and school life in general. He never took any part in oral work and often seemed 'miles away'. Well behaved and very retiring, he easily escaped attention. However, she grew so concerned about his refusal to make any spontaneous approach to her, that she went out of her way at break- and lunch-times to talk with him. After a while she began to suspect that he might be deaf; a specialist examination confirmed high frequency deafness and he was fitted with a hearing aid. Then she came to think that his vision might be defective and once again she was proved correct and he was given glasses. After two terms in her class, he had grown far less timid and worried, was willingly participating in oral work and eager to talk about his interests. The quality of some of his contributions made her wonder whether he might not be quite intelligent despite his poor educational attainments and despite the opinions held by his previous, more experienced teachers. As the headmistress appreciated the interest this young teacher had taken in Terry, she agreed to refer him to my Department for a diagnostic examination.

Family circumstances. Both parents had won 'scholarships' but family circumstances had prevented them taking advantage of a Grammar school education. Leaving school at 15, father became apprenticed to an engineering firm with whom he had remained except for war service. Mother did semi-skilled work until marriage. Their first-born, a 13-year-old girl, had always done well educationally and was now attending a Grammar school. The family seemed to be happy and closely knit with both parents sharing and stimulating their children's interests. Brother and sister were said to get on well together. No unfavourable comparisons had ever been made between their widely differing educational achievements. The only sorrow and anxiety had centred around Terry's physical disability: he had been born with a cleft palate which had necessitated seven operations before the age of five years and there were still more to come. The parents had always insisted on visiting him daily even though it led to quite a battle, especially with one hospital. Though his speech had become increasingly intelligible, the last operation had made it rather worse and continued speech therapy seemed to have little effect. The family's disappointment was all the greater since it had been hoped that no more operations would be needed; now that decision had been reversed and Terry knew he was facing yet further surgery.

Parental attitudes. Terence was a much wanted baby and when told of his handicap, the mother said she felt she would 'love him even more because he would have to suffer'. Not only did she realise that he would need all the encouragement and support that she and the father could give him, but she was also aware of the danger of over-protecting and smothering him. The parents accepted that learning to talk would be a particularly difficult task for him and therefore gave him plenty of stimulation to bring on his speech. They vividly described their frequent dilemma about how long to continue urging him to say something more clearly and when to accept what he was producing, especially since they nearly always knew what he wanted to say. However, until he started school, neither parent thought of him as a particularly dull child.

Right from the beginning Terence did not take to school. This dislike assumed serious proportions when he went up to the junior school: he clearly was reluctant to go, had frequent tummy-aches and bouts of sickness, slept badly during termtime and was obviously most unhappy. The mother became torn between allowing him to stay at home and making him go despite his pleas; she also became worried lest she had unwittingly over-protected him and given him so much love that he was now afraid to venture out and face competition. Feeling that perhaps he had been given praise at home too readily for his efforts, she taxed him with laziness and letting the family down when he brought home a particularly damning school report (which finished 'He could at least try harder'). At this Terry broke down, weeping bitterly, protesting that he had always tried and if only she would teach him at home, he would not mind working longer than at school and having no play time at all. The mother then realised the full extent of the boy's unhappiness. She went to see the head and class teacher, explaining that they had no educational ambitions for the boy and only wished that he should grow up feeling not too different from other boys; that they did not mind his being at the bottom of the lowest stream as long as he was reasonably happy at school.

Terence had started the third year in the juniors with the new young teacher previously mentioned. After only a few weeks with her, his attitude changed quite dramatically: he began to talk at home about what he was doing at school, wanted to take things to contribute to class projects, joyously mentioned that his teacher was giving him extra help so that he was now getting a few stars and that he in turn was being allowed to do jobs and run errands for her. The mother said one of her unhappiest moments came when, shortly after he had been fitted with a hearing aid, she was told he would also have to wear glasses. She felt that circumstances were increasingly singling out Terry as being, and indeed looking, different from other children. Yet he himself accepted these new burdens better than the parents had dared to hope; later they learned that his teacher had briefed his class mates not to comment on his new aids.

The child. At the beginning of his interview with me, Terence was somewhat reserved and shy. Soon, however, this was replaced by a most engaging, sensible and poised manner revealing an unexpected maturity and sense of humour. Though it was difficult at first to understand him, he willingly repeated what he had said and did not desist from making spontaneous comments. Praise and success greatly pleased him; when faced with difficult problems, he made persistent efforts to solve them and was able to accept failure in good part. His intelligence quotient was found to be 135; he did considerably better on non-verbal, practical and visuo-motor problems and was rather weaker on the verbal side. Educationally he was severely retarded, especially considering that he proved to be an able boy: at the age of $9\frac{1}{2}$ years, his reading was $2\frac{1}{2}$ years and his spelling 3 years below his chronological age; in arithmetic, his standard, though somewhat better, still only equalled that of the average 8-year-old.

Working hypothesis. Terence had been enabled by wise and loving parental handling to develop into a mentally healthy child with a good personality structure. At home all the four basic needs, discussed earlier, had been fully met. Despite severe physical handicaps, hospitalisations and the shocks of frequent surgical interventions, his emotional and social growth had been normal and his capacity for making personal relationships had remained unimpaired. Probably because he had taught himself to lip-read, his partial deafness had escaped attention at home. At school, however, none of the basic needs had been adequately met. Of course, one can see the problem of a teacher who has such a handicapped child in a class of fifty children; but one can also see the causes of the boy's failure and unhappiness at school; unable to make himself understood easily or quickly; unable to hear properly and prevented from lip-reading by the teacher's normal movements around the classroom; being scolded for laziness as his work became increasingly slower (educational backwardness being inevitably cumulative unless tackled constructively); bewildered by his failure and deeply upset by his family's disapproval. Considering the daily and cumulative impact of these experiences over a number of years on a sensitive and able child, it suggests considerable stability that a more serious breakdown was avoided. Despite having lived at school in a chronic state of insecurity, beset by failure with new experiences, lack of praise, recognition and responsibility, he could yet respond comparatively quickly to a sympathetic and understanding teacher. No doubt continued parental support and the continued enjoyment of a happy family life contributed to avoiding his sinking into complete despair or retreat.

Conference decision. Both the headmistress and class teacher attended the case conference. Though Terry was likely to benefit from remedial teaching in our Department, there were a number of contra-indicatory circumstances: he had already had much specialist attention; he was still attending a speech therapy clinic and also missing school not infrequently because of various re-examinations at the hospital, so that an additional weekly half-day's absence might be unwise; lastly there was no urgency to improve his attainments since he seemed to stand no chance of passing the 11 + examination in a year's time. It was decided to watch his progress through six-monthly re-examinations in our Department. Now that his good ability was known, his teacher was hoping to bring about quickened progress without fear of expecting too much from him. The headmistress decided to let Terry stay with the same mistress even though it would mean promotion to a B stream.

Subsequent developments. One factor everyone had underestimated was the effect of the boy's changed attitude to learning on his determination to succeed. He asked his teacher for homework and got up every morning at six o'clock to do it; he persuaded his parents and teacher to give him private coaching during the Easter and summer holidays (even offering to pay for it out of his pocket money!) Periodic re-examinations showed excellent acceleration in his rate of learning. But as he had to make up such leeway, I tried to persuade him that time was too short for him to catch up sufficiently to succeed in the examination on which he had now set his heart; I did this in an endeavour to avoid too deep a disappointment but he would not accept what to us, as educationists, seemed reason. In the event he proved to be the wiser: he won a place to a Technical School where he is now in his fifth year and doing well.

The case of Martin

IT all began with a letter from the parents saying that they had a 4½-year-old son who was mentally defective. As this had been confirmed by a number of doctors, they had accepted the verdict that he must be considered as ineducable; however, they would appreciate some guidance on how they themselves might further his education: though completely unable to speak, he could interpret the written word, following correctly instructions such as 'Fetch Daddy's papers' or 'bring Mummy her needle work box'. Further correspondence made it clear that both parents were intelligent and not trying to hawk the child from one expert to another hoping for a miracle. As I felt unable to make any suggestions without an interview, they readily agreed to bring Martin, though this involved quite a lengthy journey.

Family circumstances. Both parents were professional people, but the mother had given up her career upon marriage. Neither of them had had a particularly happy childhood and the making of personal relationships had been difficult for them. In marriage each of them had found real fulfilment and they were longing for a family. After two miscarriages, Martin was born. Labour was very long and difficult, instruments had to be used and there was some asphyxia at birth. He was a small, weak and apathetic baby who did not thrive for many months, refusing to suck and to respond positively to being alive. Because of mother's distress at having such an extremely unresponsive baby, she was advised for the sake of her own mental health to resume some of her professional activities. As a result a great deal of Martin's care was taken over by a succession of 'helps'. He failed to respond to toilet training and was still wetting and soiling himself at the age of $4\frac{1}{2}$ years. Walking was somewhat delayed but when he could not speak a single word at the age of $2\frac{1}{2}$ years, the parents sought advice about him. It was then that they were told he was mentally defective and by the time he was four years, two other doctors had confirmed this opinion.

Parental attitudes. Martin had been a much wanted baby and his lack of responsiveness had been a great sorrow to his mother; as a result she seemed to withdraw emotionally from him though taking good care of his physical wellbeing. Thus he was rarely played and romped with though a wide variety of toys were provided for him; he took no interest whatsoever in them, preferring instead to rock in his cot or on the ground; because his peculiar behaviour and his noises embarrassed the parents, he was not taken about much; and to avoid 'inflicting him' on other children, he was not given any opportunities to mix with preschool children. As a toddler he grew into an extremely active, restless and excitable child, which made it even more of an ordeal for his parents to take him about. On his fourth birthday someone had given him a plastic alphabet which the father happened to take with him on a train journey with the boy. In order to keep him sitting still, he tried drawing objects and then spelling their name with the plastic letters. Contrary to expectation, Martin was entranced by this activity and this was the start of his learning to read. When within four months he had built up a reading vocabulary of about 150 words the parents decided to seek educational advice.

The child. At first I doubted whether it would be possible to make a psychological assessment of his abilities: he charged round noisily, completely ignored people, and when placed in a chair, rocked about wildly. Clearly verbal materials (which had been used in previous examinations) were utterly useless. However, when non-verbal apparatus was presented to him, an unexpected change occurred in his behaviour: he sat still, watching the demonstration items and then himself performed the various tasks, in some cases most competently. As soon as he had finished an item, the rocking and noises would recommence to be followed by a concentrated silence while working on the next one. Perhaps the most outstanding feature was his complete failure to establish any relationship with me—indeed, I might have been a piece of furniture. By the end of the morning there was little doubt that in certain areas of mental functioning he was of at least average ability; that his lack of experience with even the simplest materials (evident from his activities in our play rooms) was bound to have had a retarding effect in addition to his lack of speech; and that there were indications that he might be profoundly deaf. An audiometric test was therefore arranged for him in the afternoon and then the parents came to discuss all the findings with us.

Working hypothesis. This was both complex and incomplete since a period of observation would have been desirable before formalising one's views. However, circumstances ruled this out.

In addition to a history of mental ill-health on one side of the family, Martin had an extremely difficult start in life physically; some brain damage during or after birth cannot be excluded though there was no definite evidence. The mother's emotional reaction to his unresponsiveness, though very understandable in terms of her own personality and all the circumstances preceding and surrounding his early life, may well have been an aggravating factor leading to the infant's further withdrawal. The audiometric test indicated that he might be profoundly deaf in both ears since he could tolerate sounds beyond the threshold of pain without flinching; against this, one had to weigh the fact that he had not cooperated well on the test and even more important, both parents were certain that there was little, if any, auditory impairment; the evidence from my own examination was rather contradictory, hence inconclusive, on this question. On the other hand there was conclusive evidence that Martin's non-verbal ability was at least average for his age, suggesting that the simple label 'mentally defective' was inappropriate. Owing to the combination of a multitude of unfortunate circumstances, none of Martin's basic needs seemed so far to have been adequately satisfied.

Conference decision. It was felt to be advisable to treat him for the time being as a deaf child. The parents were advised not to push the reading unless he himself remained interested in the activity; but that instead they should devote as much time as possible to playing with him as one does with a very young infant, also providing a good deal of physical contact of which he seemed either frightened or oblivious. Since there was no day school for the deaf in his area, yet contact with other children seemed highly desirable, it was suggested that he should be admitted to a good nursery school and allowed to stay there for at least two years. As it was quite impossible to foresee his future development and thus make long-term plans, it was decided that we would re-examine him every 6 to 9 months and that meanwhile the parents would keep in close touch with us by correspondence.

Subsequent developments. The School Medical Officer in the town where the parents lived at the time, proved most cooperative and found a nursery school willing to give Martin a trial. Needless to say full reports were sent to everyone from the beginning. The parents wrote every two or three weeks so that despite the infrequent re-examinations I was well acquainted with Martin's progress. Since we have continued to provide educational and psychological guidance for the past twelve years during which the parents in their turn kept in touch with us by sending, in addition to letters, photographs, specimens of his drawings and writing, a tremendous amount of material on his development has been accumulated. This is not the place for a detailed account nor would there be space for it. Only the bare bones of events up till now will be briefly mentioned.

Within a year Martin had stopped soiling, within two years he had stopped wetting and even more important had acquired a speaking vocabulary of about 100 words; his reading had also continued to advance. When Martin was 6 years of age we recommended that he be admitted to an infant school and again the Education Authority proved most cooperative. From then on I visited most of the schools to which Martin has been, to enlist and maintain their interest not only by correspondence but through personal contact. After two years he moved into the juniors and though he proved more difficult there because of his continued restlessness and non-conformity, other children accepted him, while his teachers found him a likeable though perplexing and fascinating boy. Subsequent audiometric tests showed less and less hearing loss until an examination when he was aged $8\frac{1}{2}$ years indicated that his hearing was normal (i.e. his previous 'deafness' had been 'psychological'). Because of the father's promotion the family had to move to another area, but once again we were fortunate in evoking interest in Martin and he was again admitted to an ordinary junior school. By now he could say and understand almost everything but his sentence construction remained highly idiosyncratic. Emotionally he was extremely sensitive, tense, timid, overactive and full of obsessional thoughts and activities. After having been allowed to stay for an extra year in the juniors, the family once more had to move, this time to an educationally very backward area; none of the available secondary schools seemed likely to cater for his needs. As by this time Martin had established quite good relationships with his parents, but still remained a very disturbed child, and since his mother was preoccupied by now with her two younger (and quite normal) children, it was felt that a boarding school for the maladjusted might be tried. A place was found for him and he stayed there for two years when circumstances once again made a move necessary. He has been in his present boarding school for senior maladjusted boys for a further two years and now once again another placement has to be found, since children leave there between the age of 15 to 16 years. Ideally I should like to find another school, preferably now for normal children, prepared to keep him for at least a further two or three years.

Throughout the past twelve years, Martin has made continuous progress on all fronts and there has been no backsliding in any aspect of his development. For this reason I suspect that he has not yet reached his ceiling or full potential growth. At the same time—despite the very considerable improvement over the years—it now seems likely that he will remain mentally handicapped and in need of special care.

Conclusion
The effect of emotion on learning needs to be given greater practical recognition, both within the home and at school. Without a feeling of security and acceptance, the most powerful incentive to maximum

learning will be absent. Whatever the level of ability and the nature of the handicap, a child needs the excitement and challenge of new experiences and the reward of approval and success. The giving of an increasing measure of responsibility also fosters the development of self-respect and self-acceptance. Divorcing or isolating the intellectual from the emotional side of life, is unlikely to lead to successful learning among any but a small minority of handicapped children. Initially the mother–child relationship provides both the incentive and the condition for learning. It is for this reason that the way to maladjustment and the way to educational failure are often along the same path. Conversely, satisfactory relationships and successful learning are shown by children who have been reared in homes where unconditional parental love and acceptance have been balanced by appropriate demands and expectations.

It has also been argued that teachers of handicapped children need to re-orientate their aims and emphasis. Even if proficiency in the three Rs were considered a sufficient aim in the education of the normal child, it would be woefully inadequate for meeting the educational needs of the handicapped.

Instead a different set of three Rs might be substituted which takes into account the fact that most handicapped children spend a period of time in ordinary schools before their educational needs are diagnosed and places are found for them in special classes or schools. These are first, rehabilitation in the emotional sphere to help overcome the sense of bewilderment and inferiority caused by current social, and, often too, by family attitudes to the handicapped. Second, remedial work in the educational field, since teaching methods appropriate to normal children are likely to have resulted in discouragement and failure; particularly since the nature of the handicap itself may have prevented the child from benefiting from many of the preschool opportunities for learning which form the basis of later educational achievement. Third, work towards the reintegration of the child into the outside community so that instead of remaining cut off in a sheltered special community he can make a place for himself in the ordinary world.

A fourth R might be added which ought to be vigorously pursued by all concerned with handicapped children: this is to press for more research. So far lamentably little time or money has been devoted to research on the learning problems of handicapped children, particularly of those with severe or multiple handicaps. The universities have been reluctant to accept responsibility for such research and they have also been slow to face the obligation of training educational and psychological specialists. Of course there are some exceptions, notably the Department of Education of the Deaf at the University of Manchester under Professor Ewing's direction. On the other hand, the vast majority of those dealing with handicapped children, whether diagnosing, treating or teaching them, have had no training in research methods. Though this need not be an insuperable hurdle, it is a very real psychological barrier. Added to this, teachers, psychologists and social workers have more than a full-time job and special classes, special schools and other establishments for the handicapped have been neither designed nor equipped to carry out research. But without a demand from teachers and informed parents, the situation is likely to remain unchanged.

It has been said that a pessimist sees a difficulty in every opportunity, whereas an optimist sees an opportunity in every difficulty. In the field of special education, there are two main difficulties: those intrinsic to the handicaps and those due to our ignorance because of lack of adequate research. Let us determine to be optimists so that we accept the difficulties as challenging opportunities.

References

ALLEN, F. H. and PEARSON, G. H. J. (1928) 'The emotional problems of the physically handicapped child', *British Journal of Medical Psychology*, **8**, 212–35.

BARKER, R. C., WRIGHT, B. A., MEYERSON, L. and GONICK, M. R. (1953) *Adjustment to physical handicap and illness; a survey of the social psychology of physique and disability.* New York, Social Science Research Council, Bulletin 55.

BOWLBY, J. (1951) 'Maternal care and mental health'. *Monograph Series of the World Health Organisation*, **2**.

CARLSON, E. R. (1941) *Born that way.* New York, Day.

CLARKE, A. D. B. and CLARKE, A. M. (1959) 'Recovery from the effects of deprivation', *Acta Psychologica*, **16**, 137–44.

CLARKE, A. D. B. and CLARKE, A. M. (1960) 'Some recent advances in the study of early deprivation', *Journal of Child Psychology and Psychiatry*, **1**, 26–36.

DAVIS, K. (1940, 1947) 'Extreme social isolation of a child', *American Journal of Sociology*, **45**, 554–65; **52**, 432–7.

MALLINSON, V. (1956) *None can be called deformed; problems of the crippled adolescent.* London, Heinemann.

MOORE, T. V. (1948) *The driving forces of human nature and their adjustment; an introduction to the psychology and psychopathology of emotional behavior and volitional control.* New York, Grune and Stratton.

PRINGLE, M. L. KELLMER and BOSSIO, V. (1958) 'A study of deprived children. Part 2. Language development and reading attainment', *Vita Humana*, **1**, 142–70.

PRINGLE, M. L. KELLMER and BOSSIO, V. (1960) 'Early prolonged separation and emotional maladjustment', *Journal of Child Psychology and Psychiatry*, **1**, 37–48.

R

PRINGLE, M. L. KELLMER (1960) 'The psychological and educational treatment of handicapped children.' *Special Education*, **49**, 17-21.

PRINGLE, M. L. KELLMER (1964) *The emotional and social adjustment of physically handicapped children*. (N.F.E.R. occasional publication no. 11.) London, National Foundation for Educational Research.

TIZARD, J. and GRAD, J. C. (1961) *The mentally handicapped and their families; a social survey*. London, Oxford University Press.

15. Psychological aspects of the changing structure and needs of the family*

Introduction

It used to be thought that rising standards of health and material prosperity would lead to a reduction in the incidence of maladjustment, backwardness and delinquency among children and adolescents. To some extent this expectation proved to be correct. For example, children whose parents have been rehoused do better at school than those who are still living in congested, and often condemned, property and the rate of delinquency is higher in slum areas than on well-established housing estates. Yet maladjustment and juvenile delinquency continue to be serious social problems. Similarly, prisons are overcrowded and half the available hospital accommodation is filled with patients suffering from various kinds of psychosomatic or mental illness. Of course statistics of these problems can be very misleading if accepted at their face value; only interpretation can elucidate their real significance. Yet changing conditions make such interpretation very difficult. The aftermath of the Second World War, a rise in the birthrate and more efficient methods of detection have probably all contributed to what appears to be a rise in the juvenile crime rate; similarly, the setting up of various treatment centres for maladjusted children may have led to a greater awareness of this condition. It may also be that the rise in standards of health and material prosperity are of too recent origin and not as yet widespread enough to show an appreciable amelioration in the incidence of social maladjustment or maladaption. And lastly, it may be that economic and social improvement do not necessarily solve these problems; they make satisfactory family and community life

* Presented at the European Seminar on 'Social Policy in Relation to Changing Family Needs' organised by the United Nations and held in Arnhem in 1961. Published by the United Nations Office of Social Affairs (Geneva) 1962.

possible, but cannot ensure it. That a general rise in material standards will not of itself abolish these social and emotional problems is strongly suggested by the high incidence of violent juvenile crime and the high consumption of tranquillisers in the most affluent of modern societies, the United States.

The last fifty years have seen tremendous changes in the scientific and economic fields which have had far-reaching repercussions on the psychological climate of the time. These changes seem to be of an unprecedented magnitude and to be taking place at a great speed, affecting all aspects of everyday life. They make very considerable demands on the adaptive powers of adults and tend to produce anxiety, since all change implies some threat to security. Yet if the challenge of the technological and social revolution is to be met successfully, deeper individual security is needed. Because it is no longer possible to bring up children with a clear idea or image of the kind of world they will have to live in—since few would dare to hazard a prediction regarding life even twenty or thirty years hence —it is all the more important to enable them at least to grow up emotionally secure as well as adaptable. Before discussing the ways in which the structure and the needs of the family have been changing, it is necessary first to discuss the psychological functions of the family.

Psychological functions of the family
By outlining first the role of the family in the personality development of the child, it will become apparent how needs, expectations and behaviour patterns are handed on from one generation to the next. We may then enquire whether these traditional ways are still applicable in the light of changing social conditions.

The basic and all-pervasive feature of parental love is that the child is valued for his own sake. In their relationship with him, the loving father and mother communicate affection through all their ways of dealing with him. The greatest impact of such love is on the development of self. Approval and acceptance by others are essential for the growth of self-approval and self-acceptance. Whether a child develops a constructive or destructive attitude to himself and to other people depends in the first place on the parents' attitude to him. In the dependency relationship of the child to the mother, later to the father, siblings and then to other people, is to be seen the primary socialising pattern, the task of learning to become a human being.

The main means of education open to the parents are the reward of love or the refusal of it (implied in punishment or frustration). It is within the family circle that the child receives his first experience of emotion: of love and hate, of irritation and anger, of cooperation and unselfishness. Not only will his most intense feelings be centring around his father and mother, but for years to come he will model his behaviour on theirs. The attitudes acquired in these first years tend to colour his subsequent social attitudes and expectations; and the structure of discipline and authority in the family both reflects and helps to determine the climate of a society. Where this structure is marked by security, recognition and respect for the individual's rights and duties, the foundation is laid for later democratic functioning.

Regardless of culture, religion, custom and tradition, the basis of all human relationships is love, mutual respect and understanding. In a list of environmental factors which influence emotional development and hence the growth of human relationships, the first and foremost place must be assigned to the family. It is within the family circle that emotional and social learning begins, long before the child has any conscious awareness of himself and others. During infancy the home is in almost complete control of his joys and sorrows; parental harmony or discord cast their spell upon him long before he understands any of the words spoken around him; parental precepts and example start to condition his feelings and attitudes long before the conscious and deliberate teachings of other institutions of society (such as the school) reach the child.

In the same way, it is within the family that, during early childhood, the basis is laid for later social and educational success. In the happy united home, an interest will be taken in and every encouragement given to the child's first experiments in learning, be it trying to walk or talk. By their delight in his efforts and progress, the parents elicit continued trial and learning. The good home also provides an ever increasing background of experiences which familiarise the child with gradually widening aspects of his environment, be they physical, social or cultural. Thus the family satisfies what are considered to be children's most important needs: the need for security, the need for emotional response from others and the need for new experiences.

Of course the family fulfils important psychological functions also with regard to its adult members. It could be argued that their needs are very similar to those mentioned above: marriage meets the need for a stable, secure relationship in which each partner is valued for his own sake and receives emotional response and support from the other; making a home and (for most couples) raising children provides the joy of new and shared experiences. In addition, the needs for recognition, independence and for responsibility find satisfaction within the family group for adults and children alike, although other groups in society make a vital contribution there (such as the school, daily work, etc). Needless to say, all these psychic needs are closely interrelated and the growth of mental stability and intellectual development depend upon their satisfaction at each state from infancy to adolescence and into adulthood. The order in which they have been mentioned indicates their relative importance during childhood. Security and affection are the essential needs of infancy; if they are not fully met, as in the case of children deprived of normal family life, there is a poor foundation for later personality development. New experiences remain throughout life the 'mental food' required for intellectual growth. The needs for recognition and independence become increasingly important as the child grows older.

There is one further factor, almost as fundamental as any of the others mentioned previously. This is the need to play. If denied the opportunity to play, the child's whole mental growth will be stunted. During the preschool years play is the major psychological means through which he begins to understand his surroundings, to learn about the physical attributes of the world, to appreciate causality and to come to terms with his emotions. In play the child can safely experience and experiment with the whole range of emotional expression without himself or others coming to harm. As he grows older, his play becomes more social and through it he learns to communicate and to cooperate with others by subordinating his self-centred, immature desires and thoughts to the interests and views of others.

In conclusion, the family gives a sense of security, of companionship and belonging to each of its members; it also bestows a sense of purpose and direction, of achievement and of personal worthwhileness. For the child it is of unique importance because it mediates between him and the world at large, providing what has been called 'a buffer, a filter and a bridge'. It thus fulfils the irreplaceable function of laying the basis for the adjustment of the individual within society. The capacity for integration, cooperation and creativity has its roots in family living.

The changing structure of the family

The factors making for change in our civilisation intimately affect the whole structure of family life. Though it is difficult to observe change while being a part of the changing scene, the more salient trends are discernible. Some of these are related to modern conditions of living and work; some to the emancipation of women and family planning; and some to new ideas about child rearing and education.

There is an increasing tendency for people to move into towns and tall flats are often replacing the small family house and garden. As cities grow and geographical mobility increases, journeys to and from work lengthen; thus shortening hours of work do not necessarily lead to the father having more time available in the evenings to be with his wife and children. Suburbs or blocks of flats do not as readily constitute a living community as did the village or small town. Social mobility is also militating against local attachment and proximity to relatives and family friends since families move house more often. Although established suburbs often develop some form of community life they do not usually integrate the whole family as a unit but rather cater for special interests (sport, politics), one sex only or certain age groups.

Next, it is no longer possible for most children to observe at first hand most of the basic processes needed for life and the work which supports their society. From being a production centre, the home has become a 'service station' into which things come ready made, processed, tinned or frozen. It is difficult for boys to identify with their father's role as breadwinners when they have only the vaguest ideas of what he actually does (except if he is a milkman, postman, pilot, shopkeeper, teacher or belongs to the few other occupations which are readily observable or otherwise easily understood). For most girls it is still much easier to identify themselves with the feminine role even where their mothers go out to work.

Now to turn to the second group of factors which are making for change in family life: the progressive emancipation of women is having a direct and increasing effect on the structure of family life. The equalising of opportunities open to men and women has led to marked changes in the relations between the sexes; most women work before marriage and many continue to do so afterwards. The experience of economic and personal independence through earning their living, leads to some conflict between a desire for this independence and the claims of domesticity and maternity. This is heightened by the economic need for women workers and an over-materialistic outlook on life, which make it appear desirable and praiseworthy for a woman to continue paid work outside her home despite family ties. To some extent this undermines the role of the father as wage earner, head of the household and authority figure. The apparent loss of status of the man and the increased self-confidence of the wage earning woman inevitably have psychological consequences on the emotional climate of the family. Being able through her earnings to provide various comforts for the house (easy chairs, carpets, TV and the like) on the one hand makes the home more attractive, so that it becomes more a centre for family living; on the other hand, housework remains to be done in the evenings and so husbands tend to share to an increasing extent domestic chores and the care of the children.

The emancipation of women may also, to some extent at least, be linked with the increase in the divorce rate. This increase could well be more apparent than real: not only was divorce socially much more frowned upon in the past, but the vast majority of wives depended solely on their husband's financial support. Greatly increased educational and vocational training for women together with the availability of legal aid, may now lead more women to break a matrimonial union which previously they would have had to endure. There is little evidence to show that such an actual break is more harmful to the children than a home broken in spirit through constant quarrels and dissension.

Family planning and a reduction in the average number of children may also be linked with the emancipation of women. This has been accompanied by a change in the composition of the average family; in the past there were not only more children, but grandparents, uncles, aunts and cousins often lived within visiting distance; thus the children gained first-hand experience not only of the very young but also of the old. The small modern family no longer provides this wide range of emotional relationships; instead family ties tend to be closer and more intense. There has also been a change in the evaluation of the age groups and in the relations between them. Instead of age carrying the prestige of wisdom, it is now considered a problem; thanks to medical advances life has been prolonged, but small flats are not conducive to the harmonious living together of three generations. Childhood and youth, on the other hand, have become periods in their own right and the subject of much study;

as a result the young are no longer thought to be merely incomplete adults.

Now to turn to the third group of factors making for change in family life: new ideas about child rearing have made their influence felt in the past thirty years or more. The impetus for this change has come from studies of both normal and exceptional children. But as tends to happen with new ideas, they have been overstated or misinterpreted (e.g. sex education being confused with mere instruction; or sensible discipline being abandoned due to misinterpreting Freudian teaching on the harmful effects of conflict and frustration, harmful only if the conflict is insoluble and the frustration inappropriate). Moreover, when parents have to unlearn some of the attitudes instilled into them through their own upbringing, they may well feel uncertain and insecure. This is likely to lead to parental anxiety and inconsistency. The conditions of presentday life also tend to intensify adult anxiety and uncertainty. To mention just a few: the increasing emphasis on economic competition; rapid and major scientific and technological developments such as atomic science and automation; a change in social and moral standards developing in the aftermath of a world war and social revolution. If parents suffer from feelings of uncertainty, conflict and doubt, these feelings are likely to be communicated to their children. The most stable and 'emotionally tough' may be able to resist the effects of an atmosphere laden with anxiety; the rest will—to a greater or lesser extent—become predisposed or conditioned to emotional instability or maladjustment.

Recent research work in the field of juvenile delinquency has produced statistical support for this supposition. The greatest 'crime proneness' was found to be associated with that birth group who passed through their fifth year either during the depression of the 1930s or during the Second World War. Scientific evidence is also accumulating about the most vulnerable periods of childhood and about the effects not only of maternal, but of paternal deprivation and of socio-economic conditions. These findings give scientific proof to the evidence of case histories with which social workers, psychologists and teachers are only too familiar, showing that matrimonial harmony and a happy, secure and dependable family life are the basis for children's emotional security and stability; conversely, that maladjustment, delinquency and school failure are closely associated with the broken home, with parental inconsistency and disharmony, and with rejection of the child.

The last factor to be mentioned which is having an effect on family structure is the steadily lengthening period of formal education and the fact that scholastic achievement rather than wealth is becoming the gateway to professional and social advancement. Similarly, as the organisation and processes of industry grow constantly more complicated, minds and hands with more developed skills are needed. The consequences for the family are twofold: there is the seed of conflict—particularly of standards and of loyalties—when children's educational level and occupational aspirations surpass to a high degree those of their parents. Secondly, there is a steady prolongation of children's economic dependence as facilities for technical, vocational and university education increase. This coincides with the earlier attainment of puberty. The delay of achieving adult status when physical adulthood has been reached is likely to be all the more frustrating when the 'psychological distance' between the generations is wider than ever before.

The changing needs of the family

Perhaps it should be stressed here that this chapter deals only with psychological aspects and touches upon other aspects, such as economic, social, or sociological, only where this is unavoidable. This is done to prevent overlap with other contributions, not through any disregard for or underestimation of their importance. At the same time the writer is convinced of the need to pay greater attention to the psychological needs of families than has hitherto been the case. During the past fifty years great strides have been made in improving material standards of life, including physical health. Better still, there is now an emphasis on the prevention of physical ills and material deprivation. The same cannot unfortunately be said regarding the preservation of mental health and the prevention of psychological deprivation. Lip service is frequently paid to the importance of a stable, harmonious family life and to the role played by parents in laying the foundations for a child's emotional adjustment and educational success. Yet rarely are the practical consequences of this view considered, and more rarely still are steps taken to translate theory into practice.

In what follows the changing needs of the family will be considered from the point of view of each of its members—the mother's first. In the process of emancipation women have been given the same educational opportunities as boys. Putting masculine ideals before growing girls carries the implication that the domestic and maternal role is somehow inferior. This view is later made explicit in Government appeals for the labour of married women, in press pronouncements and through the mass media of entertainment where work outside the home is compared favourably with being 'merely a housewife and mother'; economic factors are also responsible for the persuasive pressures directed at married women to undertake outside work. They are thus being conditioned to feel a sense of waste and dissatisfaction with the traditional feminine role of home making and child bearing. It may well be that for a small minority the daily stimulation of outside work is essential for mental stability and satisfaction. But for the great majority of women it is likely that bringing up their children and looking after husband and home is not only a full-time but also a satisfying task.

Has the time not come when it is necessary to restore in the mind of growing girls as well as in the public mind the unique importance which mothering has for the mental health of young children? There is now ample research to support the view that preschool children thrive best physically, emotionally and intellectually when they are given the almost exclusive attention of their mother or of a dependable, stable mother substitute. The best residential nursery is but a poor substitute. It is urgent to bring about a change in the climate of opinion so that mothers of young children feel confident and aware of doing a creative and essential job rather than apologetic because they are 'only full-time mothers'. Moreover, financial encouragement (possibly in the form of increased family allowances) should be given to mothers of young children so that they do not need to seek employment outside the home because of economic strain. In the long run this will prove considerably cheaper than providing facilities for difficult adolescents, be they maladjusted, delinquent, school failures or unemployable.

On the other hand, the modern educated mother, living in cramped suburban surroundings with her small children, needs a regular respite from her family which in days gone by could be provided by relatives living nearby. It should not be an impossible feat of organisation for nursery schools or play groups to make provision for preschool children to be looked after for half a day once or twice a week. Similarly, nursery school provision (to be distinguished from crèches or day nurseries) are not an educational luxury but fulfil an important function in the education of 3- to 6-year-olds living under cramped urban conditions. Again, once all her children go to school, many a mother—thanks to better educational opportunities and better health bestowed by medical advances—may feel the need to develop interests of her own outside the home. She may wish to resume a career given up at marriage or child bearing, but on a part-time basis, or to undertake some training if previously she had none. For either of these eventualities, too few opportunities exist at present (at least in some countries), especially if the mother considers that she ought to be with her children before they leave in the morning, on their return from school and during most of the school holidays. Greater flexibility will be required of industry, commerce and the professions if working mothers are to make their optimum contribution without neglecting their family responsibilities.

Next, in what ways are the needs of fathers changing? The satisfaction and security derived from possessing a craft and from having some responsibility, is increasingly denied to large sections of the working population. The challenge and joy of vocational involvement has perhaps never been available to the majority, but now—except for the professions—is available to only a small minority. Being a readily replaceable cog in the industrial machine deprives the individual of a sense of identity and personal value. To a considerable extent this loss can be restored to the breadwinner by the family. Fathers can make an indispensable contribution to the psychological development of their children, daughters as well as sons. The importance of the mother–child relationship has been so much stressed in recent years that it almost seemed fathers need merely to provide material things for their offspring. As so often happens, work with handicapped children has shown how mistaken this view is. Where fathers share responsibility for the upbringing and care of a handicapped child, the chances of his triumphing over limitations are much greater than if the mother is left to cope single-handed. The same is now seen to apply also to the normal child.

It is from and through the father that the entire family should receive a steadiness of purpose, an enthusiasm of interest, a sense of justice, an awareness of the world's problems and an inspiration to become a participant in making it a better place to live in. Through a living partnership with their wives, fathers can place before their children an example of democratic and cooperative leadership which the sons will seek to emulate and the daughters will wish to find in their future husbands. By taking some part in his children's care, finding time to play with them, later to share interests with them, fathers can enjoy and get to know them from their earliest age; delegating all care to the mother until the children are older prevents the building up of those early relationships, which are of such vital importance, and makes the father feel a stranger in his own home. It is within the family that fathers can, through being valued and needed, gain a sense of stability, personal worthiness and belonging.

Lastly, in what ways are the needs of children changing? In a world uncertain of its values, standards and even of its survival, the child's need for security is greater than ever before. Only if he finds stability, harmony and love within the family; only if reasonable, consistent and predictable demands are made on him which are appropriate to his age and stage of development; only if anxiety and frustration are kept to the necessary minimum; only then is he likely to develop the resilience and powers of adjustment required of adults in this increasingly complex and increasingly threatened world. It is also now being recognised that children's capacity to benefit from increased educational opportunities depends as much, if not more, on parental encouragement and support than it does on sheer intelligence.

The larger and even more fundamental question of how to instil in the future generation a sense of moral responsibility and a sense of values, which give meaning and purpose to life, is not the province of the psychologist but rather of the philosopher or theologist. But there can be little doubt that healthy emotional and intellectual growth is based on the child's feeling that he is loved and valued for his own sake and that this love is dependable, consistent and unconditional. The smaller the family, the more dependent is the child on such love from the parents and the greater is his vulnerability in the face of loss, be it death, desertion or divorce.

Children can cope with, or at least tolerate, a good deal of strain and tension, if their environment provides rich possibilities for all kinds of play. From earliest babyhood until at least the age of seven years, play is the major psychological means by which learning proceeds not only in the intellectual but also in the emotional and social spheres. But congested urban conditions with too small houses or flats, small gardens, if any, and dangerously busy roads, severely restrict the space and freedom for unsupervised play. Conversely, children who are allowed to roam about freely, find themselves far too readily in conflict with the law through curiosity and a sense of adventure. Making adequate provision for both indoor and outdoor playing space and facilities should not be considered a luxury. High priority must be given to it by town planners since it is one of the vital means of preserving the mental health of growing children.

Despite the marked changes that have taken place in sex roles and the relations between the sexes, sex differences are still emphasised along the same traditional patterns. It is likely that the continuation of this conventional sex typing, which starts at quite an early age, leads to confusion and uncertainty in adolescence and later: boys find men's jobs invaded by women and see their masculine role of wage earner and authority figure threatened; girls face a conflict between the security and status conferred by marriage and maternity on the one hand and on the other the desire for economic and personal independence conferred by a job. Children need to be prepared much more clearly and realistically for their future roles as parents and citizens. While increasing educational opportunities should be given to girls, particularly at the professional level, at the same time they also need more systematic guidance for their future roles as home makers. At best such guidance comes from the happy, harmonious home where a satisfactory solution has been worked out; but the schools, youth organisations and media of mass communication all have a part to play in shaping public opinion to accept these changing conditions. If girls need help in seeing how they can make a specifically feminine contribution complementary to that of men, boys must also come to see their part as husbands and fathers in a new light.

Lastly, to turn to the specifically educational needs of children: with industrial development and automation, the simpler repetitive processes are being taken over by machines and by electronic 'brains'. This leads to fewer jobs for those of limited intelligence or poor educational standard. Conversely the demand for well-trained technicians and technologists is likely to increase. Thus schooling tends to be prolonged with an emphasis on intellectual learning. Moreover, intelligent children from working class and lower middle class homes may have considerable difficulty in reconciling new norms of thought and behaviour put before them in school with what is accepted in their home and immediate group of relations and friends. This conflict together with longer dependence on parental financial support during a time when the desire for independence, for adult sex experiences and for a philosophy of life are strong, has practical implications for home and school alike. Adolescents need help to understand and work through these problems to avoid rebellion (at present tending to take ugly and violent forms) against all adult authority and standards.

A suggestion for meeting some of the psychological needs of the contemporary family

To ensure that in our complex and changing society more children grow up in the most favourable emotional and educational environment, it might help if there were available a comprehensive service or agency which is both preventive and curative. For want of a better name it might be called a family advisory service. There are several reasons why such a service seems now more urgently needed than thirty or forty years ago; perhaps chief among them is the fact that moral, religious and social standards are in the melting pot, making for parental doubts, fears and uncertainties; also during this century a beginning has been made in the systematic and scientific study of children's emotional and educational development, but, as nearly always in science, application lags at present behind discovery.

This suggested Family Advisory Service should have six functions These are briefly listed below and will be discussed in greater detail in the next chapter.

1. *Education:* to coordinate the available facilities for the dissemination of knowledge regarding children's emotional, social and educational needs; and, where necessary, to create such facilities for normal families by arranging lecture courses, discussion groups, etc.

2. *Prevention:* to make available to the usually self-reliant family a service to help them through periods of temporary strain and crisis.

3. *'Cure':* to give help to the many families suffering from some degree of defective family relationships at the earliest possible time.

4. *Long-term support:* to provide more or less continuous guidance to inadequate families to prevent a complete break-up of the home. At present no public agency can officially take action until the family fails to function as an acceptable social unit.

5. *Clearing house:* many different agencies or services are available at present to advise on various problems of normal and handicapped children. For lack of knowledge on the part of the parents, these are

often not used at all or too late. The Family Advisory Service would be competent to suggest the most appropriate specialist or body to consult in a particular case.

6. *Research:* though this may sound utopian at present, eventually this service might sponsor research, if not undertaking some itself. For certain kinds of studies it would have quite unique opportunities.

References

ANDRY, R. (1960) *Delinquency and parental pathology; a study in forensic and clinical psychology.* London, Methuen.

BOWLBY, J. (1951) 'Maternal care and mental health', *Monograph Series of the World Health Organisation,* 2.

DENNIS, W. (1941) 'Infant development under conditions of restricted practice and of minimum social stimulation', *Genetic Psychology Monographs,* 23, 143–91.

FERGUSON, T. (1951) *The young delinquent in his social setting.* London, Oxford University Press.

FORD, D. (1955) *The deprived child and the community.* London, Constable.

GOLDFARB, W. (1945) 'The effects of psychological deprivation in infancy and subsequent stimulation', *American Journal of Psychiatry,* 102, 18–33.

GOLDFARB, W. (1947) 'Variations in adolescent adjustment, in institutionally reared children', *American Journal of Orthopsychiatry* 17, 449–57.

LEWIS, H. (1954) *Deprived children; the Mersham experiment. A social and clinical study.* London, Oxford University Press.

LINTON, R. (1947) *The cultural background of personality.* London, Routledge & Kegan Paul.

MEAD, M., ed. (1953) *Cultural patterns and technical change; a manual prepared by the World Federation for Mental Health.* Paris, Unesco.

MYRDAL, A. and KLEIN, V. (1956) *Women's two roles; home and work.* London, Routledge & Kegan Paul.

PRINGLE, M. L. KELLMER (1958) 'Learning and emotion', *Educational Review,* 10, 146–68.

s

268

PRINGLE, M. L. KELLMER and BOSSIO, V. (1958) 'A study of deprived children. Part 1. Intellectual, emotional and social development', *Vita Humana*, 1, 65–92.

PRINGLE, M. L. KELLMER and BOSSIO, V. (1960) 'Early prolonged separation and emotional maladjustment', *Journal of Child Psychology and Psychiatry*, 1, 37–48.

PRINGLE, M. L. KELLMER and TANNER, M. (1958) 'The effects of early deprivation on speech development', *Language and Speech*, 1, 269–87.

STOTT, D. H. (1956) *Unsettled children and their families*. London, University of London Press.

UNITED NATIONS: *Department of Social Affairs* (1952) *Children deprived of a normal home life*. New York.

WALL, W. D. (1955) *Education and mental health*. Paris, Unesco.

WHITING, J. W. M. and CHILD, I. L. (1953) *Child training and personality; a cross-cultural study*. New Haven, Yale University Press.

WILKINS, L. T. (1960) *Delinquent generations; a Home Office Research Unit report*. London, H.M.S.O.

16. Prevention—reality or illusion

Introduction

The most glaring gap in our knowledge of child care is in the field of prevention. This is particularly the case in the prevention of emotional and intellectual neglect and deprivation of children living with their own families. While optimists believe, and pessimists deny, the possibility of preventing a good deal of socially unacceptable behaviour, whether it shows itself as emotional maladjustment, delinquency or serious educational deficiencies, there is a dearth of reliable evidence. Moreover, even if prevention is possible, effective methods of achieving lasting changes have as yet to be explored.

Two main fallacies beset current thinking about prevention: they can be summed up as 'too late' and 'too narrow'. It is generally assumed that, if a family has not asked for help, it neither needs nor wants it. Yet, according to daily experience, this is clearly not true: again and again it becomes apparent that had help been available early on—long before crisis point—the break-up of the family might have been prevented. In addition to coming too late, there is often too little done by too many. Too little in the sense that there are too few fully trained workers, too little money and too few resources for preventive measures; and there are not enough funds or plans for long-term research. On the other hand there may be too many agencies involved with a family who has problems. It seems as if neither the various workers nor certainly the family itself, are aware of the fact that their different problems all stem from one common source.

The following family situation is an example: one child is backward and truants, so the school welfare officer calls; another child is stealing, which is the concern of the police and the probation officer;

a third has a stammer and is a complete non-reader, so the educational psychologist is being consulted; the school nurse and the health visitor are frequent callers, concerned about the often dirty and neglected condition of the children; the child care officer is making arrangements for the children's temporary placement in foster homes as another baby is due shortly; there are rent arrears, which bring in an official from the housing department. Linked with all these separate problems and probably underlying them all are the family's appalling housing conditions, the father's low mentality and irregular employment, the mother's weak and ineffectual personality and the fact that her health, both physical and mental, is nearing breaking point due to the strain of coping with too many children under circumstances which would tax to the utmost a woman abler and stronger than she. Thus, at the root, there are a man and a woman whose personalities and abilities are inadequate to cope with the complexities of modern life. Though fond of their children, they are overwhelmed by the demands of parenthood. Hence their difficulties are multiple and chronic. Just as the physically disabled are permanently affected by their bodily deficiencies, so they are permanently handicapped by their mental inadequacies.

There is another aspect to the fallacy of 'too late'. Too much emphasis is given to children in their teens while the needs of the under-fives are relatively neglected. Adolescent behaviour, including delinquency, attracts a disproportionate amount of attention and money, yet action then is mainly palliative, a patching-up of difficulties whose roots go back to earlier times. It is during the preschool years that the basis is laid for personality development, moral standards and intellectual growth. There have been official investigations concerned with the needs of the 11- to 21-year-olds (Crowther, Newsom and Robbins) and now the Plowden Committee is considering the primary school child. It is significant that the most vital period, the preschool years, still awaits official exploration.

The second fallacy, summed up as 'too narrow', also has two aspects: first, the main aims of prevention are often seen as avoiding the need for taking children into care and of reducing the incidence of juvenile delinquency. Secondly, it is widely believed that preventive action is required solely among families who are seriously underprivileged economically or socially, and among so-called problem families. In fact, a child may be emotionally or intellectually deprived despite a family's high level of income, education or social class. The children of film stars are an example.

These fallacies militate against working out a broad and comprehensive concept of prevention. To enable this to be done, three questions need to be answered: what? when? and how? What ought to be prevented? When could it best be done? And how would it work?

What needs to be prevented?

The answer to this question can in essence be reduced to two fundamentals: emotional neglect or deprivation and intellectual neglect or deprivation. To put it positively, the aims should be to ensure that children acquire maximal emotional stability so that they are more resilient under the inevitable stresses and strains of life; and to promote the development of all their intellectual and educational potentialities, so that they become fulfilled as individuals and effective as citizens.

There is little reason to doubt that emotional stability, like all other human qualities, depends to some extent on genetic and hereditary factors. Over these there is as yet no control. In practice, therefore, it is environmental influences to which attention must be paid. The past fifty years have shown what attention to the physical aspects of children's growth can do. Boys and girls are now healthier, taller and heavier, and it is obesity rather than under-nourishment which has become a dietary problem. The aim should now be to achieve a similar revolution with regard to emotional health. If it succeeds, then the incidence of juvenile delinquency, mental illness and adult crime is likely to diminish appreciably in the years to come.

What, then, are the environmental influences which foster emotional resilience and health? Chiefly, the quality of personal relationships available to a child during the most formative period of his life, which is the preschool years. Growing up in a happy, stable family where each child is cherished for his own sake (i.e. irrespective of sex, appearance, personality, intelligence and other attributes or their absence); where standards are provided which are appropriate to his age and ability; and, perhaps most important of all, where the child experiences a mutually satisfying, close and lasting relationship with his mother (or a mother substitute) and his father. These factors form the basis for his later ability to make reciprocal, dependable and enjoyable relationships with an ever-widening circle of relatives and friends, children and adults.

Perhaps it needs to be mentioned that such a view of child rearing is far removed from the common misinterpretation of Freudian psychoanalytic teaching. What is being urged is not a policy of 'letting the child do as he pleases'. On the contrary: it is accepted that, unless standards of behaviour are placed before him to emulate, a child will not in fact acquire such standards. His desire to do so is prompted by the affection shown to him by significant adults whose example he wants to follow, partly to please them and partly because, loving them, he wants to become like them.

There is similarly a good deal of misunderstanding about the place and function of conflict and frustration. One could hardly bring up a child without his experiencing both—they are part of life and of growing up. Indeed, appropriate frustration and conflict help a child to mature by learning how to cope with new situations and how to master or tolerate periods of difficulties. What is harmful is conflict which permits of no solution and frustration which is allowed to become a chronic state. For example, a child whose parents have diametrically opposed expectations and ambitions for him is faced with an insoluble dilemma: if his father wants him to be a tough, independent and athletic person while his mother would like him to become a sensitive, dependent and intellectual boy, he will cause disappointment to at least one of them, whatever he strives to be. Perhaps worse still is the insoluble conflict faced by the child whose warring parents fight for his loyalty, forcing him to take sides or even to choose between living with one or the other. Similarly, there is no escape for a child of whom too much is always expected—too much in relation to his abilities or to his age; however hard he tries, the satisfaction of pleasing his parents eludes him.

Evidence shows that chronic frustration or conflict are liable to lead to mental stress and, if prolonged, to breakdown, even in adults. How much more likely that it will do so in children whose inner resources have not yet matured and who are dependent on parental approval for their sense of personal worthwhileness.

At present, there are at least three conditions propitious for preventive mental health planning. Considerable strides have been made in the past twenty or thirty years in understanding the effects of different child-rearing methods on behaviour and adjustment. Secondly, the general rise in standards of living and in physical health has brought increased awareness of the, as yet, unsolved problems of mental ill-health and social maladjustment. Thirdly, in an era of rapid and profound change in ways of living and working, a high degree of emotional flexibility and resilience is needed. The recognition of this fact has helped to bring about a climate of opinion more favourable towards research and action in the field of mental health. Today's children are growing up in a society which is in a state of flux and there is little doubt that they will continue to encounter rapidly changing conditions in the years ahead. We cannot even envisage clearly what these changes might be and so cannot prepare the growing child for them. What we can do is to provide him with the emotional stamina to face and adapt to uncertainty and to change (Wall, 1959).

The view that emotional deprivation is prevalent mainly among underprivileged and 'problem families' is still widely held. Yet social workers know that a home may be rough and ready, or even dirty and disorganised, and yet there can be real affection and a close bond between parents and children. Conversely, teachers know—because they work with all children of school age whereas social workers are mainly in contact with families who have problems of one kind or another—that pupils coming from highly respectable, educated and comfortably-off homes may yet show all the signs of emotional rejection or deprivation. Affection for and acceptance of children is not the prerogative of any social class; thus prevention needs to cut across socio-economic barriers.

There are stronger grounds for believing that intellectual neglect and deprivation are more common among underprivileged children since their parents are usually ill-educated, if not of limited ability. In recent years the part which environment plays in fostering the growth of intelligence has come to be increasingly recognised. The concept of intelligence itself has undergone an important change. It is still generally accepted that there are as considerable individual differences in intellectual endowment as there are in physical growth and eventual adult stature. However, just as, for the fullest development of physical potential, a baby's and young child's diet is of fundamental importance, so it has come to be realised that the same is true for intelligence; it, too, needs appropriate 'nourishment'. This is provided by rich opportunities for play (including environmental exploration of all kinds) and for the growth of language.

It is not merely pleasurable but positively educative for even a young baby to be played with and talked to. This lays the foundation for his desire to be active, to explore and to communicate. The pleasure his babbling gives to his mother encourages further articulation and imitation. If the home is an educated one and the children are born at intervals sufficient to enable the mother to enjoy the babyhood of each, then a tremendous amount of teaching and learning can take place which will facilitate later success at school. Conversely, in the home where language serves only the most utilitarian purposes (i.e. merely telling children what to do and not to do) much is missing: conversation, story-telling and nursery rhymes, verbal explanations which widen understanding and lead to the formation of concepts. In consequence the child remains inarticulate and stunted in language development which in turn impedes the full realisation of his intellectual potential. Lewis (1963) goes even further: 'Verbal play is a form of conduct towards others and a factor in ethical development' and 'at every successive moment the linguistic education of a child is a transformation of existing patterns of action.' Thus language and intellectual deprivation have almost as wide and far-reaching repercussions as emotional deprivation.

When should prevention start?
The first five or six years of life are vital for the prevention of emotional maladjustment, educational difficulties and delinquency. Thus special emphasis needs to be placed on this period of growth. Much remains to be discovered about what are called 'critical learning periods'. But there are suggestive leads from animal studies. These have shown that there exist critical periods of growth; if certain developments are prevented from taking place during these periods, they are unlikely to do so later. How far this is also true for the human young remains to be explored; but there is evidence that, if speech is seriously delayed or learning to read does not take place at the usual time, the achievement of either skill is much more difficult at a later stage. Whether and to what extent the same applies to the learning of emotional relationships and of intellectual concepts is not as yet known.

At present emphasis is placed on higher education, on curbing delinquency and on helping those who are handicapped physically, educationally or emotionally. Of course this must continue. At the same time it should be recognised that planning a magnificent extension of further education will leave untouched the present waste of intellectual potential if we do not build sounder foundations during the time of preschool and early school learning; and if we do not prevent early emotional and intellectual deprivation. The effectiveness of early prevention can hardly be in doubt. To patch up and repair damage is more difficult than to prevent its occurrence. In the physical and medical field, this has come to be accepted almost as a commonplace; adequate pre- and post-natal care as well as preventive measures during early childhood (such as a balanced diet, vaccinations, etc.) have met with quite spectacular success.

The fostering of the same preventive outlook in the psychological care of children is the logical next step forward. A similar concern must be developed for their early emotional, social and educational wellbeing as that now taken for granted with regard to physical health. Early and comprehensive preventive action is now possible under the Children and Young Persons Act 1963. But it is neither inevitable nor compulsory that such action will in fact be taken. It will entirely depend upon whether the Act is interpreted in the broadest possible sense or whether it will only be used to prevent disaster such as the break-up of families or serious delinquency. Section 8 of the Memorandum on the Act limits the powers of the Authority to 'family difficulties and domestic problems [where] there is some reason to suppose that these may create a risk of children having to be received into or committed to the care of a Local Authority'. Such an interpretation seems circumscribed: the range of conditions where preventive action may be needed is conceived too narrowly and the concept of 'being at risk' is too limited.

The problem family does not spring into being fully fledged nor does the maladjusted, backward or delinquent child do so. Most of the danger signs which signal a breakdown of an individual or of a family are well known to teachers and to social workers. These danger signs must be heeded earlier than has been the case hitherto. Though more time-consuming and thus more expensive in the short run, it is bound to be more economical, both in time and money, in the long run. Taking action early will prevent more serious and intractable difficulties later. Moreover, taking a child into care or placing him in an approved school creates problems of its own, quite apart from being very costly.

The broad categories of 'children at risk' are sufficiently well known to make truly preventive early action possible. Briefly, there are five groups: families where there is serious or irreversible physical or mental illness or a disabling handicap; homes which are broken in spirit or in fact; fatherless families, whether because of illegitimacy, divorce, desertion or death; homes where overcrowding, a lack of basic amenities and too frequent child-bearing are overtaxing the mother's physical and mental resources; and lastly, sudden and disrupting crises which may befall any family, such as accidents and bereavements. In all these circumstances parental care may become inadequate unless outside support is made available long before the possibility of taking children into care needs to be considered. Of course, at times, this will still have to be done.

The figures speak for themselves (Home Off., 1964): 25,000 children, or half the total taken into care in 1963, were short-term cases due to the mother's confinement or short-term illness; in the same period, 5,000 children, or 10 per cent, came into care because of the family being made homeless; reception into public care is three or four times as great for children under school age. Of the total number of children in care, 35 per cent are illegitimate whereas the incidence in the population as a whole is only 5·4 per cent. There are three-quarters of a million fatherless children, a third of whose fathers are dead and half of whom have parents who are separated or where one partner deserted the family (Wynn, 1964).

These facts and figures suggest that it may not be paradoxical or unrealistic to help families who are normally quite happy and stable but whose resources are inadequate at times of crises; and that long-term support should be available to all parents whose children are liable to be at risk long before crisis point is reached, otherwise disintegration of the family unit may be a likely consequence. Not only is such comprehensive preventive action wiser, but it would be an investment for the future. At present many children from unsettled, disrupted and inadequate families grow up to become themselves the inadequate parents of another generation of deprived children. And thus the pattern of unsatisfactory relationships, emotional maladjustment and educational backwardness is perpetuated.

To advocate the need to concentrate on the very young preschool child within the normal family in no way implies giving up hope for the long-term rehabilitation of problem families. Recent work with those severely handicapped mentally and with patients in mental hospitals, who have reorganised themselves into therapeutic communities, has produced encouraging evidence. This shows that even those suffering from severe or chronic mental handicaps can be helped by new methods of re-education, training or therapy. The same is true of the ill-effects of deprivation (Clarke and Clarke, 1959 and 1960; Trasler, 1960). 'Community care' has become almost a catch phrase but it will only become a reality if as a community we are willing to care early enough and comprehensively enough.

How would prevention work?

The only honest answer to this question is that at present no one knows exactly how to set about it, partly because there is not even agreement on objectives. The new Children and Young Persons Act provides a unique opportunity for experiment and study. Some authorities are at present evolving schemes for setting up preventive services. Others are in the process of doing so. Probably different schemes will be developed in different areas to suit local needs and resources. The undertaking of some action research now could be of direct practical value.

Whether prevention can be translated into reality by reorganising existing services, both statutory and voluntary, or whether some new structure or organisation is required, is still an open and controversial question. Those who believe that the existing machinery is adequate may be either too optimistic or take too narrow a view of prevention. It is possible that a new framework needs to be created. This has been put forward by the L.C.C., the Fabian Society, the Fisher group (in their report to the Ingleby Committee) and the Home Secretary (to judge from his foreword to the most recent report of the Children's Department). Various labels have been suggested for such a new preventive service: family bureaux; family consultation centres; family welfare clinics; or family advice centres. Whatever the administrative structure, prevention will need to be comprehensively based and should evolve from cooperation between existing statutory and voluntary services.

What areas of work and what kind of activities should a preventive service cover? Here it is useful to think of two broad aspects: (a) primary prevention, concerned with the child living with his family, and (b) secondary prevention, concerned with the child who comes into residential care for long periods or permanently. Primary prevention should have four main aims: (1) to achieve a general rise in children's resilience under emotional strain by encouraging the full development of their emotional and intellectual potential; (2) to help families through periods of temporary strain and crisis; (3) to improve and supplement the quality of child care for underprivileged children and (4) to prevent the disintegration of the family unit. As well as sharing the general aims of primary prevention, secondary prevention would plan to minimise, as far as possible, any harmful effects of coming into and being in care. Some of the provisions which need to be included in a fully comprehensive service will be briefly considered.

a. *Primary prevention*
To bring about a general rise in children's emotional stability and to develop fully their intellectual potentialities, advice on questions of child care and upbringing must be readily available to all parents, irrespective of social class, educational background or income. Ignorance and prejudice concerning children's psychological needs can be found among middle-class and intellectual parents, just as emotional neglect is by no means confined to underprivileged families. Though considerable advances have been made in the past twenty years in our knowledge of children's development, application always lags behind research findings. Fear and prejudice about mental health (and ill-health) still linger on: a feeling that to need advice on emotional, social and educational aspects of a child's growth is either being fussy or confessing to failure.

There is, however, a growing recognition among parents of all classes that advice and discussion with informed experts can be of value. Radically different circumstances and rapidly changing conditions no longer make grandmother's advice as pertinent as it used to be; moreover, often she no longer lives near enough to offer it. What must be fostered is a climate of opinion where mothers are as ready to seek advice on psychological aspects as they are now to seek reassurance on a child's physical development. The parents of handicapped children have very special needs in this respect (Tizard and Grad, 1961).

Next, a speedy and effective service is required to help the usually self-reliant family through periods of temporary strain and crisis. Social mobility and smaller families can make such 'first aid' essential when there is a confinement, physical or mental illness, an accident or a bereavement. A recent letter from a young man who is a dancer in one of our well-known ballet companies typifies the present situation in many areas: 'Three months after our third son was born, my wife developed asthma. She was rushed to hospital very ill indeed. The next day I was to start touring with the company. It was the most bitterly desperate moment of my life. With the family spread all over the country and most wives in jobs, I could see no way of getting the babies looked after at home. After well over a week the 'home help people' notified me that they were coming to 'investigate'. When I was a child there were always grannies and aunts to look after us if mother was ill.'

In addition to such practical help, skilled case work may also be needed; for example, to support a mother through the shock of her husband's sudden death or to assuage fears in a family where one of the parents has become mentally ill (Irvine, 1961 and 1964). Though it has been argued that because of heightened awareness and tension, a crisis may provide a particularly fruitful period for intervention (Caplan, 1962), this view is not universally accepted.

To improve the quality of child care among underprivileged and incomplete families, a number of ancillary provisions, including financial ones, need to be made. For example, fatherless families remain among the very poorest (Wynn, 1964) and this forces many a mother to seek outside employment. She then finds herself and the infant open to exploitation by the unscrupulous because provision for the preschool child's day care is quite insufficient.

To facilitate the fullest emotional and intellectual development of the underprivileged child means compensating him for missing the opportunities for all-round growth available in the happy, educated home. This entails adequate provision for play and for fostering, deliberately and systematically, language and intellectual development. Preschool play groups are making a valuable contribution, but they are not an adequate substitute for nursery schools. Even the latter may have to rethink their methods; experiments which are being carried out in Israel with culturally deprived immigrants may have some relevance here. Adequate nursery school facilities would in addition, relieve mothers who are overburdened by too many pregnancies, financial strain and adverse housing conditions, from caring for their children during part of each day. This may well result in making them feel less harassed and thus less impatient; as a consequence the quality of their mothering might improve. Being given the opportunity to watch their children's activities in the nursery school and to discuss the meaning and aims of what is being done, could also be an educative influence.

During the primary school stage, opportunities need to be provided for all those educational and cultural experiences of which under-privileged children are commonly deprived. Here one has in mind opportunities for the give and take of conversation and discussion with interested, intelligent adults; guidance to read good books and to talk about films, radio and TV programmes; visits to places of interest such as museums, airports, fire stations; going to concerts, theatres, travelling, camping, etc. These aspects of a child's informal education exert a stimulating influence on his intellectual and scholastic development. Socially underprivileged children are penalised in the educational race partly by their parents' inability to cater for these needs.

If such children do begin to experience educational difficulties, their parents usually fail to take action; indeed, often they are neither aware of, nor concerned about, their child's school failure. Early provision of remedial facilities in the school; opportunities for super-vision of some home work in quiet rooms; and an informed interest in the nature of the child's learning difficulties, might prevent these from becoming increasingly serious and eventually irreversible. The link between educational failure, behaviour difficulties, truancy and delinquency is too well established to need elaboration.

During the secondary school stage, the focus of preventive work should shift from the child within the family to his increasing emanci-pation from it; adequate preparation for and appreciation of the role of wage earner, citizen and future parent should now be the aim (Wall, 1948 and 1959). During this stage of growth there is a heightened state of emotional receptiveness during which questions of human relationships become of absorbing fascination. A sym-pathetic but neutral outsider is more likely to be the recipient of con-fidence than the involved parent, particularly where there are or have been serious family tensions. Easy opportunities for talking in-dividually with adults (preferably those who have some knowledge of the young person's family background) as well as for taking part in discussion groups should be provided.

Topics would range from factual ones, such as leisure time activities, local training opportunities, the implications of changing from being a pupil to becoming a worker and budgeting (whether it involves pocket money, weekend earnings or wages), to a considera-tion of the relation between the sexes, courting, marriage and the effect of children on the relationship between the parents.

Engaged and newly wed couples are another group who are in a receptive state of mind; a comprehensive programme of 'education for family living' is likely therefore to make a real impact.

b. *Secondary prevention*

Here the aim would be to counteract or at least mitigate, the effect of previous or present damaging emotional and social experiences among children in long-term care. Handicapped children, who have to attend boarding schools and thus also live in residential care for the major part of their lives, would be included. There is a good deal of evidence now on the likely ill effects of prolonged substitute care on emotional, linguistic and intellectual development and some knowledge of how to ameliorate them. But the comparative merits of various types of substitute care need study as well as the most effective ways of providing a culturally and educationally enriched environment.

Another aim of secondary prevention would be the early detection of emotional and educational difficulties and the provision of skilled treatment before these become intractable. The facilities needed for underprivileged children living in their own homes are similarly required for many of those who are 'in care'. In addition, they have some special problems. These can be divided into two groups, those connected with the child's own family and those relating to 'being in care'.

Emotional problems connected with the child's own family. Removal from home is almost inevitably a shock and may make the child feel abandoned. The younger he is, the more difficult the task of preparing him adequately and of explaining why it has to happen. To children their parents appear to be all-powerful, even if in fact they are quite inadequate. This belief makes it difficult for the child to accept that events are beyond parental control. In consequence he tends to feel that he has been sent away as a punishment for being naughty or that his own bad behaviour is in some way responsible for whatever disaster has led to the family's break-up. When physical or mental illness or desertion have been the cause, anxiety about the parent's fate is an added fear. In cases where brothers and sisters have remained at home, there may also be resentment and jealousy. Even when he is old enough to be given a full explanation, this must still fall short of a true understanding of the situation. In the words of one 8-year-old: 'No one told me what it would really feel like to be without my mum and dad.' If the child is permanently 'abandoned' by his family, this often has a devastating effect on his self-confidence and self-image: feeling guilty and unworthy, he comes to think of himself as rejected and unloved; this makes him less able to form new bonds of affection.

If, on the other hand, his family do keep in touch with him while he is in care, then he has to learn to make a new relationship with his parents and other relatives. No longer are they part of his daily life; they are now occasional visitors who spend a few hours with him but have no share in everyday happenings. Feckless and unreliable parents add to his difficulties by making promises they do not keep, be it failing to visit, to write letters, to send gifts or to take him back home. Such behaviour either forces the child to face the fact that his parents are inadequate and untrustworthy or else—if this is too painful for him to accept—makes him shift the blame on to 'them', a hostile authority.

By the nature of the complex circumstances which result in a child's being taken into care, he has also to come to terms with the problem that his personal future may be uncertain, for a shorter or longer period. No one may know exactly when or whether he will be able to go home; and whether and how soon he is to be moved from the reception centre to a children's home or to a foster home. According to the child's temperament and past experience, uncertainty will engender unrealistic hope, apathy, depression or black despair. It may also lead to evasiveness or lying since he is unable to talk truthfully to other children in school about his own family and what is to happen to him.

When he does return home, becoming reintegrated within the family poses new problems of adaptation. Chief among them are overcoming his resentment about having been 'abandoned' and learning to live with his 'real' parents rather than the idealised picture of them which he is likely to have built up during the separation.

Emotional problems connected with 'being in care'. Coming to live in unfamiliar surroundings provokes feelings of bewilderment and loss, even in adults. Children's feelings of security depend in great measure on familiar surroundings and on a familiar routine. Different standards of living and of conduct, new food, unfamiliar sounds, sights and smells are all confusing and frightening, the more so the younger the child. Though improved physical care and a regular daily routine will be of benefit in the long run, their immediate impact may have the opposite effect. While still 'mourning' the loss of his parents and adjusting to new surroundings, the child has simultaneously to learn to make several new relationships: with the child care officer; with the reception centre staff or house staff of the children's home; with foster parents; and with other children. Moreover, these relationships are rather different from those he had known in his own home: they are inevitably less personal; the ratio of children to adults is higher than in the average home; and the adults change, going on and off duty, or leaving altogether for new jobs. In many cases the child will also be attending a new school with all the stresses this can involve in adjusting to different teaching methods, standards of behaviour and general atmosphere; and again new relationships have to be made with teachers and class mates.

Among children who remain in care for considerable periods or permanently, three conditions make the formation of stable relationships difficult: the high turn-over of house staff; children's frequent change of placement (on average, once every two years); and the continual 'coming and going' of other children. This state of flux is likely to give the children a sense of impermanence and change, heightening their feelings of insecurity and uncertainty: it may seem safer then not to make close ties and to avoid emotional involvement. Moreover, residential homes often lack a father figure. This makes identification with a male difficult—though needed by both boys and girls; it also excludes the opportunity of learning about harmonious relationships between adult men and women by living in an atmosphere where these exist. For these reasons alone, fostering must be considered more satisfactory and conducive to the emotional adjustment of long-term cases. Unfortunately there is a shortage of suitable foster homes, particularly for disturbed and handicapped children. This is a serious problem in the field of secondary prevention.

Perhaps the most urgent need is for more information and knowledge on which action can be based. Local authorities are now empowered to spend money on research and thought needs to be given to how this might best be done. There would seem to be some disadvantages in research work being done wholly or solely by local authority staff: few, if any, have training in and experience of such work; partly due to the shortage of personnel and partly because of the demanding nature of child care work itself, there is little time for research; also it is open to doubt whether those closely involved in

T

case work could at the same time adopt the more detached attitude essential to sound research work; lastly, there may be a danger of some findings not seeing the light of day if they conflict with the policy or criticise the practice of the employing local authority.

Yet, unless local conditions are known and taken into account, research findings may be misinterpreted. Perhaps the pattern of collaboration which has evolved in the educational field could be a useful model: this consists of research being initiated by Institutes of Education and by the National Foundation for Educational Research on the one hand and practising teachers on the other hand; at the same time, trained research workers are given access both to records and to children so as to carry out projects which require specialised skills and knowledge.

Many problems of secondary prevention still await systematic investigation. For example, what are the comparative advantages and shortcomings of various types of substitute care for children of different ages? How frequent are the emotional problems discussed earlier and how adequately are they being dealt with? Whose job should it be to help children to come to terms with them—child care workers, residential staff, psychiatrists, psychologists? What are mentally healthy ways of coming to terms with such problems and what are the most effective methods—individual or group play therapy, individual or group discussion, role playing, environmental therapy? Are children allowed adequate opportunity and time for grief and mourning on separation and are they adequately supported through this period? What is the ultimate fate of children who have been in care for long periods—how do they make out in work, marriage and as parents?

There is one problem which can be solved only by close collaboration between administrators and field workers but which also requires the skills of experienced researchers. This is the mundane yet vitally important question of records. At present much valuable and basic information remains inaccessibly buried because the way in which records are kept does not allow systematic collation or comparison between one area and another. Record-keeping and form-filling are delicate, if not explosive, topics. They are bedevilled by their time-consuming nature, the need for confidentiality, and inter-departmental barriers for their exchange. Yet few would deny that records are as fundamental and indispensable in the field of child care and education as they are in medicine.

In child care, records serve two closely related purposes. First, to provide a continuous picture of a child's life story: who looked after him, where, for what period of time and for what reasons; if changes occurred, when and why they took place and how they were presented to the child. When there are gaps in this background information, which at present is often the case, it is difficult to make new plans; and gaps may hinder, or even prevent, the understanding of a child's needs as well as of his behaviour. The second purpose of records is peculiar to children who are deprived of a normal home life for long periods or permanently: it is to help them to acquire and maintain a sense of personal identity. Normally a child acquires this sense through living with his family. The link with his own past is established by his parents talking about events he cannot remember, reinforced by photos and other mementos from his infancy; while the link to his future is provided by the family's long-term educational and vocational plans for him. The recurring phrase 'when you are older' represents the forging of this link. The opportunity for continuous and long-term identification with the parents also plays a vital part in acquiring this supremely important sense of personal identity.

Because of the inadequacy of most current systems of record keeping, the child 'in care' has often large gaps in his knowledge about himself and his family, which no one is in a position to fill. The more unsettled a child's home life has been and the more changes of placement and of staff he has experienced, the greater the difficulty of his acquiring and maintaining a sense of personal identity. When no one can provide him with a continuous story of his own past; when his future is equally uncertain; and when he lacks the opportunity for unbroken and long-term identification with parental figures; when he has failed to develop a sense of personal worthwhileness; is it surprising then that he often remains unable to make relationships and to give his trust?

Those who have the daily task of keeping and dealing with records are best fitted to decide on the basic minimum which must be obtained and on what is the practically possible maximum which it would be desirable to record. Thus child care workers and administrators need to do the initial thinking and planning. Research workers could advise on the design and layout which make for ease and economy in recording and which facilitate later analysis and collation. Pilot studies of various types of records would then need to be evaluated both by the practitioner and by the researcher before an agreed decision can be reached. Of course better records will not by themselves improve child care practices but they could contribute to them.

Conclusions

Primary prevention needs to be seen as a far-reaching and comprehensive concept. Whether existing services are able to undertake this work or whether some kind of new service, such as family advice centres, should be created for the purpose, may be largely an administrative issue. Whichever way is adopted, the basic nature of what requires to be done will not be affected. The essence of primary prevention lies in dealing with the total situation of the whole family at the earliest time possible. Its main tasks can be summarised under six headings:

1. *Education.* To coordinate available facilities for the dissemination of knowledge regarding children's emotional, social and educational needs; where necessary, to create such facilities for normal families (as well as for engaged couples) by arranging lecture courses, discussion groups, etc. This work would aim to raise the general level of child care and to promote the full development of children's intellectual and emotional potentialities.

2. *First-aid.* To make available to the usually self-reliant family a service to help them through periods of temporary strain and crisis, such as physical or mental illness or bereavement.

3. *Early prevention.* To give help to families suffering from some degree of defective family relationships and to supplement the quality of child care for underprivileged children. This needs to be done at the earliest possible time, recognising that early learning is basic and that defective family relationships are not confined to any one strata of society. While poor housing and financial strain contribute to or may cause impaired relationships and intellectual neglect, the converse is not true: the absence of these adverse factors does not ensure adequate intellectual stimulation or harmonious family relationships.

4. *Long-term support.* To provide more or less continuous support for incomplete or inadequate families to prevent neglect, deprivation or a complete break-up of the home. Here one has in mind the unmarried, widowed or deserted mother or the 'problem family' where one can predict that it will have in-built difficulty in functioning as an acceptable social unit. In such cases the parents have themselves

often been the victims of broken homes or of inadequate parental care. To prevent their children from becoming the problem parents of the next generation would be one of the aims of such continuous guidance and support. If successful it should bring about greater emotional stability and more resistance to stress in successive generations.

5. *To be a clearing house.* Nowadays many different agencies and services are available to advise on the problems of normal and handicapped children. Lack of knowledge on the part of parents (maintained sometimes by the prejudice of those who should know better) often results in these services not being used at all or too late. A preventive service should be competent to suggest the most appropriate specialist or body to consult in a particular case.

6. *Research.* In addition to being itself an experimental project, a Family Advice Service could sponsor, or possibly itself undertake, some investigations. It would have unique opportunities for certain kinds of studies: for example, an examination of the composition of families who seek its advice; the kind of questions, relating to children's growth, that are most commonly raised by mothers; the problems which are specific to the incomplete family, especially the mother who is without a husband's support; the effect of having a physically or mentally handicapped child in an otherwise normal family; and the kind of situations that spark off crises, threatening the break-up of the family as a viable unit.

Perhaps a recent article in *The Times* (12 October 1964) neatly sums up the case for primary prevention: 'It is amazing that, on economic grounds alone, preventive work should have taken so long to get legislative support. In this country, there is a strong tradition of charity towards those less well off, but it seldom goes so far as to providing them with equal opportunities. Well-to-do families have always had the resources to do their own preventive child welfare; with solicitors, doctors, psychiatrists, headmasters, bank managers and the rest of the family to call on, their children are seldom sent away anywhere but to boarding school.'

Now to turn to secondary prevention which must also be broadly conceived. There can be little doubt that the responsibility for it should lie in Children's Departments and that they possess both the legal power and the administrative machinery for embarking on a comprehensive preventive programme. Its main pillars would seem to be personnel and training. Paradoxically the more effective primary prevention becomes, the more disturbed and handicapped will be those children who have finally to be taken into care, since they will come from the hard core of families too unstable and inadequate to function even with maximum long-term support. The children will tend to be long-term cases since other provision than removal from home should be available for short-term cases. In education it is now accepted practice that emotionally disturbed and other handicapped children should be placed in much smaller groups than normal pupils if they are to be taught effectively and remedially. The view is gaining ground that in addition all teachers of the handicapped need additional training. In the same way it will have to be accepted in the child care field that smaller groups will be needed for the more disturbed and handicapped children who will make up the future population of residential Homes. This will mean not only more but better trained staff. At a time when untrained people are not only accepted but by their presence prevent the collapse of residential services, this may sound unrealistically utopian. A possible alternative to increasing the number of residential personnel may be to plan for a very considerable increase in foster homes. This would be more realistic since residential work as a career has become increasingly unattractive to women. However, more foster homes will only be found if appropriate conditions and incentives, including financial ones, are provided. Acting as a foster parent needs to be presented as what it really is: a social service demanding personal maturity, devotion to unloved, and often unlovable, children, and perseverance in the face of unresponsiveness, distrust and repeated backsliding. In fact, it is a challenge to compassion, experience and knowledge.

A corollary is the jettisoning of two traditional views: first, that any warm-hearted woman who has successfully brought up her own family is fitted to take on this task. Second, that only sufficient payment should be given to cover the child's keep so that fostering is not undertaken merely for financial gain. Why adopt such a puritanical view regarding fostering when all others who professionally care for children are rewarded financially (albeit often at too low a level, as in the case of house parents)? The devotion of teachers to the interests of their pupils is not doubted because of the salary claims made by the profession; nor does anyone question the devotion of paediatricians because they are adequately remunerated.

It is likely that many women would prefer to look after one or more children in their own homes rather than to seek outside employment in factories, shops or offices. Particularly mothers, whose own children are growing up so that they have time and energy to spare, may be attracted to such work. Fostering should be regarded as a vital social service and as a job much more difficult than bringing up one's own family: it involves getting to know a strange child whose past experiences are likely to have made him difficult to understand and to handle; whose own parents will in most cases retain the right of access; and who may well continue to unsettle him and to interfere, consciously or unconsciously, in his building a satisfactory relationship with his foster parents.

What is involved in fostering, then, is not only loving care but the rehabilitation of an emotionally disturbed or even damaged child. Such work is much more responsible than being in a factory or shop; it also, like any mother's day, allows of no set hours or well-defined duties. It is a job which demands a professional attitude of mind as well as compassion; knowledge as well as affection; a willingness to accept problems which may interfere with one's own family life; and determination to persevere even when a child is slow to respond. If these facts are accepted, three practical consequences follow: most foster mothers will need some training as well as the continued support of adequately trained child care staff; remuneration must be adequate; and careful selection will have to be made so as to exclude those who would undertake such work primarily for financial reward. The present shortage of foster parents means that there cannot be much selection. The suggestions made here are likely to lead to a considerable increase of suitable people offering to undertake this work so that selection would be needed. Experiments would then be required to discover appropriate selection methods.

Another practical issue relating to effective secondary prevention is the classification of children who are removed from their own homes. Present administrative arrangements have a number of shortcomings and the labels given to children are based on a rather artificial classification. They suggest real differences when in fact none or few exist. Whether a child is labelled maladjusted, requiring care and protection, delinquent, or needing to be taken into care, depends less on his behaviour than on the agency by which and to which he gets referred. These in turn are determined by a combination of chance, local circumstances and social class.

There are a number of people whose concern for a child may lead them to take action: a head teacher, a school welfare officer, a policeman, a child care officer or a parent himself. What action they take will depend on administrative convenience, local facilities and other chance factors. Thus a head teacher may refer a child to the school psychological service or to the children's department; if the child comes from a middle class home the head teacher is likely to call up the parents to discuss some delinquent behaviour whereas the boy from a problem family is more likely to find himself before the juvenile court (his family often being already known to the police and the probation officer). Not only is the child's label often fortuitous but his placement too will depend on chance factors. Thus there is very considerable similarity between children who find themselves in rather different establishments: attending a child guidance clinic; going to a day school for the maladjusted; living in a hostel or residential school for the maladjusted; in a reception centre; a children's Home; a remand Home; or in an approved school. Even how they get there differs markedly: a parent will take the child weekly to the clinic; if he goes to a residential hostel or school, he will be prepared for it beforehand and then travel to it with his parents; a child care officer—whom he is likely to have known for some time—will take him to the reception centre or children's home; while, if sent to a remand home, he will be escorted only by police officers straight from the court hearing. Yet the fundamental reasons why the intervention of outside agencies is needed are basically the same: some inadequacy in one or both parents or defective family relationships which have had an adverse effect on the child's personality development.

If one of the aims of secondary prevention is to make removal from home as constructive an experience as possible then it must become a more rational and positive procedure. One way of achieving this might be to set up observation centres for all children who have special needs or problems which can only be examined by their removal from home. Otherwise the diagnosis of their difficulties can be done much more satisfactorily while the child remains in familiar surroundings. The purpose of the observation centres would be threefold: to arrange a thorough medical check, including minor ailments, minimal neurological involvement and psychiatric conditions; to carry out a thorough psychological examination, including emotional and social development; and to have a thorough educational examination, including language development and scholastic attainments. The team responsible for this comprehensive investigation would include all the staff of the observation centre from teachers and houseparents to cleaners and the handyman.

To be effective, these centres will need to be liberally staffed by well-trained people who stay in the job. Diagnostic work is notoriously difficult. One of the legacies of having starved the social sciences of money for research is the dearth of reliable tools for accurate measurement and prediction. Shortage and turnover of staff lead to a lack of feedback of information; yet this is essential if experts and observation centre staff are to learn both from the success and the failure of their recommendations. The setting up of such comprehensive observation centres might lead to the abolition of our present rather meaningless labels. Then we may come to regard some children as being in need of special care just as we consider now that some are in need of special education.

Prevention—can it become a reality or is it merely an illusion? The only way to find out is by giving preventive services a fair chance to prove themselves. Too often in education, in child care and in social work, new schemes are attempted halfheartedly with too little money and too few staff. Then it is concluded that these 'new-fangled ideas' do not work. In the educational and social services, short-term experiments are of very limited value. What is needed is a number of preventive services which are allowed to run for at least twenty years and which have a programme of action research built into them to evaluate what is being achieved. If successful, then the focus of problems may change, just as children's earlier physical maturation has posed new problems. For example it may well be that if children's language and intellectual potentialities are realised to a greater extent, then schools will need to adopt more stimulating and demanding teaching methods.

Quick answers cannot be expected from any preventive programme. But, if successful, then the children who have benefited from it will in their turn become better parents and better citizens, thus more than repaying the investment society has made in them.

References

CAPLAN, G., ed. (1961) *Prevention of mental disorders in children*. London, Tavistock.

CLARKE, A. D. B. and CLARKE, A. M. (1959) 'Recovery from the effects of deprivation', *Acta Psychologica*, **16**, 137–44.

CLARKE, A. D. B. and CLARKE, A. M. (1960) 'Some recent advances in the study of early deprivation', *Journal of Child Psychology and Psychiatry*, **1**, 26–36.

HOME OFFICE (1964) *Report on the work of the Children's Department, 1961–1963*. (H.C. 155.) London, H.M.S.O.

IRVINE, E. E. (1961) 'Psychosis in parents; mental illness as a problem for the family', *British Journal of Psychiatric Social Work*, **6**, 21–6.

IRVINE, E. E. (1964) 'Children at risk', *Case Conference*, **10**, 293–6.

LEWIS, M. M. (1963) *Language, thought and personality in infancy and early childhood*. London, Harrap.

PRINGLE, M. L. KELLMER (1961) 'The incidence of some supposedly adverse family conditions in schools for maladjusted children', *British Journal of Educational Psychology*, **31**, 183–93.

PRINGLE, M. L. KELLMER (1962) 'The long-term effects of remedial education: a follow-up study', *Vita Humana*, **5**, 10–33.

PRINGLE, M. L. KELLMER (1962) 'Backwardness and underfunctioning in reading during the early stages of the junior school', *Special Education*, **51**, 14–23.

TIZARD, J. and GRAD, J. C. (1961) *The mentally handicapped and their families; a social survey*. London, Oxford University Press.

TRASLER, G. (1960) *In place of parents; a study of foster care*. London, Routledge & Kegan Paul.

WALL, W. D. (1948) *The adolescent child*. London, Methuen.

WALL, W. D. (1959) *Child of our times: cultural change and the challenge to healthy mental growth*. (National Children's Home, Convocation lecture) London, N.C.H.

WYNN, M. (1964) *Fatherless families; a study of families deprived of a father by death, divorce, separation or desertion before or after marriage*. London, Joseph.

17. Summary of findings and recommendations

1. Language development among children in care was found to be more seriously affected by deprivation than any other aspects of development and achievement. This was due to a multiplicity of interacting and adverse circumstances. (Chapters 3, 4, 5, 7.)

2. The use of group tests of intelligence and of reading are likely to underestimate the abilities of deprived children. In common with the majority of maladjusted and educationally backward pupils, their emotional condition and unfavourable attitude to learning mitigate against sustained effort and attention in a group situation. (Chapters 2, 3.)

3. The most fruitful time for the prevention of language and later educational difficulties among the emotionally and culturally deprived is during the preschool years. (Chapters 3, 7, 10, 16.)

4. The provision of nursery schools for children from overcrowded, underprivileged homes and the addition of a trained nursery school teacher in every residential nursery, are urgent needs. (Chapters 7, 10, 16.)

5. Smaller classes and remedial teaching provision are of particular importance for the culturally and emotionally deprived child. (Chapters 3, 6.)

6. In residential homes of all types and for all ages, much greater emphasis should be placed on conversation, on reading to and with the children, and on employing every means to awaken and develop the child's ability to express ideas, thoughts and feelings. Culturally enriching experiences need to be regarded as furthering the same aims and not simply as 'treats'. (Chapters 3, 7, 10.)

7. Increased practical recognition should be given to the fact that every child in care needs the opportunity to make a stable, lasting

relationship with a dependable adult; a relationship which is maintained regularly and reliably over a period of years. (Chapters 4, 5, 11, 12.)

8. The effects of emotion on learning need to be given much greater practical recognition, in work with both normal and handicapped children. (Chapters 8, 9, 13, 14.)

9. The structure and needs of the family have been changing and are still in a state of flux. This produces tensions and strain in children as well as in those who care for them. There is a need for new concepts and new services to meet the challenge of rapid social and scientific changes. Suggestions are made for a preventive service which should be much broader and more comprehensive than is envisaged at present. Among its aims would be the fostering of children's intellectual, emotional and social potentialities, the long-term support of inadequate or incomplete families, the mitigation of the effect of past damaging experiences once children are taken into care and to make being in care as constructive an experience as possible. (Chapters 15, 16.)

Bibliography

ADLER, A. (1932) *What life should mean to you.* London, Allen & Unwin.

AINSWORTH, M. D. and BOWLBY, J. (1954) 'Research strategy in the study of mother–child separation', *Courrier de Centre International de l'Enfance*, **4**, 105–31.

AINSWORTH, M. D. and others (1962) *Deprivation of maternal care; a reassessment of its effects.* (Public Health papers, 14.) Geneva, World Health Organisation.

ALDRICH, C. A., SUNG, C. and KNOP, C. (1945) 'The crying of newly born babies, I. The community phase', *Journal of Pediatrics*, **26**, 313–26.

— — — (1945) 'The crying of newly born babies, II. The individual phase', *Journal of Pediatrics*, **27**, 89–96.

— — — (1945) 'The crying of newly born babies, III. The early period at home', *Journal of Pediatrics*, **27**, 428–35.

—, NORVAL, M., KNOP, C. and VENEGAS, F. (1946) 'The crying of newly born babies, IV. A follow-up study after additional nursing care had been provided', *Journal of Pediatrics*, **28**, 665–70.

ALLEN, F. H. and PEARSON, G. H. J. (1928) 'The emotional problems of the physically handicapped child', *British Journal of Medical Psychology*, **8**, 212–35.

—, TIBOUT, N. H. C. and FREUD, A. 'Aggression in relation to emotional development, normal and pathological', in: *International Congress on Mental Health, 1948, vol. 2. Proceedings of the International Conference on Child Psychiatry*, 4–23.

ANDRY, R. (1960) *Delinquency and parental pathology; a study in forensic and clinical psychology.* London, Methuen.

AUSUBEL, D. P., SCHIFF, H. M. and GOLDMAN, M. (1953) 'Qualitative characteristics in the learning process associated with anxiety', *Journal of Abnormal and Social Psychology*, **48**, 537–47.

BARKER, R. G., WRIGHT, B. A., MEYERSON, L. and GONICK, M. R. (1953) *Adjustment to physical handicap and illness; a survey of the social psychology of physique and disability*. New York, Social Science Research Council, Bulletin 55.

BEIER, E. C. (1951) *The effect of induced anxiety on flexibility of intellectual functioning*. Psychological Monographs, **65**, no. 326.

BERNSTEIN, B. (1960) 'Language and social class', *British Journal of Sociology*, **11**, 271–6.

— (1961) 'Social structure, language and learning', *Educational Research*, **3**, 163–76.

BEVAN, R. T. and JONES, B. (1961) 'Signs occurring in childhood, which indicate a poor social prognosis', *Case Conference*, **7**, 206–11.

BIRCH, L. B. (1949) 'The remedial treatment of reading disability', *Educational Review*, **1**, 107–10.

BODMAN, F., MACKINLEY, M. and SYKES, K. (1950) 'The social adaptation of institution children', *Lancet*, **258**, 173–6.

BOURNE, H. (1955) 'Protophrenia; a study of perverted rearing and mental dwarfism', *Lancet*, **269**, 1156–63.

BOWLBY, J. (1946) *Forty-four juvenile thieves; their characters and home life*. London, Baillière, Tindall & Cox.

— (1951) 'Maternal care and mental health', *Monograph Series of the World Health Organisation*, **2**.

— (1954) *Child care and the growth of love*. Harmondsworth, Penguin.

— AINSWORTH, M. D., BOSTON, M. and ROSENBLUTH, D. (1956) 'The effects of mother–child separation; a follow-up study', *British Journal of Medical Psychology*, **29**, 211–44.

BOWLEY, A. H. (1947) *The psychology of the unwanted child*. Edinburgh, Livingstone.

— (1951) *Child care; a handbook on the care of the child deprived of normal home life*. Edinburgh, Livingstone.

BRODBECK, A. J. and IRWIN, O. C. (1946) 'The speech behaviour of infants without families', *Child Development*, **17**, 145–56.

BROSSE, T. (1950) *Homeless children; report of the proceedings of the conference of directors of children's communities, Trogen, Switzerland*. Paris, UNESCO.

BURLINGHAM, D. and FREUD, A. (1954) *Infants without families; the case for and against residential nurseries*. London, Allen & Unwin.

297

BURT, Sir C. (1944) *The young delinquent*. 4th edn. London, University of London Press.

— (1946) *The backward child*. 2nd edn. London, University of London Press.

CALIFORNIA STATE BOARD OF CONTROL (1918) *Intelligence of orphan children and unwed mothers in Californian charitable institutions.* Sacramento, California.

CAPLAN, G., ed. (1961) *Prevention of mental disorders in children.* London, Tavistock.

CAREY-TREFZER, C. J. (1949) 'The results of a clinical study of war-damaged children who attended the Child Guidance Clinic, Hospital for Sick Children, Great Ormond Street, London', *Journal of Mental Science*, **95**, 535–59.

CARLSON, E. R. (1941) *Born that way*. New York, Day.

CASTLE, M. (1954) 'Institution and non-institution children at school', *Human relations*, **7**, 349–66.

CLARKE, A. D. B. and CLARKE, A. M. (1954) 'Cognitive changes in the feeble minded', *British Journal of Psychology*, **45**, 173–9.

— ed. (1958) *Mental deficiency; the changing outlook*. Methuen.

— (1959) 'Recovery from the effects of deprivation', *Acta Psychologica*, **16**, 137–44.

— (1960) 'Some recent advances in the study of early deprivation', *Journal of Child Psychology and Psychiatry*, **1**, 26–36.

— and REIMAN, S. (1958) 'Cognitive and social changes in the feeble minded; three further studies', *British Journal of Psychology*, **49**, 144–57.

CLIFFORD, W. (1960) 'Professionalism and vocation in residential work', *Child Care*, **14**, 1, 9–10.

CRISSEY, O. L. (1937) 'Mental development as related to institutional residence and educational achievement', *University of Iowa Studies in Child Welfare*, **13**, no. 1.

DAVIS, K. (1940, 1947) 'Extreme social isolation of a child', *American Journal of Sociology*, **45**, 554–65; **52**, 432–7.

DAWE, H. C. (1942) 'A study of the effect of an educational programme upon language development and retarded mental functions in young children', *Journal of Experimental Education*, **11**, 200–9.

DENNIS, W. (1941) 'Infant development under conditions of restricted practice and of minimum social stimulation', *Genetic Psychology Monographs*, **23**, 143–89.

DOLL, E. A. (1935) 'A genetic scale of social maturity', *American Journal of Orthopsychiatry*, **5**, 180–90.

— (1937) 'The inheritance of social competence', *Journal of Heredity*, **28**, 152–65.

— (1953) *Vineland Social Maturity Scale*. Minneapolis, Educational Test Bureau.

— (1953) *The measurement of social competence; a manual for the Vineland Social Maturity Scale*. Educational Test Bureau, Minneapolis, U.S.A.

DUNSDON, M. I. (1947) 'Notes on the intellectual and social capacities of a group of young delinquents', *British Journal of Psychology*, **38**, 62–6.

DURRELL, D. D. (1940) *Improvement of basic reading abilities*. Yonkers on Hudson, New York. World Book Co.

EDMINSTONE, R. W. and BAIRD, F. (1949) 'Adjustment of orphanage children', *Journal of Educational Psychology*, **40**, 482–8.

FEINBERG, H. (1954) 'Achievement of children in orphan homes as revealed by the Stanford Achievement Test', *Journal of Genetic Psychology*, **85**, 217–29.

FERGUSON, T. (1951) *The young delinquent in his social setting*. Oxford University Press.

FERNALD, G. M. (1918) *The mental examination of 75 children at the 'Y' House*. Sacramento, California State Board of Control.

— (1943) *Remedial techniques in basic school subjects*. New York, McGraw-Hill.

FLEMMING, V. V. (1942) 'A study of Stanford–Binet vocabulary attainment and growth in children in the city of Childhood, Mooseheart, Illinois, as compared with children living in their own homes', *Journal of Genetic Psychology*, **60**, 359–73.

FITZGERALD, O. W. S. (1948) 'Love deprivation and hysterical personality', *Journal of Mental Science*, **94**, 701–17.

FORD, D. (1955) *The deprived child and the community*. London, Constable.

FREDRICSON, E. (1950) 'The effects of food deprivation upon competitive and spontaneous combat in C57 black mice', *Journal of Psychology*, **29**, 89–100.

FRIEDMANN, S. (1958) 'A report on progress in an L.E.A. remedial reading class', *British Journal of Educational Psychology*, **28**, 258–61.

GATES, A. I. (1941) 'The role of personality maladjustment in reading disability', *Journal of Genetic Psychology*, **59**, 77–83.

GATEWOOD, M. C. and WEISS, A. P. (1930) 'Race and sex differences in newborn infants', *Journal of Genetic Psychology*, **38**, 31–49.

GESELL, A. and AMATRUDA, C. S. (1947) *Developmental diagnosis; normal and abnormal child development; clinical methods and pediatric applications.* 2nd edn. New York, Hoeber.

GINDL, I. and HETZER, H. (1937) 'Unangemessenheit der Anstalt als Lebensraum für das Kleinkind', *Zeitschrift für Angewandte Psychologie und Psychologische Sammelforschung*, **52**, 310–58. Leipzig.

GOBB, M. (1922) 'The mentality of dependent children', *Journal of Delinquency*, **7**, 132–40.

GOLDFARB, W. (1943) Infant rearing and problem behaviour', *American Journal of Orthopsychiatry*, **13**, 249–65.

— (1943) 'The effects of early institutional care on adolescent personality (Graphic Rorschach data)', *Child Development*, **14**, 213–23.

— (1945) 'The effects of psychological deprivation in infancy and subsequent stimulation', *American Journal of Psychiatry*, **102**, 18–33.

— (1947) 'Variations in adolescent adjustment in institutionally reared children', *American Journal of Orthopsychiatry*, **17**, 449–57.

GOLDMAN-EISLER, F. (1958) 'Speech analysis and mental processes', *Language and speech*, **1**, 59–78.

GRAY, P. G. and PARR, E. A. (1957) *Children in care and the recruitment of foster parents; an enquiry made for the Home Office.* London, Social Survey.

GROSSACK, M. M. (1954) 'Some effects of co-operation and competition upon small group behaviour', *Journal of Abnormal and Social Psychology*, **49**, 341–8.

HALLGREN, B. (1950) 'Specific dyslexia ("congenital world-blindness"); a clinical and genetic study', *Acta Psychiatrica et Neurologica*, supplementum 65. Copenhagen.

HATTWICK, B. W. and STOWELL, M. (1936) 'Relation of parental over-attentiveness to children's work habits and social adjustments in kindergarten and the first six grades of school', *Journal of Educational Research*, **30**, 169–76.

HOGGART, R. (1957) *The uses of literacy; aspects of working class life, with special reference to publications and entertainments.* London, Chatto & Windus.

HOME OFFICE (1946) *Report of the Care of Children Committee.* (Cmd. 6922) London, H.M.S.O. (Curtis report.)

U

HOME OFFICE (1964) *Report on the work of the Children's department. 1961–1963* (H.C. 155) London, H.M.S.O.

— *The needs of young children in care; a memorandum prepared by the Home Office in consultation with the Advisory Council on Child Care.* London, H.M.S.O.

IRVINE, E. E. (1961) 'Psychosis in parents; mental illness as a problem for the family', *British Journal of Psychiatric Social Work*, **6**, 21–6.

— (1964) 'Children at risk', *Case Conference*, **10**, 293–6.

JANIS, I. L. and FESHBACH, S. (1953) 'Effects of fear-arousing communications', *Journal of Abnormal and Social Psychology*, **48**, 78–92.

JERSILD, A. T. (1954) 'Emotional development', in Carmichael, L., ed., *Manual of Child Psychology*, Chapter 14, 833–917. London, Chapman & Hall.

KLEIN, E. (1945) 'The reluctance to go to school', *Psychoanalytic Study of the Child*, **1**, 263–79.

KIRK, S. A. (1958) *Early education of the mentally retarded.* Urbana, Illinois, University of Illinois Press.

LAWRENCE, E. M. (1929) 'An investigation into the relation between intelligence and inheritance'. Ph.D. Thesis, London University.

LEAGUE OF NATIONS. Advisory Committee on Social Questions (1938) *Enquiry into measures of rehabilitation of prostitutes. Part 1. Prostitutes; their early lives.* Geneva.

LEEDS. Education Committee (1953) *Report on a survey of reading ability.* Leeds, Education Department.

LEVY, D. M. (1943) *Maternal overprotection.* New York, Columbia University Press.

LEVY, R. J. (1947) 'Effects of institutional versus boarding home care on a group of infants', *Journal of Personality*, **15**, 233–41.

LEWIS, H. (1954) *Deprived children; the Mersham experiment. A social and clinical study.* Oxford University Press.

LEWIS, M. M. (1963) *Language, thought and personality in infancy and early childhood.* London, Harrap.

LINDGREN, H. C. (1956) *Educational psychology in the classroom.* London, Chapman & Hall.

LINDQUIST, E. F. (1940) *Statistical analysis in educational research.* Boston, Mass., Houghton Mifflin.

LINTON, R. (1945) *The cultural background of personality*. New York, Appleton-Century-Crofts.

— (1947) *The cultural background of personality*. London, Routledge, & Kegan Paul.

LITHAUER, D. B. and KLINEBERG, D. (1933) 'A study of the variation in I.Q. of a group of dependent children in institution and foster-home', *Journal of Genetic Psychology*, **42**, 236–42.

LITTLE, M. F. and WILLIAMS, H. M. (1937), 'An analytical scale of language achievement', *University of Iowa Studies in Child Welfare*, **13**, 47–78, 88–94.

LOWRY, L. G. (1940) 'Personality distortion and early institutional care', *American Journal of Orthopsychiatry*, **10**, 576–85.

LURIA, A. R. (1961) *The role of speech in the regulation of normal and abnormal behaviour*. London, Pergamon Press.

LYNN, R. (1957) 'Conditioning and the psychopathic personality.' Paper given to the British Psychological Society.

— (1957) 'Temperamental characteristics related to disparity of attainment in reading and arithmetic', *British Journal of Educational Psychology*, **27**, 62–7.

MCCARTHY, D. A. (1930) *The language development of the pre-school child*. Institute of Child Welfare Monographs, No. 4. Minneapolis. University of Minnesota Press.

— (1947) 'The psychologist looks at the teaching of English', *Independent Schools Bulletin*, **5**, 3–11.

— (1952) 'Language and personality development', *Reading Teacher*, **6**, 28–36.

— (1952) 'Organismic interpretation of infant vocalisations', *Child Development*, **23**, 273–80.

— (1953) 'Some possible explanations of sex differences in language development and disorders', *Journal of Psychology*, **35**, 155–60.

MACMEEKEN, M. (1939) *Ocular dominance in relation to developmental aphasis; certain facts and interpretations arising out of an investigation into incidence of reading disability and the nature of the difficulties involved in such disability*. London, University of London Press.

MALLINSON, V. (1956) *None can be called deformed; problems of the crippled adolescent*. London, Heinemann.

MANDLER, G. and SARASON, S. B. (1954) 'A study of anxiety and learning', *Journal of Abnormal and Social Psychology*, **47**, 166–73.

MASLOW, A. H. (1954) *Motivation and personality*. New York, Harper.

302

MATHEMATICAL ASSOCIATION (1959) *Mathematics in secondary modern schools.* London, Bell.

MEAD, M. ed. (1953) *Cultural patterns and technical change; a manual prepared by the World Federation for Mental Health.* Paris, UNESCO.

MIDDLESBROUGH. Education Committee (1953) *Report of a survey of reading ability carried out in the schools of the authority during 1951 and 1952 by the Middlesbrough Head Teachers' Association in co-operation with the officers of the Authority.*

MILNER, E. (1951) 'A study of the relationship between reading readiness in grade one school children and patterns of parent–child interaction', *Child Development,* **22,** 95–112.

MINISTRY OF EDUCATION (1950) *Reading ability; some suggestions for helping the backward.* (Pamphlet no. 18) London, H.M.S.O.

— (1957) *Standards of reading, 1948–1956.* (Pamphlet no. 32) London, H.M.S.O.

MONROE, M. (1932) *Children who cannot read; the analysis of reading disabilities and the use of diagnostic tests in the instruction of retarded readers.* Chicago, University of Chicago Press.

MONTAGU, M. F. Ashley (1957) *The direction of human development; biological and social bases.* London, Watts.

MONTAGUE, E. K. (1951) 'The role of anxiety in serial rote learning'. Ph. D. Thesis, University of Iowa.

MOORE, J. E. (1939) 'Sex differences in speed of reading', *Journal of Experimental Education,* **8,** 110–14.

MOORE, J. K. (1947) 'Speech content of selected groups of orphanage and non-orphanage pre-school children', *Journal of Experimental Education,* **16,** 122–33.

MOORE, T. V. (1948) *The driving forces of human nature and their adjustment; an introduction to the psychology and psychopathology of emotional behaviour and volitional control.* New York, Grune and Stratton.

MORGAN, C. LLOYD (1900) *Animal behaviour.* London, Arnold.

MOWRER, O. H. and KLUCKHOHN, C. (1944) 'Dynamic theory of personality', in Hunt, J. McV., ed., *Personality and the Behaviour Disorders,* New York, Ronald Press, **1,** 69–135.

MUNDY, L. (1957) 'Therapy with physically and mentally handicapped children in a mental deficiency hospital', *Journal of Clinical Psychology,* **13,** 3–9.

MYRDAL, A. and KLEIN, V. (1956) *Women's two roles: home and work.* London, Routledge & Kegan Paul.

Neale, M. D. (1958) *Neale analysis of reading ability. Manual of directions and norms. Test Booklet*. London, Macmillan.

O'Connor, N. (1956) 'The evidence of the permanently disturbing effects of mother/child separation.' *Acta Psychol.*, **12**, 174–91.

Oliver, J. N. (1958) 'The effect of physical conditioning exercises and activities on the mental characteristics of E.S.N. boys', *British Journal of Educational Psychology*, **28**, 155–65.

Opie, I. and Opie, P. (1959) *The lore and language of schoolchildren*. Oxford, Clarendon Press.

Piaget, J. (1959) *The Language and Thought of the Child*. London, Routledge and Kegan Paul.

Pringle, M. L. Kellmer (1950) 'A study of Doll's Social Maturity Scale'. Ph. D. Thesis, London University.

— (1951) 'Social maturity and social competence', *Educational Research*, **3**, pt. 1. 113–28; pt. 2, 183–95.

— (1956) 'The backward child, Part I', *Times Educational Supplement*, 12 October, 1956.

— (1957) 'The educational needs of deprived children', *Child Care*, **11**, 4–9.

— (1957) 'Differences between schools for the maladjusted and ordinary boarding schools', *British Journal of Educational Psychology*, **27**, 29–36.

— (1958) 'Learning and emotion', *Educational Review*, **10**, 146–68.

— (1961) 'Emotional adjustment among children in care.' Parts 1 and 2, *Child Care*, **15**, 5–12, 54–9.

— (1960) 'The psychological and educational treatment of handicapped children.' *Special Education*, **49**, 17–21.

— (1961) 'The incidence of some supposedly adverse family conditions in schools for maladjusted children.' *British Journal of Educational Psychology*, **31**, 183–93.

— (1962) Backwardness and underfunctioning in reading during the early stages of the junior school.' *Special Education*, **51**, 14–23.

— (1962) 'The long-term effects of remedial education: a follow-up study.' *Vita Humana*, **5**, 10–33.

— (1964) *The emotional and social adjustment of physically handicapped children*. (N.F.E.R. occasional publication no. 11.) London, National Foundation for Educational Research.

— and Bossio, V. (1958) 'A study of deprived children, Part 1, Intellectual, emotional and social development', *Vita Humana*, **1**, 66–92.

— — (1958 'A study of deprived children. Part 2, Language development and reading attainment', *Vita Humana*, **1**, 142–70.

— — (1960) 'Early, prolonged separation and emotional maladjustment', *Journal of Child Psychology and Psychiatry*, **1**, 37–48.

— and SUTCLIFFE, B. (1960) *Remedial education; an experiment. An account of two years' work by a remedial unit for maladjusted and deprived children at the Caldecott Community*. University of Birmingham and Caldecott Community.

— and TANNER, M. (1958) 'The effects of early deprivation on speech development', *Language and Speech*, **1**, 269–87.

RAVEN, J. C. (1948) *Mill Hill Vocabulary Scale*. London, H. K. Lewis.

— (1951) *Controlled projection for children*. 2nd edn. London, H. K. Lewis.

REYMERT, M. L. and HINTON, R. T. (1940) 'The effect of a change to a relatively superior environment upon the I.Q.s of one hundred children', in National Society for the Study of Education, *Yearbook*, **39**, 255–68. Bloomington, Ind., Public School Publishing Co.

RIESSMAN, F. (1962) *The culturally deprived child*. New York, Harper & Row.

RHEINGOLD, H. L. (1943) 'Mental and social development of infants in relation to the number of other infants in the boarding home', *American Journal of Orthopsychiatry*, **13**, 41–4.

ROUDINESCO, J. and APPELL, G. (1950) 'Les répercussions de la stabulation hospitalière sur le développement psychomoteur des jeunes enfants', *Semaine des Hôpitaux de Paris*, **26**, 2271–3.

SAMUELS, F. (1943) 'Sex differences in reading achievement', *Journal of Educational Research*, **36**, 594–603.

SCHONELL, F. J. (1942) *Backwardness in the basic subjects*. Edinburgh, Oliver and Boyd.

— and SCHONELL, F. E. (1956) *Diagnostic and attainment testing. (Silent Reading Test B)* 3rd edn. London, Oliver & Boyd.

SHIRE, Sister M. L. (1945) 'The relation of certain linguistic factors to reading achievement in first grade children'. Ph.D. Thesis, Fordham University.

SIMONSEN, K. M. (1947) *Examination of children from children's homes and day-nurseries by the Bühler–Hetzer developmental tests*. Copenhagen, Busck.

SKELLS, H. M., UPDEGRAFF, R., WELLMAN, B. L. and WILLIAMS, H. M. (1938) 'A study of environmental stimulation; an orphanage pre-school project'. *University of Iowa Studies in Child Welfare*, **15**.

SMITH, H. P. and HIXON, L. (1935) 'A comparative study of orphanage and non-orphanage children', *Elementary School Journal*,
36, 110–15.

SMITH, M. E. (1935) 'A study of some factors influencing the development of the sentence in pre-school children', *Journal of Genetic
Psychology*, **46**, 182–212.

SNYGG, D. and COMBS, A. W. (1949) *Individual behaviour: a new
frame of reference for psychology*. New York, Harper.

SOBEL, F. S. (1948) 'Remedial teaching as therapy', *American
Journal of Psychotherapy*, **2**, 615–23.

SONTAG, L. W. (1941) 'The significance of fetal environmental differences', *American Journal of Obstetrics and Gynaecology*, **42**, 996–1003.

SPENCE, J. C. (1946) *The purpose of the family; a guide to the care of
children*. (National Children's Home Convocation lecture.)
London, N.C.H.

— (1947) 'The care of children in hospital', *British Medical Journal*,
4490, 125–30.

SPITZ, R. A. (1945) 'Hospitalism; an inquiry into the genesis of
psychiatric conditions in early childhood (I)', in *Psycho-analytic
study of the child*, **1**, 53–74. London, Imago Publishing Co.

— and WOLF, K. M. (1946) 'Anaclitic depression; an enquiry into
the genesis of psychiatric conditions in early childhood (II)', in
Psycho-analytic Study of the Child, **2**, 313–42. London, Imago,
Publishing Co.

STALNAKER, J. M. (1941) 'Sex differences in the ability to write',
School and Society, **54**, 532–5.

STOTT, D. H. (1956) *Unsettled children and their families*. London,
University of London Press.

— (1956) 'The effects of separation from the mother in early life',
Lancet.

— (1958) *The social adjustment of children; manual to the Bristol Social
Adjustment Guides*. London, University of London Press.

STROUD, J. B. and LINDQUIST, E. F. (1942) 'Sex differences in
achievement in the elementary and secondary schools', *Journal of
Educational Psychology*, **33**, 657–67.

SULLIVAN, H. S. (1948) *The meaning of anxiety in psychiatry and in
life*. New York, The William Allanson White Institute of Psychiatry.

SYMONDS, P. M. (1949) *The dynamics of parent–child relationships*. New
York, Bureau of Publications, Teachers College, Columbia University.

TANSLEY, A. E. and GULLIFORD, R. (1960) *The education of slow-learning children.* London, Routlege & Kegan Paul.

TERMAN, L. M. and WAGNER, D. (1918) 'Intelligence quotients of 68 children in a Californian orphanage', *Journal of Delinquency,* **3,** 115–21.

— and MERRILL, M. A. (1937) *Measuring intelligence; a guide to the administration of the new revised Stanford–Binet test of intelligence.* London, Harrap.

THEIS, S. VAN SENDEN (1924) *How foster children turn out; a study and critical analysis of 910 children who were placed in foster homes by the State Charities Aid Association and who are now eighteen years of age or over.* (Publication no. 165) New York, State Charities Aid Association.

TILTON, J. W. (1951) *An educational psychology of learning.* New York, Macmillan.

TIZARD, J. and GRAD, J. C. (1961) *The mentally handicapped and their families; a social survey.* Oxford University Press.

TRASLER, G. (1960) *In place of parents; a study of foster care.* London, Routledge & Kegan Paul.

TYLER, R. W. (1948) 'Co-operation and conflict in the mental development of the child', *Mental Hygiene,* **32,** 253–60.

UNITED NATIONS. Department of Social Affairs (1952) *Children deprived of a normal home life.* New York.

VERNON, M. D. (1957) *Backwardness in reading; a study of its nature and origin.* Cambridge University Press.

VYGOTSKY, L. S. (1962) *Thought and language.* New York, Wiley.

WALL, W. D. (1948) *The adolescent child.* London, Methuen.

— (1955) *Education and mental health.* Paris, UNESCO.

— (1959) *Child of our times; cultural change and the challenge to healthy mental growth.* (National Children's Home Convocation Lecture.) London, N.C.H.

WATTS, A. F. (1944) *The language and mental development of children.* London, Harrap.

WECHSLER, D. (1949) *Wechsler Intelligence Scale for Children.* New York, Psychological Corporation.

WHITING, J. W. M. and CHILD, I. L. (1953) *Child training and personality; a cross-cultural study.* New Haven, Yale University Press.

WILKINS, L. T. (1960) *Delinquent generations. A Home Office Research Unit report.* H.M.S.O.

WILLIAMS, H. M. and McFARLAND, M. L. (1937) 'Development of language and vocabulary in young children', *University of Iowa Studies in Child Welfare*, **13**.

WOODWORTH, R. S. (1941) 'Heredity and environment; a critical survey of recently published material on twins and foster-children', *Social Science Research Council Bulletin*. **47**.

WOOTTON, B. (1959) *Social Science and Social Pathology*. Allen & Unwin.

WYNN, M. (1964) *Fatherless families; a study of families deprived of a father by death, divorce, separation or desertion before or after marriage.* London, Joseph.

YEDINACK, J. G. (1949) 'A study of the linguistic functioning of children with articulation and reading disabilities', *Journal of Genetic Psychology*, **74**, 23–59.

Author Index